The International Library of Sociology

THE SOCIOLOGY
OF PROGRESS

Founded by KARL MANNHEIM

The International Library of Sociology

SOCIAL THEORY AND METHODOLOGY
In 22 Volumes

THE SOCIOLOGY
OF PROGRESS

by
LESLIE SKLAIR

First published in 1970
by Routledge

Reprinted 1998, 2001
by Routledge
2 Park Square, Milton Park, Abingdon, Oxon, OX14 4RN

Transferred to Digital Printing 2007

Routledge is an imprint of the Taylor & Francis Group

British Library Cataloguing in Publication Data
A CIP catalogue record for this book
is available from the British Library

The Sociology of Progress
ISBN 0-415-17545-3
Social Theory and Methodology: 22 Volumes
ISBN 0-415-17818-5
The International Library of Sociology: 274 Volumes
ISBN 0-415-17838-X

Publisher's Note
The publisher has gone to great lengths to ensure the quality of this
reprint but points out that some imperfections in the original
may be apparent

Contents

Acknowledgments

I should like to record two types of debts. The first is to those who have directly helped me in the writing of this book and the second is to those whose help has been indirect.

The University of London doctoral thesis of 1969 which forms the basis of the book was supervised by Professor Donald MacRae whose guidance and encouragement played a large part in its completion. For this I am very grateful indeed. Professor Morris Ginsberg commented on Part One and Chapter IX and Professor Sambursky gave me the benefit of his views on the idea of progress in antiquity.

My principal indirect debt is to Herminio Martins who, as a teacher and friend, has set the highest standards of both intellect and enthusiasm in sociology for me. Many others, those with whom I studied at the University of Leeds, and those with whom I presently teach at the London School of Economics, in particular, have helped me in ways too complicated to specify.

Lastly I must acknowledge the social context in which this work was written. If the *events* at the London School of Economics over the past few years have had any worthwhile consequence then it has been, for me, the atmosphere that has been generated in which teacher and students have come closer in the certainty that each has something to learn from the other and that both, in sociology at least, are engaged in the same critical enterprise. I have benefited greatly from my teaching experiences.

It is customary to relieve all the aforementioned from responsibility (or guilt) for the subsequent contents. This I have no hesitation in doing, as most of them disagree with me in any case. The same applies to my wife, Freda, who nevertheless showed commendable patience and good humour most of the time.

L.S

Introduction

This study is divided into two parts, of which the first is mainly historical and the second is mainly theoretical. In the first part I have attempted to trace the history of the idea of progress and the theories built around it, in a sociologically relevant manner. Thus, I have been interested less in precise contextual analysis of what writers have said about progress than in picking out the general direction of thought amongst those who wished to understand social life and to explain social phenomena. Part One, therefore, cannot be presented as a comprehensive history of the idea of progress, but rather as a selective account of certain major trends in social thought, organized around the concept of progress in human affairs, and intended to highlight the development of sociology. Indeed, one of the main themes implicit here is that the idea of progress and the idea of sociology were mutually reinforcing aspects of the movement in thought of the last few hundred years that has made each man as conscious of his fellows as he has always been of himself.

In Part Two a sociological theory of progress is articulated. This is set out in three stages, the sociological, the moral and the applied. Here it is argued that sociology, by its very nature, is morally *relevant*, and that the findings of sociologists and other social scientists about man and his societies can make significant differences both to our moral judgments and to our moral actions. Progress is nothing if it is not a moral concept, and to decide whether or not a particular social phenomenon represents progress is a moral decision. The gist of my argument in the second part of this book is that the social sciences can provide sound evidence on which to base such moral decisions, and that it is the continuing task of a responsible sociology to see itself in this light. However, it is essential to emphasize even at this early stage that one class of moral and sociological problems may prove insurmountable to any theory of progress. And this is the point where the two parts of this study interact.

Any study of the history of the idea of progress will plainly indicate that there are many ideas of progress, some so wide apart that it seems strange to identify them by the same generic term. Two major types of progress are identified in this study, partly as a response to the variety of theories discussed in Part One, and partly as a response to the theoretical needs of Part Two. These are characterized as *innovational* and *non-innovational* progress (for want of better terms), and though they do occur from time to time within one theory of progress, they are usually expressive of quite distinct styles of social organization. This distinction between innovational and non-innovational progress, generalized to distinguish societal types, provides a basis for the analysis of the dynamics of modern and non-modern societies. Thus, the history of various theories of progress, the moral significance of progress, and the sociological categories of innovation and non-innovation, provide the key to a sociological theory of progress.

I have attempted to build a sociological theory of progress from historical fact, theories about history and generalizations about the aspirations of man in society—concentrating on the first two of these in Part One and the last in Part Two. Chapter I looks briefly at some of the roots of the idea of progress before the eighteenth century, and suggests that although it never emerged *fully* before this time, it has appeared in one form or another since antiquity. The contemporary orthodoxy that progress is an invention of the 'modern' world is true only in so far as we mean what I have termed 'innovational progress', for 'non-innovational progress' (that which is not based on new things, ideas or processes) stems from antiquity.

In Chapter II the crucial period of the age of enlightenment in Europe is discussed. It is perhaps more accurate to speak of the European enlightenment*s*, for in the eighteenth century there were at least three national flowerings of interest in the idea of progress—in France (most importantly), in Germany and in Britain (especially in Scotland). This chapter reflects the current interest in the Scottish thinkers whose social thought strikes so many chords familiar to the modern sociologist. It is they, I argue, who at this early stage drew attention to the political implications of a theory of progress.

Here, around the end of the eighteenth century, is located a social process of great importance for the idea of progress and its future development—the institutionalization of science. This book is not a study of the history of science as it would need to be to substantiate fully the hypothesis linking the changes in the idea of progress in the nineteenth century with the changes in the social status of science and technology. What I have attempted to do is to suggest this link and to prepare the way for the more detailed analysis of the very special role that science and technology have played and continue to play in the development of theories of progress. This more detailed analysis takes place particularly in Chapters VI, VII and XIII. The precise dating of the institutionalization of science does not affect the sociological theory of progress in Part Two, although the nineteenth-century theories of progress point strongly to the decades around 1800 as the most likely time for this process to have taken place.

The title of Chapter III, 'Progress through Order and Progress through Revolution: Comte and Marx', tells concisely the story to which I have been alluding. In Comte and Marx, as much as in any other individuals in this study, are exemplified the styles and para-doxes of the idea of progress, and its interaction with societies in the midst of revolutionary but structured modernization. The section on Comte's ideas of progress in the hands of his many and various followers illustrates the power of such a doctrine at a crucial his-torical period.

Chapter IV deals with the often very complex relations that grew up between progress and evolution, especially as it affected Social Darwinism (so-called) and the work and influence of Herbert Spencer. This is indeed one of the most fascinating periods in British intellectual history, and it is especially important for the sociologist and the social anthropologist to pause now and again and cast a backward glance at the intellectual ferment in Victorian England; not only history is to be found there.

For my purposes a key figure of this time is T. H. Huxley, and it is on his warnings about the frailty of human progress that the chapter on progress and evolution is ended. As Huxley might have foretold, the notion of progress and theories of progress ran up against a great volume of opposition in the twentieth century, and there is no doubt that the optimism of the eighteenth and nineteenth centuries, among the intelligentsia at least, suffered a setback of such pro-portions in the twentieth century that it is still not yet clear whether progress as a traditional social ideology has recovered. It is my con-sidered opinion that the idea of progress as it has been presented in the first four chapters of this book has not fully recovered from the events of the present century, and my selection of material for Chapters V and VI is intended to reflect this view of the matter.

Chapter V examines what are the first modern sociological analyses of social progress and related issues. Neither Weber nor Durkheim can properly be regarded as a 'progress theorist' in a nineteenth-century sense, although they were concerned with the same general problems as their predecessors. The difference lies in their treatment of social change. With Spengler and Toynbee (and to some extent Sorokin) this difference is further highlighted, and the latter belong more to the previous era in this context. The rather gloomy and pessimistic character of these writings does not seriously misrepresent the tone of much social thought of the period.

The critics of progress discussed in Chapter VI come from a variety of sources, and although there is no specific anti-progress school of thought that can be isolated, the opposition to the machine and the reaction against technological society seems to me a theme important enough to spell out in some detail. Thus, it is in the works of men like Jacques Ellul that the idea of progress, and particularly that of innovational progress, is currently being modified in strictly contemporary ways.

The first part of the book ends with a series of questions, and it is important that I make clear the point of these questions, for they are admittedly not those that are most commonly asked in modern sociology. They concern some large problem areas, such as the issues around the direction of history, the dynamics of social change and the development of modern society in its ethical as well as its empirical aspects. They also concern some more immediate and intimate issues, such as the moral meaning of social life for men in communities and the criteria of everyday ethical decisions. The point of asking such questions is that sociology, as a human and social science, must make morally relevant statements and must back them up with sound evidence. The sociological theory of progress, in short, attempts to establish good reasons for value-judgments about social life and social change.

Progress is therefore defined as 'the end point, temporary or permanent, of any social action that leads from a less to a more satisfactory solution of the problems of man in society'. This definition, derived to some extent from the theories of progress discussed in Part One, is primarily intended for use in Part Two. On the basis of this definition, Chapter VII distinguishes two types of progress, innovational and non-innovational progress. These types are defined as follows: *innovational progress* is progress by means of the production of new things, ideas and processes, with maximum *impact* on society. *Non-innovational progress* is progress by means of the maintenance and diffusion of familiar things, ideas and processes, with minimal *impact* on society.* The term *impact* is used in a special sense to signify the effect that the different types of progress have on social structures.

With the establishment of the innovational/non-innovational progress distinction, elements of which can be found scattered in the works of some classical thinkers and Rousseau, Comte and Ellul for

---

* The definitions are introduced here so that the treatment of the idea of progress in Part One can be more readily understood.

example, the next task is to set up the value-standard whereby one can judge what count as 'more and less satisfactory solutions of the problems of man in society'. And this is the sociological ethic, which is elaborated in three parts.

Chapters VIII and IX deal with the basis of such an ethic in human conduct and our accumulated knowledge of social relations. The main argument here is that it is _morally_ relevant to discover the conditions that must be fulfilled for man and society to exist. Various moral strategies are mentioned, and as the definition of progress focuses on problem-solution in society, the way in which certain problems tend to be redefined is discussed.

Reasons are presented for the utility and the significance of the sociological ethic, and then, in Chapter X, some sociological attempts to find the previously suggested basis for this ethic are reviewed. The works of Malinowski, Aberle et al., Levy and Parsons are critically assessed for their contributions to the analysis of the requisites of individuals and societies.

In Chapter XI, I present my own list of individual and social requisites for human society, retaining some of the items of these functionalists and rejecting others. In addition, arguments are forwarded to save this analysis from identification with a 'survival ethic' through the distinction between human and inhuman societies. In any case, a crucial social requisite is what I term _preference-structures_, and this by itself is a bulwark against inhuman society.

The loose structure of the sociological theory of progress is completed in Chapter XII. In the remaining chapters the theory is applied to some textbook criticisms of progress and some problems of the sociology of science—a particularly vital problem area.

In Chapter XIV there is a summary of the conclusions reached in this study, and more importantly, a brief statement of its limitations and some of its implications.

A word on the relationship between Part One and Part Two is in place here. There are two extreme modes of writing about the development of social thought or a specific idea like that of progress. On the one hand, we may trace out the ways in which ideas have developed from thinker to thinker, from country to country, in chronological and/or geographical succession. On the other hand, we can set up analytical categories and classify all incidences of the idea in question in either/or and perhaps mixed classes. Neither of these two extremes is satisfactory, and in this study of progress as a social concept I have tried to retain the best of each method, although leaning to the former.

Fundamentally, any sociological concept, and especially a notion like progress, must be seen in its historical development, and in relation to the sociological conditions of this development. Thus, although this is not a work in social history or the history of science, it is essential that some attention should be paid to these areas. The idea of progress cannot be properly understood in isolation from such matters.

Nevertheless, some analytical order is necessary that we might better organize the many ideas and theories of progress and so better understand them. The distinction between innovational and non-innovational progress is not an attempt to pigeon-hole, but rather a response to the difficulties that some of the subtler theorists of progress have come up against in their writings. Thus, a selective study of some sociological uses of the idea of progress has suggested that there are two basic modes of progress, and that they characterize two basic modes of society. These remarks are intended in an ideal-typical sense; it is metaphorical to speak of innovational or non-innovational societies, and perhaps it would be safer to speak only of societies whose major institutions operated mainly on an innovational or non-innovational mode of progress.

Part One and Part Two complement each other in so far as history and theory are in constant interaction. We interpret history in terms of our theories, and our theories develop and change in terms of our views of history. In this book *progress* is seen as the vital link that binds history and sociological theory to the conduct of men in society.

part one

The history of
the idea of progress

I   The roots of the idea of progress

The idea of progress is often considered to have emerged fully only in the seventeenth or eighteenth centuries, although it appears consistently, if obscurely, in the literature of antiquity and in the Middle Ages. Therefore, this chapter is not to be regarded as some kind of ritual homage, but as a necessary first step in an historical account of the development of the ideas and the theories of progress that form the basis of this study. Wherever the break between the pre-modern world and the modern world is made, it is useful to compare the social thought of each period in order to decide whether or not the break is so dramatic that it gives us a false picture of events and obscures a real measure of continuity in thought. In this spirit I shall examine the classical and the medieval roots of the idea of progress.

The classical roots
As Flint pointed out in his *History of the Philosophy of History*, practically all views may be discovered in Greek and Roman thought, and indeed strange combinations of ideas often appeared in seemingly untroubled co-existence. Anaximander and Empedocles, Lucretius and Virgil all combined notions of progress with notions of decay. The somewhat pessimistic Horace could combine a wish to return to old and frugal standards with a recognition of material progress, amidst the troubles of his times.[1]

The most systematic attempt to reveal the sources of the idea of progress in antiquity is contained in Ludwig Edelstein's posthumous book, published under the title of *The Idea of Progress in Classical Antiquity*.[2] This brief work represents only half of the task, covering the period often referred to as the Hellenistic Age from about 323 to 30 B.C., but Edelstein's scholarship unearths a multitude of references to the idea of progress and even to phases in its development. In

3

this interpretation, such figures as Seneca and Posidonius come through very strongly, and although both are objects of considerable controversy, it is now almost impossible to deny that *some* notion of progress was discussed and accepted by many influential thinkers in classical antiquity.

Seneca and Posidonius are portrayed by Edelstein as men who reinforced the role of progressivism in Stoic thought—men who had few doubts as to the possibilities of new knowledge. Posidonius, particularly, lived out some such belief through an active interest in natural phenomena and a quest for knowledge about them. The life of Seneca is an altogether fascinating affair, and in at least one respect, the relations between masters and slaves, his thinking can be deemed socially progressive for the times in which he lived.*

Nevertheless, it would be fanciful to imagine that beneath every ancient boulder and within every antique manuscript there lurked a meaningful idea of progress. As Edelstein implies, it is not merely mentions of terms like progress that we should be looking for, but, just as importantly, we should attempt to find some deeper structures of thought within which such ideas could derive meaning and could develop. The history of ideas can be written, like the history of wars and politics, in many ways, not all of them entirely free from the human frailties of historians who wish to project stories of the past consonant with expected presents and hoped-for futures. Those who look for the genesis of ideas with peculiarly modern connotations in the thought of antiquity are prone to these difficulties, particularly the historian of the idea of progress. It is with this ever-present possibility of our 'inventing the past' in mind, that I must turn to examine some relevant strands of ancient thought.

There were at least two major conceptions in the thought of antiquity that can be linked to the subsequent growth of later theories of progress, and I shall deal briefly with each of these in turn.

The first of these conceptions presented history as an endless series of cycles—an inevitable regress from some golden age to a state of utter despair and misery, and then just as surely society would be regenerated and progress to the golden age once more.

---

* Bertrand Russell in his *History of Western Philosophy* (London: Allen and Unwin, 1961, p. 267), perhaps the best and certainly the most stimulating book of its kind, gives an amusing thumbnail sketch of Seneca's life and tribulations. Russell comments on the great riches of this Stoic, purportedly partly derived from money-lending in Britain, and possibly as a consequence of this—Boadicea's revolt—'a rebellion against capitalism as represented by the philosophic apostle of austerity'! Seneca, however, was also the principal exponent of the enforcement of the duties of masters towards their slaves and of legal rights for them. (See W. E. Lecky, *Rationalism in Europe*, London: Longmans, Green, 1884, vol. 2, 235 ff.)

This process would continue to the end of time, and within the limits of the golden age and the age of misery, all is the same. 'All things from eternity are of like forms,' says Marcus Aurelius, 'and come round in a circle ... it makes no difference whether a man shall see the same things during a hundred years or two hundred, or an infinite time.'[3] The dimension of optimism is necessary for the development of any full-fledged idea of progress, and this was a dimension that did not always have an important place in classical thought.

Lucretius, who was born at the beginning of the first century B.C., about two hundred years before Marcus Aurelius, had even rejected the notion of a golden age. He too believed in the inexorable decline of man from some higher stage, and shared the pessimistic resignation of the Emperor. Nevertheless, it is worth quoting a passage from Lucretius' great work, *De Rerum Natura*, to show how open in fact he was to the possibility of temporary progress in the short term, notwithstanding his doubts about it in the longer term:

Tillings of fields, walls, laws, and arms, and roads,
Dress and the like, all prizes, all delights
Of finer life, poems, pictures, chiselled shapes,
Of polished sculptures—all these arts were learned
By practice and the mind's experience,
As men walked forward step by eager step.
Thus time draws forward each and everything
Little by little into the midst of men,
And reason uplifts it to the shores of light.
For one thing after other men did see
Grow clear by intellect, till with their arts
They've now achieved the supreme pinnacle.*[4]

The implication of 'achieved the supreme pinnacle' will not escape those who are involved in an attempt to keep abreast of the developments of any branch of knowledge at the present time!

This brings up the crucial issue of the position of science in antiquity, for it is a reasonable assumption that if anything would break into the closed system of ever-recurring cycles it must be science and its power to effect social change through technology. Our stock of knowledge about ancient science is steadily building up both in terms of the general outlines over many fields as exemplified in Sarton's monumental reviews and in the close detail of particular enterprises, such as Sambursky's meticulous studies of Greek

---

* Lucretius uses the term '*progredientis*' (progress) here. See the present translation in line 6 of the passage quoted. Edelstein, op. cit., pp. 146-7, has a useful discussion of the genesis of the term.

physics.[5] There seems to be little doubt that significant science did occur in antiquity, especially in the Hellenistic period, and that this movement declined and remained in decline for many centuries thereafter.

Edelstein goes so far as to say that during this period the scientists, who were generally speaking still the scholars and the philosophers, even attempted to popularize scientific findings, citing Lucretius' *Of the Nature of Things*, from which I have just quoted, as a prime example of this activity. Emphasizing the role of the scientist as influential expert, Edelstein claims that 'the belief in progress held by the scientist was accepted and cherished by many'.[6] Until we have much more information about the impact of science and technology on the societies of antiquity, however, it is difficult to speculate confidently about the relations between science and the idea of progress, though this is a theme that will recur often in the following pages when I come to discuss the idea of progress in later centuries. What is certain, in the words of Sambursky, is that 'Despite the level of scientific sophistication and maturity reached at the close of antiquity the world had to wait for many centuries for the continuation of the story of science'.[7] This would suggest that the science that there was could not have been institutionalized as an ongoing part of the structure of these societies. (For a further discussion on this point, see pages 32-3.) This, in turn, suggests that a belief and confidence in the activity of science need not necessarily spill over into a belief and confidence in progress as a whole. Thus, important figures in the development of ancient science and philosophy, like Plato and Aristotle, though they cannot be characterized bluntly as indifferent to general progress, cannot be assumed to have supported it fully. Both Plato and Aristotle probably subscribed to a general theory of cycles, and neither suggested that our knowledge or our moral capacity were limitless. Plato, in the *Timaeus*, developed a mild theory of development within cycles that might be characterized as a precursor to later conceptions in which the image of the spiral replaced that of the cycle. Aristotle, in the *Nicomachean Ethics*, makes an interesting observation that was to be reflected often in later ages in discussions of moral and material progress:

> Happiness must be a kind of Contemplative Speculation; [he says] but since it is Man we are speaking of, he will need likewise External Prosperity, because his Nature is not by itself sufficient for Speculation, but there must be health of body, and nourishment, and tendance of all kinds.
>
> However, it must not be thought, because without external goods a man cannot enjoy high Happiness, that therefore he will require many and great goods in order to be happy.[8]

Indeed, the pursuit of moral progress as an ideal superior to material progress emerges from both Plato and Aristotle, particularly in Plato's most famous work and arguably the most famous work of philosophy ever written, *The Republic*. Here Plato sets out what we might now characterize as an ideal type of moral city, founded on his conceptions of justice in the relations that bind men to men and all to the community. There are endless arguments as to whether Plato was a 'progressive' or to the extent of his belief in one sort of progress or another, but the very fact that in *The Republic* and also in *The Laws* he took the trouble to consider how best societies might be organized to accommodate all the citizens is enough to demonstrate that he thought some improvement to be possible and desirable. However much we may disagree with some or all of his conclusions, his enterprise is undoubtedly relevant to the sources from which later theories of progress derived. But this attempt to specify the good society was the result of reflection rather than experiment, and was a reflection that concluded in something like certainty. This is strikingly confirmed by Edelstein in the case of Aristotle too: 'Man's craving for infinity can be satisfied not by striving endlessly for more things and new insights but only within the confines of his inner life by thinking the truth, i.e., thinking immortal thoughts.'[9] Thus must the statement above be interpreted.

Though this attitude is not necessarily hostile to science as such, it would appear to lead to some types of science and methods rather than others. The Greek predilection for deduction, more true for Plato than Aristotle, led to a general underestimation of inductive and probabilistic reasoning. There was no Greek science of statistics, and the Greeks did not fully conceive of technology in terms of man's control over nature. They did not interfere with nature.*

These complex interrelations amongst strands in some ideas of progress in antiquity are balanced by what appears to be a genuine anti-progressive school of thought which developed around the Cynics, and especially from the founder of the school, Diogenes, who lived in the fourth century B.C. Diogenes, who resembles no one more than Rousseau in his reasons for and expressions of disapproval towards the arts and science, or science and technology as we would say nowadays, advocated the attainment of simple virtues through the living of the simple life. The story told of his reply to Alexander the Great when the latter asked if he desired any favour attests to his sincerity and also provides *one* model of the relations between the intellectual and the state. Diogenes said to the great man: 'Only to stand out of my light.'

* I am indebted to Professor Sambursky for a most illuminating discussion of these topics and particularly for these last points.

Apart from the very important context of the role of science and technology in the increasing destructiveness of warfare, it is not clear exactly what deleterious effects of science and technology Diogenes had in mind. The complete rejection of civilization that the Cynics saw as the only way to full virtue, entailing that they live (literally) like dogs, is an extreme form of anti-progressive thought that functions usefully to throw the various and modified forms of progress that we have observed into a proper perspective.

It is probably true to say that, in the final analysis, the motivation for any ideas of progress that have been found in the thought of antiquity did not come principally or even to any very substantial degree from ancient science. As has been suggested, this is in no way to deny the significant achievements of ancient science, but to insist that the relations between science and technology and the structure of society were minimal.

Perhaps a more weighty motivation for ideas of progress lay in the second great historical conception of antiquity—a belief that some messianic intervention in human affairs would bring salvation to men. In its most highly developed form this is, of course, the particularly Judeo-Christian contribution to the movements of thought that both promised progress and at the same time prevented men from fully articulating theories of progress.

Jules Delvaille emphasizes the progressive role of the Hebrew prophet in contrast to the supposed resignation of the Greeks and the Romans. The prophet, Delvaille claims, 'did not admit this humiliating resignation to exterior events; he felt in himself the liberty to choose between good and evil, to realize the one and to diminish the other. For that, he is a man of progress'[10] (my translation).

The importance of this notion of salvation or that of Providence cannot be overrated for the subsequent development of the idea of progress, especially with regard to the case of the *philosophes* of eighteenth-century France. The most powerful formulation of this theological world-view is to be found in the work of the fifth-century churchman, Saint Augustine, and particularly in *The City of God*. This need not be looked upon as a non-progressive (much less as an anti-progressive) tract, for the whole point of the distinction between the earthly city, the domain of evil, and the heavenly city, the domain of spiritual good, is that the latter represents an improvement over the former. It is not my intention to grapple here with the metaphysics of Augustine's system, but it should be pointed out that the journey from the city of man to the city of God, even on earth, was a journey of moral and spiritual progress. Material progress, in this scheme, is somewhat irrelevant.

The whole topic of Utopian thought, very much a part and at the same time a source of Millenarian ideas, played a not unimportant role in the background of the idea of progress up to and including the eighteenth century,[12] though in some forms the idea of progress has outgrown its Utopian heritage. It is after all hardly possible to enunciate a Utopian theory without subsuming some idea of progress, though it is perfectly possible once having attained an idea of progress to reject any utopian notions. There is a relation of one-way implication between utopia and progress.

Yet another impetus to the development of the conditions for an idea of progress is furnished by the reaction to primitivist thought. George Boas has shown how anti-primitivism can be construed as suggesting notions of progress in the works of the Christian poet Prudentius, of the fifth-century John Scotus and of others, while Origen and Saint Augustine actually praise technical progress as such.[13] Generally, however, these intimations of progress are more often than not concerned with religious progress as in the theory of Joachim of Florus, who envisaged the development of man through an age of the flesh, by way of a transitional age, to the final age of the spirit.

In spite of the large number of instances when something approaching an idea of progress seemed imminent before the sixteenth century, it would be churlish to disagree *completely* with Bury's view that the idea (in some forms at least) is ideologically excluded by the conditions of the ante-modern, that is the pre-sixteenth-century, world. However, a more reasonable and more accurate portrayal of the situation is given by Flint when he asserts:

> It was only with that radical change in the attitude, direction, and methods of thought, of which the Renaissance and the Reformation were the first conspicuous manifestations, that the idea of progress could enter into the stage of development in which *its significance in all departments of science and existence* has gradually come to be recognized [my emphasis].*[14]

In the ten centuries that span the divide between the city of Athens and the city of God, the spirit of pessimism slowly gave way to one of spiritual optimism. Just as some Ancient Greeks had explained their degeneration by the legend of the theft of the arts by

---

* Recent classical scholarship tends to support this position. Books by Havelock, Guthrie and Cole (in addition to that of Edelstein discussed above) argue that the Greeks and the Romans did have *some* meaningful and important notions of progress. The matter is put in a sober perspective by E. R. Dodds (in his review of Edelstein's *The Idea of Progress in Classical Antiquity*) in *Journal for the History of Ideas*, 29 (1968), pp. 453-7.

As I shall go on to argue in Chapter VII, the distinction between innovational and non-innovational modes of progress, defined in the Introduction, helps in an understanding and resolution of this type of controversy. (See also Chapter VI.)

Prometheus from the wrathful gods, the Christians took heart from the promise of an indefinite but certain redemption, and could look forward to an eternal paradise of the soul if not the body. The ideology of decline had to be replaced by an ideology of providential salvation before man could properly start to conceive in any permanent fashion of the improvement of his moral and spiritual lot and his material conditions.*

The threshold of the 'modern' world

There is a gap of about one thousand years from the time of Saint Augustine to what can be considered the threshold of the modern world. It is not until the sixteenth century and the work of Jean Bodin that a real advance can be said to have been made in the study of history.

However, it is only proper to mention the names of Roger Bacon, for his contributions to medieval philosophy of science, and Ibn Khaldun, the great Berber historiographer, for his analysis of, amongst other things, the place of conflict in social change and development. But they were of another, previous, world.

The French historiographer of the sixteenth century, Jean Bodin, was perhaps the last of the philosophers of history who was not fully aware of the implications of a theory of progress. Progress there had been, as Bodin both realized and specifically pointed out, but in the past and in the present. His three-stage geo-political theory of the development of mankind nowhere breaks through to the essential intuition of speculation on future states of affairs, and so he is left with a theory of cycles rather than one of progress as such.

What Bodin did accomplish, on the other hand, was very important for the subsequent development of history and the historical approach to the idea of progress.[15] Franklin presents a most convincing case to the effect that Bodin's methodology of history can be interpreted as a bulwark against historical 'pyrrhonism', which Bodin found necessary to refute in order to build up his reconstructed juristic science on the basis of a sound universal history. Of the sixteenth-century Pyrrhonists, Francesco Patrizzi was by far the most subtle. Patrizzi had argued that accurate history is quite impossible, as the 'good' historian, who must be both an original author and a neutral to prevent bias, is hardly likely to be told anything of real import. Neutrals have access to the public annals, it is true, as do

---

* I am content to leave the last word on this issue with Robert A. Nisbet, who says in *Social Change and History: Aspects of the Western Theory of Development* (New York; Oxford University Press, 1969, p. 41): 'I can think of no single misapprehension greater than that which says the Greeks were lacking in a sense of distant past and future, of slow, gradual and cumulative change in time.'

later historians, but, Patrizzi claims, no sensible statesman is going to disclose his secrets to either the neutral historian or the public annals.

The attempts of Melchior Cano and François Baudouin, contemporaries of Bodin, begged rather than answered the vital questions. Bodin himself did face the problem and in his proposed solution, contained in *Method for the Easy Comprehension of Histories* of 1566, he set forth what can accurately be called a methodology for the science of history.

Not only did Bodin give a comprehensive guide for the practice of historical research itself, but he also took the crucial step of condemning value-judgments in history. In this connection Bodin worked out a socio-psychological scheme whereby the value-bias of sources might be discovered. It is interesting to note that he considered that it was necessary on the basis of his methodological advances to reject all theories of historical decadence, but it is to a cyclic rather than a progress theory that he turns for his universal history.

Francis Bacon's architectonic *The Advancement of Learning* (first published in 1605) provided one of the models for the Encyclopaedia of d'Alembert and Diderot a century and a half later. Bacon's major contribution was to insist that utility is the proper end of knowledge. In this I would agree with Bury, but when he goes on to argue that Bacon falls short of a fully articulated theory of progress on the grounds that he never speaks of the indefinite duration of this progress, the question becomes debatable. Bacon comments (as Bury himself quotes) on 'an expectation of the further proficience and augmentation of all sciences; because it may seem they are ordained by God to be coevals, that is, to meet in one age.'[16] On the other hand, in Bacon's imaginary utopia, the New Atlantis, he describes a situation in which in spite of all the wonders of Salomon's House of scientific treasures, there are no less than *nine* categories of men devoted to further scientific research of one kind or another. Thus, if the Merchants of Light, the Depredators, the Mystery-men, the Pioneers, the Compilers, the Benefactors, the Lamps, the Inoculators, and the Interpreters of Nature are all necessary in the scientific utopia, it is surely reasonable to assume that Bacon did not consider the coevality of the sciences in some state of perfection to be at all imminent in sixteenth-century England.

It is not so much that Bacon almost achieved a theory of progress that is important, but that he introduced what has been called the 'New Philosophy', whose actual significance for the development of science has been coupled with the work of Newton. Lord Macaulay, a most severe critic of Bacon's character, puts this in the following words:

Some people may think the object of the Baconian philosophy a low object, but they cannot deny that, high or low, it has been attained. They cannot deny that every year makes an addition to what Bacon called 'fruit'. They cannot deny that mankind have made, and are making, great and constant progress in the road which he pointed out to them. Was there any such progressive movement among the ancient philosophers?[17]

Benjamin Farrington, in his study of Bacon as the philosopher of the emerging industrial society, concurs in Macaulay's judgment—that knowledge ought to bear fruit in science and industry is the great conception that Bacon bequeathed to the modern world. It is in Bacon more than in anyone else that the fundamental core of the Positivist method as propounded by Comte two hundred years later is to be found. Both men gave up the deeply disturbing problems of knowledge that had haunted the metaphysicians, and concentrated exclusively on observing the connections between things— what Macaulay suggested that some people might call a 'low object'.

Bacon's claim to have developed a full theory of progress is championed by Farrington, who asserts that 'he knew very well and repeatedly insisted that material progress would bring men no happiness at all unless it were governed by the sovereign virtue of love'.[18] Notwithstanding this statement, and indeed the testimony of Delvaille that Bacon had 'given a scientific theory of Progress',[19] Bury's more reserved judgment must stand. While no one would deny that Bacon had achieved a very clear notion of scientific progress, there is still a great deal of doubt as to whether he had any clear conception of social and moral progress, and the loose structure of Farrington's argument does not satisfy on this point. A perusal of the sections on conjugate and civil knowledge, towards the end of the *Advancement of Learning*, contrasts with the enlightened and progressive nature of Bacon's plans for the development of science in no uncertain manner. However, Bacon is certainly an important figure in the development of the idea of progress.

While carrying out a refrigeration experiment in 1626 Bacon caught a chill and died. Just eleven years later Descartes' *Discourse on Method* was published, possibly one of the most important books in the history of thought, and certainly a crucial work in the history of the idea of progress. In a sense, Descartes' argument for the supremacy of reason clinched the Battle of the Books for the Moderns (a battle, incidentally, which could hardly have been lost) before it began. As one commentator remarks, the debilitating theory of nature's decay, 'the antithesis of the idea of progress . . . bred a despairing resignation to an inexorable decree of fate',[20] on which the future of the West was balanced, and which the West largely rejected.

12

The method of Descartes may be split into two parts. Firstly, we must doubt everything of which we are not certain, and if we apply this principle to history and not simply to the present world around us, we can thereby derive the necessary strength to shake off the unwanted effects of the past. As Descartes himself says, 'We cannot better demonstrate the falseness of Aristotle's principles than by pointing out how they have been followed for several centuries without causing any progress in knowledge.'[21] Therefore, we reject those things that have no epistemological pay-off in certainty as well as those that have no scientific pay-off in utility. Once we have found something certain, in Descartes' case the *cogito*, then we may start to rebuild knowledge on this firm and confident foundation.

The second part of Descartes' procedure consisted in the claim that the criteria of the *cogito* were the clearness and the distinctness of the idea involved. Thus, he generalized this into the methodological principle that all clear and distinct ideas were true. Notwithstanding the very real philosophical difficulties of the notion of clear and distinct ideas, many of which Descartes himself recognized, the method of doubt and its complementary establishment of certainty cannot be overestimated in the history of Western thought. In many ways, for example in the standard of scientific parsimony that prefers the simpler and clearer explanation to the more complex and convoluted, the Cartesian Revolution did stand at the threshold of *modern* thought. Though Descartes nowhere articulated a theory of progress, the method of doubt and the criteria of clear and distinct ideas, almost a recipe for simple reason as compared to the elaborate niceties of scholasticism, suggested a break with the past. This break, on one level, was so complete that men could look only to the future to comprehend fully the changes that were about to take place in science, in the societies in which they lived, and in their ways of looking at the world.

The repercussions of the philosophy of Descartes were both particular and general. His own particular applications, especially in mathematics, were very important, and his influence on the subsequent discussion of a whole host of philosophical and scientific issues is marked.

However, it is with the more general repercussions that I am concerned here. The major of these was that theories of progress, specifically of science at first and then in a much wider scope, became almost inevitable. Already in or around 1647 Blaise Pascal was confidently saying that:

not only does each man advance from day to day in the
sciences, but all mankind together make continual progress in
proportion as the world grows older, since the same thing

13

happens in the succession of men as in the different ages of
single individuals,[22]

and this despite Pascal's Jansenist opposition to Descartes' religious
views.*

Also interesting in this context is the work of Perrault, whose
contribution to the Battle of the Books came down very firmly
though respectfully on the side of the moderns. Fontenelle, too,
expressed few doubts as to the scope of man's progress, and he even
improved on Pascal's optimism. Humanity, he exclaimed, 'will have
no old age . . . in other words, and to drop allegory, men will never
degenerate.'[23]

We are now of course well into the age of Protestantism, and no
examination of the idea of progress would be complete without some
mention of the Puritan notion of progress, and more particularly, of
the crucial shift from what might be termed the theological to the
secularized concept of progress that the *philosophes* in large part were
to complete in the eighteenth century.

In a most interesting study of theological attempts to construct a
theory of progress in the early eighteenth century, Ronald Crane
argues that progress was conceived of by the Anglican Apologetics
as a weapon against the anti-religious sentiment that was informing
a great deal of European philosophy at the end of the seventeenth
century.[24] This seemingly contradictory doctrine of conservative,
religious progressivism may be traced back to Tertullian and on
through the rejection of perpetual decay in the writings of Augustine
and Aquinas, to a large and almost forgotten work of George
Hakewill, published in 1627. The men who took the idea of progress
from this tradition, notably John Edwards, William Worthington
and Edmund Law, are in a significant sense the first group of thinkers
to articulate a complete theory of progress, in intent if not in fact.
These Anglicans, following Hakewill, were to take the crucial step of
distinguishing material from moral progress.

None of them denied the fact of progress in the arts and in the
sciences, indeed it was all around for them to see. 'Thus we surpass
all the times that have been before us; and it is highly probable that
those that succeed will far surpass all other epochs . . .,' suggests
John Edwards, and goes on to ask the rhetorical question, 'Why may
there not be expected a proportionable improvement in Divine
Knowledge, and in Moral and Christian Endowments?'[25] Religious
progress for these thinkers was of course something of a special case,
and on this account, Edwards' statement quoted above might be
ambiguous. Moral endowments, it might be argued, are Christian

---

* The fact that Pascal became less optimistic at a later date perhaps reflects the
very explosive and liberating influence that the ideas of Descartes had.

endowments, for Edwards. Crane, however, writing on Worthington, presents a more clear-cut picture. Accepting material progress, Worthington further held that 'a gradual improvement had also taken place in man's moral and spiritual condition and that the time would come when, even on this earth, all traces of the wickedness and corruption induced by Adam's original disobedience in Eden would disappear from human nature'.[26]

From this statement it is clear that religious progress, though certainly related in an important fashion to moral progress, and also not unrelated to material or scientific progress, is not the same thing as these others; it is separate but interconnected.[27] Perhaps, most significantly, for the first time it becomes possible to speak seriously of some total concept of progress that is seen to operate in the divergent spheres of human existence. The relations between the different aspects of progress are as yet only crudely spelled out, but the lines of future theoretical development of the idea of progress are by now established.

The separate category of religious progress that complicates the efforts of the Anglican Apologetics is an almost exclusively English* variety of the idea of progress. 'It was not, as in France, among the enemies of the church that the new philosophy chiefly took shape,' Crane concludes, 'but rather among its friends.'[28] It was to the *philosophes*, who in general had no need of the specific category of religious progress, that the task fell of constructing and disseminating the fuller and simpler, and eventually most influential, idea of progress, and it is to them that I turn in the next chapter.

---

* The difficulties of a Roman Catholic idea of progress are too obvious to require further comment. This, of course, does not prevent the Catholic thinker from holding some vague secular notion of progress.

II Progress and the European enlightenment

The eighteenth century, known in Europe as the age of enlightenment, by popular agreement marks something of a watershed in the history of thought. This is especially so with respect to social thought, and what are termed philosophies of history. In this chapter I shall examine the thought of this era in its distinctive French, German and British modes.

The philosophes

The French enlightenment, the age of the *philosophes*, has been characterized as 'the moment when the French rationalist movement made its juncture with the British empirical-analytic movement . . . primarily through Voltaire and at about 1730'.[1] It was not only the empiricist philosophy of Locke and his followers that impressed the French, but also the style of English society and the evident progress that had taken place there as compared to the stagnant French polity. It was not merely the achievements of the aged Newton that had excited Voltaire and his contemporaries, but also the respect in which the intellect and science were held in England. If it can be argued that no theory of progress could have been fully accepted in the Dark Ages because little actual progress could be seen, then, conversely, the progress in the sciences and in civil society that appeared clearly in England and to a lesser degree in other parts of Europe by the middle of the eighteenth century ensured the success of such theories.

The Royal Society in England and the Academy of Sciences in France were both well established by this time and, as a German historian of technology has said: 'quantitative natural science, based on the combination of experiment and reason began its triumphal march. . . . In this way a systematic rational technology, built on scientific discoveries, began its career in the cultural history of man.'[2]

The combination of the rise of science and the decline of certain forms of religion must be considered together in the complex development of the idea of progress. The theories of progress of the *philosophes* can be understood partially though not totally in terms of a reaction against centuries of religious intolerance and the stifling of thought that the medieval church had imposed. Collingwood explains that 'by the Enlightenment, *Aufklarung*, is meant that endeavour, so characteristic of the early eighteenth century, to secularize every department of human life and thought. It was a revolt not only against the power of institutional religion but against religion as such.'[3]

It was not only institutional religion that suffered at the hands of the new philosophers, but also the old establishment throughout French society. Pierre Bayle, the great sceptic of the seventeenth century, had done his work of destructive analysis well. His ruthless exposure of the weaknesses of the Ancients and the dogmatic Moderns had cleared the ground for the ideological revolution which was to lead, ninety years after his death, to the violent collapse and traumatic rebirth of France. 'Intellectual liberty,' Lecky says of Bayle, 'was the single subject which kindled his cold nature into something resembling enthusiasm.'[4] This could be the motto of the French enlightenment.

The mood of France in the middle of the eighteenth century, therefore, was one that was ripe for bold, new ideas, and the exponents of such ideas were rather less reticent about elaborating them in public than had been the case for many years. Flint dramatizes the situation as follows:

> Under Louis XIV the displeasure of the king involved ruin;
> under Louis XV, to criticize and ridicule the constituted
> authorities with dexterity and effect was the shortest and easiest
> route to fame.[5]

The decades around 1750 accordingly brought out an unprecedented array of social philosophies.

It was around this time that the extraordinary Abbé de Saint-Pierre was developing his projects for universal peace into what Bury was to describe as the point when 'we first find the theory widened in its compass to embrace progress towards social perfection'.[6] Saint-Pierre has stimulated recent interest due to the almost prophetic nature of his enlightened views on the importance of international organization and assembly for the maintenance of peace,[7] and his views on progress were just as original and significant. The motivating force of his progressivism lay in the numerous schemes for reform that he optimistically put forward, encouraged by the advances in science and its practical application. When men turned their sharp

C

attention to ethical and political matters, he argued, then the human race would see the full fruits of its progress.

Sainte-Pierre, however, was a pre-*philosophe*, for as Bury suggests his impact was minimized by his absorption in many partial projects, and his ideas, many of which were developed by the *Encyclopaedistes*, failed to cohere into the overall view of mankind that was the hallmark of those in France who followed him.

Three works in particular suggest these new conceptions of history from which subsequent theories of progress were to emerge. In 1748 Montesquieu's *Spirit of Laws* appeared, followed two years later by Turgot's *Discourses at the Sorbonne**, and in 1756 Voltaire published his *Essay on the Manners and Spirit of Nations*.

In some ways Montesquieu and Voltaire were very much opposed, in spite of the shared critical spirit that stimulated their works. Montesquieu contributed to the study of history (perhaps even more in his *Persian Letters* than in *Spirit of Laws*) a profoundly relativist approach. This was to have important consequences for the general critique of the idea of progress at a later stage, though Montesquieu himself never utilized this notion. Voltaire, on the other hand, emphasized the possibility of progress for the individual mind, and his attack on institutionalized evils, especially the church, is largely an attempt to point out the obstacles to progress that existed in his society. Any theory of progress that Voltaire might have wished to construct would have been somewhat empty, however, as he attributed a very prominent role to chance in the historical process. Perhaps Voltaire's attitude is best summed up in his own words. At the end of a discussion on the relative merits of the Ancients and the Moderns, in a very real sense the battle for the idea of progress, Voltaire comments with admirable balance: 'happy is he who is sensible to the merits of the Ancients and the Moderns, appreciates their beauties, knows their faults, and pardons them.'[8]

Giambattista Vico, the Italian who attempted to establish a New Science of history, was another writer whose ideas, published in the first half of the eighteenth century, provided some framework essential for treating history in terms of knowable laws. Although not widely read in France, Montesquieu seems to have known of him. Vico's cyclical theory of history is in no important sense a theory of progress. However, along with Montesquieu and Voltaire, his reflections helped to set a scene in which the development of theories of progress might take place.

Most scholars are agreed that the first really 'modern' and complete theory of progress is to be found in Turgot's lectures on the successive advances of the human mind, delivered at the Sorbonne. All the

---

* Delivered in 1750, these discourses were not published till the nineteenth century.

necessary elements of a theory of progress, each previously advanced at one time or another but never before welded together into a full theory, are present. Turgot held that culture was continually evolving due to the interaction of several factors, and though he recognized the diversity of mankind and of the circumstances in which men lived, he posited the essential unity and fixity of human nature. Neither is he blind to the undeniable historical fact that the course of progress is rarely smooth and that men advance at widely differing rates. Not only progress in the past and present, but also the inevitable and ultimately the perfect progress of the future awaited man. The law of three stages, popularized by Comte almost a century later, is to be found, albeit in a less systematic form, in the pages of Turgot.

The basic and simple epistemological insights that run through this theory of progress, and are most important for any theory of this nature, are the distinctions between the good and the evil in human institutions and between the essential and the accidental in things. On these criteria, which of course themselves require internal criteria, Turgot achieves a conception of social progress as a consequence of intellectual achievement.

A notable and original element in Turgot's theory of progress is the realization that the advance of the sciences and the arts actually relieves man from his bondage to nature, and that the progress of society thus becomes a self-perpetuating process. Progress engenders

> ... that leisure whereby genius, relieved of the burden of caring for primal needs, emerges from the narrow sphere where they confine it and directs all its energies towards the cultivation of the sciences; hence that more vigorous and more rapid advancement of the human mind, which bears along with it all parts of society, and which, in turn, receives new energy from their perfection. The passions develop along with genius. [9]

Here, then, a more fully articulated idea of progress has emerged: it not only echoes the reflections on the development of knowledge in general and the sciences in particular that have been noted in the work of Francis Bacon, but it also begins to trace out the wider social consequences of this progress in a serious fashion. The problem of moral progress and its relationship to material progress does not arise in any form other than the superficial recognition that not all change need necessarily be for the good.

Turgot shied clear of the implications of this position, as indeed did all of the eighteenth-century French progress theorists, and it was precisely this relation between material or intellectual progress and social or moral progress on which the nineteenth-century Positivists were to cut their teeth.

One can do no better than to follow Bury in his analysis of the development of the idea of progress among the Encyclopaedists. Both his emphasis on the 'anthropocentrism' of man at this period and his selection of the empiricist epistemology of Locke, turned to a more extreme sensationalism as the basis of the view of human nature, are extremely well founded. The latter point is particularly important. With the great increase in knowledge (whether trustworthy or not) of a vast number of societies, most of them primitive even by the standards of eighteenth-century Europe, it was natural that the *philosophes* should speculate as to the possibilities of cosmic universal progress, as contrasted with local and by now fairly obvious development. Bury writes:

> This doctrine of the possibility of indefinitely moulding the characters of men by laws and institutions—whether combined or not with a belief in the natural equality of men's faculties— laid a foundation on which the theory of the perfectibility of humanity could be raised. It marked, therefore, an important stage in the development of the doctrine of Progress.[10]

Diderot, Helvétius, the Baron d'Holbach, to mention only the most prominent, elaborated the theory of progress as found in the work of Turgot. The task of the Encyclopaedists, in this as in their major endeavour, was to spread the enlightenment rather than to create new knowledge, and to disseminate and to establish rather than to pioneer.

Of all the thinkers who influenced the French Revolution, none is more paradoxical nor has been more liable to stimulate contrary interpretations of his work than Rousseau. Both Flint and Bury see him as something of a cold hand on the warm heart of the enlightenment. Flint bluntly presents Rousseau defending the view that 'scien ces and arts had depraved the morals and the manners of mankind',[1] while Bury suggests that he was an optimist on the question of human nature and a pessimist on the question of civilization. Lovejoy, on the other hand, attempts to expose what he calls the 'supposed primitivism' of Rousseau's thought. He argues that the infamous state of nature is really best seen as a pre-political stage, and in fact this stage has four divisions, only the first of which is the 'state of nature'. Rousseau goes so far as to posit a 'law of necessary and gradual progress through natural causes',[12] which results in a transition from the state of nature into some other state. Rousseau of course saw the drawbacks of the inevitable and universal progress as advocated by those around him, and Lovejoy vividly portrays the dilemma: 'primitive man was healthy, placid, and good-natured, but absolutely stupid, non-social, and non-moral; ... civilized man is highly intelligent and morally responsible, but profoundly *méchant*, insincere, restless, and unhappy.'[13] Rousseau would wish that progress might ensure the best of both of these conditions, but feared that civilization was bringing about a sad combination of the worst. It must be concluded that Rousseau was probably as convinced of progress as the Encyclopaedists themselves but was more realistic in regarding it as, pragmatically, a mixed blessing. The idea of progress elicited no reactions of blind faith and unquestioning loyalty from Rousseau.

This is wittily expressed in a 'Dialogue on Progress' between Diderot and Rousseau written by Maurice Cranston and broadcast in 1966. In spite of the fact that Cranston presents Diderot as a little too optimistic and Rousseau as a little too pessimistic on the consequences of progress, the differences between Rousseau and the less critical representatives of eighteenth-century French thought are well caught by the following excerpt:

Diderot: ... knowledge has languished because religion, which is based on superstition, is hostile to science.

Rousseau: It is right to be hostile. Science grows up with men's vices. Indeed every science you can name has its roots in some moral defect. Arithmetic springs from avarice, physics from idle curiosity, mechanics from ambition. And this evil origin appears again in their purposes. If men were not unjust, what use would they have for jurisprudence? ...

Diderot: The value of science is clearly explained by Bacon: ... to diminish the poverty of man's life on earth by creating a new abundance.

Rousseau: Abundance? But that is to make things worse. Luxury is an evil in itself, and it has always been recognized by the wisest men as an especially corrupting evil. Frugality is necessary to a good and upright life in an individual, and for a strong and healthy state, ...

Diderot: 'Luxury' is your word. I did not use it, and neither did Bacon. ...[14];

And so on! But it was not only with Diderot and the Encyclopaedists that these differences arose.

The contrast between Rousseau and the last of the *philosophes*, as we might properly characterize the Marquis de Condorcet, is open and very pointed. Condorcet, who wrote his *Sketch for a Historical Picture of the Progress of the Human Mind* in 1793 while under great duress from pursuing revolutionaries, sums up the contemporary case for progress with unusual clarity, and, considering his precarious situation, with astonishing equanimity. Dividing the history of the world into ten stages, nine in the past and the tenth in the future,

Condorcet displays no doubt whatsoever of the inevitability of progress in all aspects of life on earth. By the power of reason and on the evidence of historical fact, Condorcet claims to have shown

> That nature has assigned no limit to the perfecting of the human faculties, that the perfectibility of man is truly indefinite; that the progress of this perfectibility, henceforth independent of any power that might wish to arrest it, has no other limit than the duration of the globe on which nature has placed us.[15]

Material progress, progress in the sciences and in the intellect in both scope and power, will lead without question to moral progress, to the good society which will make possible and inevitable equality between the nations and equality within the nations. Condorcet is hardly expressing original thought in his *Sketch*, but he does bring together many strains of the idea of progress into one powerful expression. There is, however, a point of special interest only hinted at by Condorcet, but nevertheless of crucial importance for the later development of the idea of progress in France. This was the role that history was to play in the theory.

In revolutionary times, and especially when the revolution is carried out on 'rational' premises, ideas as well as men tend to go through great changes of both a permanent and a temporary nature. Condorcet, as has been noted, based his reflections on future progress largely on past historical data. The key to the future, one might claim for him, lay in the past. The social revolution of 1789 fitted into this scheme as a culmination of the trends of the historical past, and paradoxically engendered the notion that progress operated best in conditions of stability and order. There was not long to wait before Comte had grasped this firmly, and was constructing a social theory on the twin bulwarks of order and progress.

It is a difficult task to attempt to sum up one of the most exciting and fruitful periods of social philosophical thought in recorded history—and this is no exaggerated account of the *philosophe* movement in eighteenth-century France. Certainly, the heuristic use of the idea of progress as an organizing principle of such a summary is in no way out of place. If the seventeenth century witnessed an investigation of progress in the sphere of natural knowledge, then as Sampson says, the philosophers of the eighteenth century 'extended the belief to include man's capacity to achieve moral and social progress'.[16] When treating the period in France as a whole, several general points in connection with the development of the idea of progress clearly merit attention.

It is necessary to investigate the ontological status of the concept as understood by the mainstream of the eighteenth-century French philosophers. The general impression that the enlightenment tends to give is that philosophy had become a very much more secular business. No longer is the philosopher necessarily the man of God; no longer is knowledge the possession solely of the divine. The rise of science and technology, unquestionably the single most important factor in the genesis of the 'modern' world, are usually taken to be inextricably bound up with this wholesale ideological revolution. It is, therefore, vital for an understanding of the thought of this period that its most cherished idea should be scrutinized to see exactly how far the theological past had been shaken off.

The *locus classicus* for this debate is to be found in Carl Becker's short but explosive *The Heavenly City of the Eighteenth Century Philosophers*. The main burden of Becker's polemic, having important implications for the sociology of knowledge as well as for the philosophy of science, is to demonstrate that:

the underlying preconceptions of eighteenth-century thought
were still, allowance made for certain important alterations
in the bias, essentially the same as those of the thirteenth
century ... the Philosophes demolished the Heavenly City of
St. Augustine only to rebuild it with more up-to-date materials.[17]

There are at least two aspects of this complex proposition, and it is as well to separate them at the start. On the one hand, Becker is suggesting that the supposedly pure, non-metaphysical, empirical 'hopes' of the *philosophes*, when confronted with the apparent wonder of experimental science, are sadly mistaken. This notion of the inevitability of metaphysical assumptions for science, or indeed for any human enterprise, is of direct relevance for the subsequent history of the idea of progress. On the other hand, Becker's argument leads one to entertain the strongest doubts about the success with which the *philosophes* managed to abolish God and general theological props in their enunciation of the eighteenth-century theories of progress.

As I have shown with reference to the Anglican Apologetics of the early eighteenth century, as documented by Crane, a theological basis is not necessarily inconsistent with a theory of progress, and religious progress may be conjoined with both material and moral progress. Therefore, it would seem to be a perfectly legitimate enterprise to investigate enlightenment theories of progress with an eye to detecting the smuggling-in of any theological notions; this is precisely the mode of Becker's attack.

The fulcrum of this attack was the notion of posterity, which, by the admission of Diderot himself, played the same role in enlightenment philosophy as the other world had played in religious philosophy. Under the heading of 'The Eschatology of Progress' Sampson sets this issue out in an illuminating fashion:

> If the *philosophes* were to succeed in their attempt to transfer men's aspirations from the eternal to the temporal, it was necessary that they should at least continue to affirm that life was not devoid of purpose and that there was reasonable hope of that purpose being brought to an earthly fulfilment. That they did in fact continue to affirm that the human story is one with a happy ending, is a tribute not to their insight into the psychology of the mass receptivity of ideals, but to the fact that their own fundamental assumptions had been irrevocably shaped by the very tradition they sought to repudiate.[18]

Posterity then was not an arguable point; it was an unquestioned assumption and the overriding optimism of the enlightenment could do nothing but attribute to it the most positive value. In a sense, the belief in posterity *was* the eighteenth-century optimism. It remains to be seen how far we can consider this as a 'heaven-substitute'.

If we take heaven to represent simply the place where everything works out properly, an important component of this being the distribution of just deserts, then posterity is clearly a heaven-substitute. When we link this up with the notion of providence, the force that inevitably directs the good man to heaven and makes heaven the place for good men, or the condition in which good men will spend eternity, then in the same way we may speak of progress as the inevitable force that directs men in the direction of an ever-more perfect posterity. There are of course differences as to the processes involved, the *philosophes* would no doubt claim. Condorcet for one suggests that reason is the total criterion of progress and that lack of social and moral progress comes under the same category as, say, error in the natural sciences. Reason, not faith, the enlightenment declares, is the shift involved in replacing heaven with posterity, providence with progress. But as Hume had shown with such relentless clarity, the methods and logical devices on which the natural sciences themselves are based, however operationally successful they might be, are in the same ultimately leaky boat of uncertainty and prejudice as were the more obviously intuitionist and revelatory methods of the theologians.

The so-called historical sciences, proto-scientistic social philosophy in particular, were in the worst possible situation. They had generally neither the heuristic claims of the natural sciences nor the traditional, albeit battered, authority of religious doctrine. On this view, the idea of progress is the 'good fairy' of the enlightenment philosophers!

This is, admittedly, an extreme position, but one that is a necessary corrective to the loose and self-deceiving 'humanist' optimism of the eighteenth-century *philosophes*. Part of the trouble, especially connected to the lack of rigour of the various theories, is the fact that the pre-revolutionaries were unable to take the large step back which would have enabled them to cast a long cool look on science as their nineteenth-century counterparts, the Positivists, were able to do.

Reason, the intellect or the human mind itself were taken as the essential data in the explanation of progress, rather than the institution of science as such, though science was constantly, though very often obscurely, called upon to illustrate the largest points. Perhaps the *philosophes* were too near the undeniable conquest of experimental science to appreciate its institutional significance fully, and perhaps they were too much a part of the early sociology of science to be able to construct a sociology of science for themselves.

The ontological status of the idea of progress in eighteenth-century French philosophy was therefore much nearer that of the traditional theology than the *philosophes* either intended or admitted.

Germany and Britain

While the idea of progress undoubtedly received more attention in France in the eighteenth century than in any other European country, it was not by any means completely absent in the thought of German and British writers of this period. First let me briefly examine the incidence of the idea in German social philosophy.

What might nowadays be termed a conflict theory of progress appears in a short work by Kant, published in 1784. This is a series of nine propositions, each of which is augmented by a commentary, tending towards a view of history as a teleological and gradually evolving process in which the species as a whole rather than man in the particular instance progresses. In his fourth proposition Kant speaks of 'the mutual antagonism [of men] in society' as the means whereby nature develops all the capacities of mankind, and through which, on the attainment of order 'regulated by law', human progress occurs.

Kant is noticeably far more conscious of the actual role of social and political institutions in this process than his French counterparts, but still displays the metaphysical reliance on some higher, almost mystical helping hand which guides and gives purpose to man's perennial search for progress in the material and moral spheres. His eighth proposition expresses these points well:

> The history of the human race, viewed as a whole, may be
> regarded as the realization of *a hidden plan of nature* to bring
> about a political constitution, internally, and, for this purpose,
> also externally perfect, as the only state in which all the
> capacities implanted in her by mankind can be fully developed[19]
> [my emphasis].

The direct stimulus for Kant's foray into the darkness of the philosophy of history was the publication of the first volume of a massive universal history, *Ideen zur Philosophie der Geschichte der Menscheit*, by his former pupil at Konigsberg, J. G. Herder. It is with this historically underrated figure that, in many respects, we can begin to note some significant development away from the most obvious naïveties of the enlightenment philosophers of history. Space does not allow me to do more than mention in passing the strikingly modern aspects of Herder's anthropology and his reflections on nationalism. In his theory of progress the temper is clearly an advance on those with which I have previously dealt.

In the first place, Herder makes a supreme attempt to rid himself of the crude ethnocentrism that plagued European 'universal' histories. As Walsh has noted, it may be said that Herder invented the idea of *a* civilization, against the notion of civilization as such,[20] and this was to have special importance for his conception of progress. Each nation, Herder argued, bound by its common language and general cultural tradition, must be seen and evaluated on its own terms. It is significant here that Herder completely rejected the notion that the past was all darkness and the present was all light, and also propounded the methodological dictum that the only possible objectivity was a *relative* objectivity in matters of historical interpretation. It is not surprising then that he did not commit himself to a theory of inevitable linear progress.

The theory to which he did commit himself hovered between an 'identification of the idea of development with the idea of moral progress',[21] and a more considered analysis of the relationship between reason and knowledge on the one hand and the happiness of mankind on the other.

> In proportion as reason increases among mankind [he asserts in the *Ideen*] men must learn from their infancy to perceive that there is a finer greatness than the inhuman greatness of tyrants, and that it is better as well as harder to cultivate a country than to ravage it, to found a city than to destroy one.[22]

This learning is essentially what he means by *Humanität*, the manifestation of human striving, of which progress is, in the words of a recent commentator on Herder, 'a relative operative ideal'.[23]

The strength of Herder's idea of progress is perhaps best demonstrated when it is pointed out that he not only anticipated Kant, who incidentally reviewed the *Ideen* in a most hostile and sarcastic fashion, but that he also anticipated Comte, though these make uncertain bedfellows and their combination gives an apparent ambiguity to Herder's account. He shared with Kant an appreciation of the part that conflict was to play in any theory of progress of mankind, and with Comte he shared an appreciation of the role of tradition and order. It is most striking that Barnard, who does not note the similarity with Comte in this respect, should characterize Herder's position in the following words:

> For progress, if it was to have enduring effects, had to be a concomitant of social *growth*; it had to emerge, that is, out of a given social tradition. Without tradition, progress was like a plant without roots ... tradition without progress was like a plant without water.[24]

It is difficult, therefore, to concur entirely with Professor Berlin when he suggests that Herder struck a blow at the idea of progress.[25] That Herder rejected the naïve optimism of the *philosophe* view of progress is indeed true, as was noted above, and there is no doubt that he set out consciously to undermine the complacency that underlay this attitude to social change. But in doing this, vague and diffuse and vacillating as he was, he made a beginning in the arduous and (it may be added) traumatic task of delivering the idea of progress from its largely idyllic childhood into the hard world.

The single most important aspect of Herder's theory of progress is his attempt not simply to assume its inevitability in one form or another but to give some guide as to how one might empirically identify it. That this guide is in characteristically problematical terms of the 'effect of changing influences and conditions upon the formation and development of human propensities and to establish whether these reveal a degree of continuity in their purposive direction',[26] is less significant than the fact that he did initiate a sort of 'inductive sociology' to deal with the problem of progress.

Herder did not draw a firm line between material and moral progress, though it is fair to comment that he was aware that they were to be distinguished and not identified or carelessly run together. The line of his theory of progress, however, shows a development of thought in the question of what is to count as progress that was to be taken up and elaborated unacknowledged, or more probably unwittingly, by the positivist philosophers and, as so often happens in the history of ideas, very much transformed.

Of the remaining German philosophers of this period only Schiller, Fichte and Schelling can be briefly mentioned here. Schiller and Fichte tread the same mainly progressive paths as Kant, who exerted great influence on them both. Schiller's major original contribution lies in his elaboration of the institutional bases of human progress, whereas Fichte may be regarded as a half-way stage between Kant and Hegel, primarily through his introduction of what Collingwood terms 'the dynamic plan' in history. Schelling, closely related intellectually to Hegel, breaks through finally to the notion of history as the absolute, a notion that Hegel was later to build into one of the most powerful philosophies of history of the nineteenth century.

The philosophy of history was a rather less serious affair in Britain than in either Germany or France in the eighteenth century. Once again Bury's remarks throw light on why this should have been so. England as compared to France, Bury says, 'had her revolution behind her ... enjoyed what were then considered large political liberties ... [and] English thinkers were generally inclined to hold, with Locke, that the proper function of government is principally negative.'[27] The idea of progress, however, appeared usually in a mild form, either as a modification of the French optimism, as in the speculations of Gibbon, or as a more home-grown product like the theory of economic and social progress that burst out with the publication in 1776 of Adam Smith's *The Wealth of Nations*.

The French Revolution inspired lively and important debates in England. Burke, Paine and Godwin are only the most prominent of those whose philosophical works were directly or indirectly stimulated by the events of 1789. Godwin, the most original of the three, had followed the initial pessimism of Rousseau concerning the ways in which civilization tends to corrupt man, but, bolder than Rousseau, he goes on to draw out a theory of the perfectibility of man. Godwin claims that government, not civilization as such, is the evil—eliminate this and progress and perfectibility are assured. Godwin's anarchism and unflinching faith in future good did not wait long for an answer. Before the century was over an English clergyman had given notice of possibly impending doom.

Thomas Robert Malthus wrote his *Essay on the Principle of Population*, first published in 1798, as a counter-argument to the Godwinian views expressed by his own father. The great weakness in the theory of Godwin, and in most of the French attempts to construct theories of progress, Malthus argues, is the neglect of the *problem* of population. Both Godwin and Condorcet blatantly gloss it over and refuse to acknowledge that upon its solution rests the viability of their theories. Malthus puts the case very simply: the means of subsistence on earth increases in arithmetic ratio, the population increases in geometric ratio, thus in three hundred years the population would be to the means of subsistence, starting from unity at intervals of twenty-five years, as 4,096 to 13. Something was obviously required to be done about this catastrophic state of affairs, and Malthus advocates on the preventive side 'moral restraint' on the part of individuals to bring down the birth rate, and further opines that vice and misery, what he terms the 'positive checks', will do the rest to ensure survival. Put in these terms it is plain that Malthus can be regarded as a forerunner of some important notions to be found more fully developed by the Social Darwinists.

As Levin has pointed out in a recent study,[28] it is mistaken to be overwhelmed by Malthus's pessimism. It is instructive to call attention to the similarity of the theory of Malthus to that of Kant. Both men realize that progress is not to be easily or cheaply attained. Kant shows clearly that conflict is necessary for progressive development. Likewise, Malthus sees that difficult obstacles have to be overcome before progress, in which he most certainly believes, can properly take significant effect. The issue of population for Malthus, and the difficulty of men finding good government for Kant, exemplify the possibilities of limited rather than inevitable and indefinite progress as these two thinkers conceived it.

Even more important than the intellectual development in England in the eighteenth century was that which occurred to the North, and has come to be known as the 'Scottish Enlightenment'. Were it only for David Hume and Adam Smith, the greatest philosopher and the greatest political economist of the century respectively, this period in the thought of Scotland might most justly be noted, but in fact there were several contemporaries of Hume and Smith who made important contributions to the idea of progress. Not least amongst these was Adam Ferguson, the Edinburgh professor who has been hailed by a number of historians of ideas as one of the important precursors of modern sociology.[29] It is in his theory of progress that the general trends of the thought of this school can be found.

Ferguson organized his treatment of social development around the three stages of savagery, barbarism and civilization, and he argued that to pass from one stage to the next societies had to meet the needs that these changes called forth. But this was by no means a simply automatic process, for there were two main obstacles to progress, namely inclement physical or environmental conditions and despotism, a form of government that was almost wholly inimical to progress. Where neither of these limiting conditions was present then progress would take place. Ferguson was not entirely content to leave matters in this state and he attempted to give some reason why progress should take place at all.

> What does the species gain [he asked] in the result of
> commercial arts, and at the expense of so much invention and
> labour . . . we may observe, that progress itself is congenial to
> the nature of man; that whatever checks it is distress and
> oppression; whatever promotes it, is prosperity and freedom.[30]

This statement points to a most significant fact about the whole school of eighteenth-century Scottish social philosophers. These men considered that the foundation of a science of social man waited upon a satisfactory analysis of human nature, and so it was with human psychology and social psychology that the fundamentals of their

29

systems lay. The *nature of man*, therefore, is the mechanism behind human progress for Ferguson. I must add, however, that some speculations about the God of the eighteenth century lay behind the nature of man for Ferguson. Further, there is more than a suggestion that Ferguson's idea of progress was a basically conservative one, and conservative with respect to the commercial form of society in which he lived. The Scottish Enlightenment had gone hand-in-hand with a terrific development of the industrial and commercial life of Scotland.[31] Kettler in his recent study suggests that Ferguson's concept of 'virtue' in this context appears to be tailor-made for business society, and that Ferguson even 'suggested that the striving after "new things" was in itself a part of virtue'.[32] However, as Kettler goes on to make clear, Ferguson was not willing to call any change, commercial or otherwise, progress by definition, but insisted that the moral judgment always had to be made.

As was mentioned above, Ferguson considered that despotism presented an insufferable obstacle to progress, but he went on to choose 'mixed monarchy' rather than democracy as the form of government most suited to commercial development. It is not so much this choice of political system as the fact that he felt obliged to elaborate the *political* concomitants of progress that is significant here, and it is interesting that two other members of this school felt the same need.

David Hume, in his essay, 'Of the Rise and Progress of the Arts and Sciences', first published in 1742, takes the opposite choice to that of Ferguson. 'It is impossible,' Hume asserts, 'for the arts and sciences to arise, at first, among any people, unless that people enjoy the blessing of a free government.'[33] He goes on to comment that refined taste, the polite arts, prosper under a monarchy, whereas the arts and sciences, which include religion, politics, metaphysics, morals and mathematics and natural philosophy, succeed best in a republic.

Again, Dugald Stewart, writing at the end of the century, opines that 'the provisions which nature has made for the intellectual and moral progress of the species, all suppose the existence of the political union'.[34] Stewart's theory of progress though not as specifically thought out as that of Ferguson, is not unlike it in its reliance on the progressive account of human nature guided by some 'invisible hand'.[35] But what links these three philosophers together in their conception of progress, and indeed runs through the whole school, is the explicit recognition of the political or what we would certainly today call the sociologically political concomitants of progress in society.

It has been said that the study of man consists in the picking out of the obvious. Be this as it may, it is highly significant that one of the vast array of obvious facts rather than another is selected by any individual or school for special attention. It is with the Scottish Enlightenment, and perhaps most particularly with the work of Ferguson, that the idea of progress begins to take on a specifically sociological significance in contrast to what may be termed the 'philosophy of history' approach it had up till then followed.*

There is, it is true, still no systematic attempt to distinguish material and moral progress in the works of the Scottish philosophers, but it can be said that they, along with Herder, were poised on the brink of the deeper analysis of progress that was to appear in the efforts of some of the nineteenth-century writers who benefited from the successive sharpening of the ways in which the problems were set out.

One or two further points should be made in this context. Hume, for example, shows the not uncommon tendency to vacillate between a cyclical theory of progress, as in his essay on Arts and Sciences referred to above, and a more linear theory, which may be derived from his 'Political Discourses' of 1752.[36]

Lord Kames, another member of the school, is notable for his reconciliation of a mild primitivism with a fairly ardent progressivism on the basis that the catastrophe attendant on the tower of Babel justifies these apparently contradictory positions.[37] This line of reasoning sounds less blatantly fanciful in an age threatened with the mass extinction of the human race through particular scientific progress and the general failure of human communication than it otherwise might.

Even Lord Monboddo, the most primitivist member of the school and perhaps its most eccentric, was not so totally out of touch with his contemporaries that he did not espouse a mild theory of progress. Gladys Bryson sums up the matter well, when she says:

> with the Scots, the conception of progress was the more
> favoured [than that of primitivism], though they were not
> always logically consistent in their judgment, and were frequently
> regretful that progress seemed to bring in its train some very
> undesirable concomitants.[38]

It is true to say that by the end of the eighteenth century the idea of progress was part of the intellectual vocabulary of Europe. It is also true to say that for all but a very few the notion of progress was an assumption, implicit or explicit, without which no work in social philosophy and history could begin. Even Burke, the most adamant critic of the French Revolution and the principles it purported to

* Thus, I must conclude that Bury's remark that an analysis of the work of Ferguson would not help the student of the development of the idea of progress who had already consulted Hume and Smith (Bury, op. cit., p. 221) is misleading.

embody, operates on a mild theory of progress, a gradual social evolution, in which future progress evolves from the tradition of the past and the wisdom of political experience. Taking into consideration the local differences and variations for which reasons have been suggested, it is legitimate to look at the idea of progress as it swept Europe as a whole and to inquire further into the more important factors in its flowering at that time.

The most obvious and the most widely documented factor is of course the rise of science and technology. Not surprisingly, most thinkers used at least a rough model of scientific progress for the explanation of social and moral progress, as has been documented briefly in the foregoing review. It is thus pertinent to make a few observations on this crucial topic before turning to its extreme and particular development in scientistic positivism.

Science, broadly and loosely speaking, has a lasting and diffuse effect on society only when it is institutionalized. Science and technology can be said to be institutionalized when their organization is linked in important ways to the organization of other major social institutions like education, the occupational structure, the economy, the military, and so on, and where the consequences of activities within science and technology are important for these other institutions and vice versa. This is not to say that individual scientists and craftsmen-inventors working alone or under specific sponsorship cannot do important and influential things. But for science to develop internally, then certain external factors relative to what might be termed 'the social system of science' must come into operation. In a sense, scientific progress is a superfluous expression; progress appears to be redundant here, for it is almost, if not entirely, impossible to conceive of a non-progressive science. (One highly popular methodology argues that the task of science is a continual attempt to falsify hypotheses and would certainly claim that this is progressive by nature.)[39] Therefore, scientific progress is to be understood in this context as the progress of society under the impact of science, leading simply to material progress. Material progress then entails scientific progress, but the relation does not hold in the opposite direction, and the institutionalization of science is the most important condition of material progress. Conversely, given the institutionalization of science then scientific progress will lead inevitably to material progress. The degrees of such progress and the time scales involved are empirical problems of great importance for the study of social change in modern societies.

Although it is extremely difficult to fix dates to such a large event, there is evidence to suggest that the decades around the year 1800 may be considered the period of the institutionalization of science in Europe. The French Revolution had brought the scientists Carnot and Monge into government and had thus opened the door to a collaboration between these two sectors of social life that was to grow to enormous proportions.[40] Secondly, also in France at this time, a decisive step was taken to set the pattern for scientific education that was to provide this collaboration between science and government with trained manpower. In 1795 the *Ecole Polytechnique* was opened as a school for technical and scientific study, and before long most of the major cities in Europe had followed the lead of Paris and had set up their own equivalents.[41]

Therefore, although it is fair to say that science and the particular methods it used were established during the period of the *philosophes* and the eighteenth-century theorists of progress generally, the actual *institutionalization* of science took place after the French Revolution and almost certainly as a consequence, to a greater or lesser degree, of precisely these theories of progress and the progressive intellectual climate that they could not but engender. In pointing out that none of the eighteenth-century theorists succeeded in painting a very convincing picture of the ways in which scientific progress, as material progress, could lead to moral and social progress, I must emphasize that as yet science was only minimally institutionalized. By the middle of the nineteenth century those who wrote about society were in a position to elaborate a theory concerning the relations between scientific and social progress from an entirely different, and in some ways more endowed, point of view.

It is to these, the proponents of the idea of progress in the nineteenth century, that I now turn in the next chapter.

III Progress through order and progress through revolution: Comte and Marx

The fortunes of the idea of progress in the nineteenth century, for it was not yet to meet up with any significant misfortunes, are principally bound up with three major intellectual figures and the movements of thought which they willingly or unwillingly fathered. Accordingly, the discussion of this chapter will revolve around Comte and the growth of positivism and Marx and the growth of Marxism. In the next chapter, Darwin and what came to be known as social Darwinism will be examined. If Marx is supposed to have said to the workers of Amsterdam, 'Je ne suis pas marxiste', it is even more certain that Charles Darwin would have vigorously disclaimed paternity of the excesses of some of his self-titled disciples.

Different as the original theories of these three men were in both content and intention, it is nevertheless true to say that each in its fashion was an attempt to grapple with the problems of human and social development and the directions that they took.* It was therefore inevitable that each of these theories operated with some conception of progress, and in fact, each made extremely important contributions to its history. The major contribution, and one which paradoxically led in no small measure to the subsequent wholesale rejection of the optimistic eighteenth-century view of progress, was the uneasy realization that the relation between material and scientific progress on the one hand, and social and moral progress on the other, did present a problem. It is the proposed solutions to this problem, with which the eighteenth century was replete, that this chapter sets out to investigate and to begin to evaluate.

* This is not strictly true of Darwin himself, though it is certainly true of the social Darwinists. Perhaps the name of Spencer might be substituted here for that of Darwin.

*Comte and the idea of progress**

It is no overstatement of the case to say that the idea of progress is the cornerstone of the Comtean system. It is certainly the basis of his Law of the Three Stages, and without it one cannot fully appreciate his notion of the hierarchy of the sciences. Furthermore, his distinction between the static and the dynamic aspects of sociology is in its most important sense a working out of the distinction and the relations between order and progress.

Comte defines progress, in the *System of Positive Polity*, as 'a gradual amelioration of some fundamental Order, by a series of modifications gradually tending to the completion of one design'.[1] Three elements may be derived from this definition and each is developed at great length throughout the volumes of positivism. The first element, a natural condition that is to improve, is inherent in the Law of the Three States. Briefly stated, it is 'that each of our leading conceptions—each branch of our knowledge—passes successively through three different theoretical conditions: the Theological, or fictitious; the Metaphysical, or abstract, and the Scientific, or positive'.[2] There is no doubt whatsoever that Comte approved of this inevitable and iron law of the progression of the human mind and of the societal types that it necessarily engenders. For Comte, industrial and scientific society follows from theological society as surely as communist society follows from capitalist society for Marx.

The second element in the definition of progress, really an aspect of the first, 'the completion of one design', is illuminated with reference to the classification of the sciences that Comte ambitiously sets up. The hierarchy of the sciences is intended to show the order in which the basic divisions of human knowledge can reach the positive stage. Comte places mathematics at the top of the list, followed by astronomy, physics, chemistry, biology, and finally social physics or sociology. The volumes of *The Positive Philosophy* are an elaboration on this theme: a history of the sciences as they have progressed from the theological stage to the positive by way of the transitional metaphysical state. As each discipline shakes off the fetters of the theological past, it becomes a true science, one that operates through the positive method, the only method of true science. This consists in the knowledge that 'the Positive Philosophy ... regards all phenomena as subjected to invariable natural *laws*', and that rather than vainly chasing after first causes, its 'real business is to analyse accurately the circumstances of phenomena, and to connect them by the natural relations of succession and resemblance'.[3] The reason why one science becomes positive, that is scientific, before another is to be found in the nature of the phenomena with which it is particularly

* An extended version of this section is published in *Inquiry*, 11 (October 1968), pp. 221-31.

concerned. The hierarchy can be set up, Comte claims, because the development of each science depends on the development of the one above it in the hierarchy.

The classification of the sciences is therefore a progression through a progression. Each science progresses internally through the three states of knowledge and takes its turn in the general progression of the whole substantive body of knowledge. In Comte's view all the sciences had become positive by the time that he wrote, and sociology had become positive by dint of his own efforts.

The third element in the definition of progress is the reference to the gradualness of the change. The motto of positivism is 'Progress through the development of Order', and this epigram sums up the approach that Comte took towards sociology as a science. Sociology, Comte suggested, was made up of social statics and social dynamics, the study of order and the study of progress. Social statics is in fact the essential link between biology, the preceding science, and social dynamics, the final science of society.

For someone who claimed to be the harbinger of the greatest revolution in thought in the history of man, Comte was fairly conservative—at most he was a gradual reformer of whom Burke might have approved. There is nothing in Comte to give the impression that the future has to be wrenched from the past, rather the development of society is to be seen in terms of 'Continuity in change and also of Unity in nature'.[4] Statics, and not dynamics as in the positive philosophy, is to be the primary emphasis of the *Positive Polity*, Comte's handbook of sociology. In sociology, however, one can make no strict split between statics and dynamics; they are to be seen as different sides of the same coin, the one meaningless without the other. They are, Comte says, 'in intimate harmony', and 'the statical study, and the dynamical study tend gradually to unite in one'. The conclusion to which Comte readily accedes is that 'we explain alternately the laws of Order by those of Progress, and the laws of Progress by those of Order'.*[5]

One weakness in Comte's thought in this respect should be pointed out. There appears to be nothing in his system that shows the necessity for sociological change to be gradual, 'a series of modifications', as he says in his definition of progress. In his *Preliminary Discourse on the Positive Spirit*, prefixed to his work on astronomy, Comte explains that 'the true Positive Spirit consists, above all in seeing in order to foresee, in studying what *is* in order to infer from it what *will be*, in accordance with the general dogma of the invariability of natural laws'.[6] This insistence on 'the general dogma of the invari-

---

* It is interesting to note the criticism of Comte in Parsons' *Structure of Social Action*, in which Comte's interest in both statics and dynamics is compared unfavourably to Durkheim's concentration on the former.

ability of natural laws' is not so much logically incompatible with a belief in gradual social change by means of a 'series of modifications', as sociologically unconvincing. Assuming that Comte considered these modifications to be within the power of man to achieve, and this seems to follow from the possibility of the positive method, then it appears that Comte combines a belief in social engineering with a belief in invariable natural laws operating in society. The difficulty in this position concerns the status of social experimentation and 'controlled change'.

It is difficult to reconcile the albeit properly scientific hit-and-miss attitude of the social engineer with Comte's view in the *Positive Polity* that 'Civilisation progresses according to a necessary Law . . . [and it] has, under every aspect, made constant progress'.[7]

The idea of progress, then, is essentially bound up with three of the most important points of Comtean thought. It is now in order to examine the different types of progress that Comte recognizes. In *The Positive Philosophy* it is suggested that 'the only idea of progress that is really proper to the revolutionary philosophy [Comte is probably referring specifically to the work of Condorcet], is that of the continuous extension of liberty; that is, in positive terms, the gradual expansion of human powers'.[8] However weak and limited this idea is, it seems to Comte to be the one most worth developing, for, as he goes on to say, 'this school [the revolutionary] is the only one that is always open to new action on behalf of progress.'[9] In fact, he does develop it in a most unexpected fashion.

As an initial concept-staking claim, Comte asserts in both *The Positive Philosophy* and the *Positive Polity* that, on the basis of his system, 'it is thus evident that the conception of progress *belongs exclusively* to the positive philosophy'[10] (my emphasis). This seemingly preposterous statement takes on a new and much more convincing light when we note that Comte is speaking not of one idea of progress, but of three. These are Practical progress (almost but not quite material) whose agency is Activity, Theoretical progress whose agency is Intellect, and Moral progress whose agency is Feeling. One would expect, on the basis of the positivist spirit, that practical progress would be unassailable as the true end of man. But no! And here Comte's work takes an important and far-reaching turn. 'Feeling,' exclaims Comte, 'is not only the essential spring of true progress, but also its main end, since our Moral amelioration is of much more importance, public as well as private, than any advance in either Speculation or Action.'[11]

Feeling, Affection, the Moral influences, then, are the 'main end' of progress—the rationale for the whole system. To celebrate this discovery Comte goes so far as to add a new science to his hierarchy of the positive branches of knowledge, that of the true science of Man, though this science ought ever to retain its sacred name of Morals . . . a sound Cerebral Theory, for Positivism, more than almost any other philosophy, emphasises the uses to which Knowledge can be applied in the world, the seventh and last gradation in the grand Hierarchy of Abstract Science is as distinctly defined as any of the others.[12]

Thus, when the positive stage has been reached, theory and practice both progress, as do all the sciences, towards the pinnacle of moral science attained through the progress of feeling. The three hierarchies—the Law of the Three States, the classification of the sciences, and the agencies of Activity, Intellect and Feeling—therefore indicate the complexity and fullness of Comte's idea of progress.

If sociology is the science of the collective mind or mental evolution, then Moral science will deal more with the individual mind and will be the logical conclusion to the search for knowledge—the measuring-rod for the progress of civilization.

In this progression of civilization, Intellect (theoretical progress) and Activity (practical progress) are to be considered as the handmaidens in the development of morals, in the evolution of Feeling. In a statement reminiscent of Hegel's view of the historical development of Freedom, Comte insists that 'The Social Instinct had to be purely civic in Antiquity, collective in the Middle Age, and universal in the Final State'[13] (italics in the original). We are justified in assuming, therefore, that in the way that the theological and the metaphysical states are as one compared to the vast difference between them and the positive scientific state, the practical and the theoretical modes of progress are as one compared to the moral progress brought about by the revolution in Feeling. The basis of this revolution in Feeling is generally taken to be material progress, taken in one place to be a fourth *type* of progress and in another to be almost a framework within which theoretical and practical progress operate.[14] The latter interpretation follows unmistakably from the contention that 'progress depends *directly* on the intellectual and active faculties alone'.[15]

Comte, therefore, either holds or is forced into holding the view that material and moral progress are the two essential types of progress, and that there is some necessary connection between them. *It is on this necessary connection that the Positivist case rests.* Several very important consequences for the idea of progress follow from Comte's views.

In the first place, the traditional (and to some extent the contemporary) distinction between material and moral progress must be redefined. In Comte's scheme the difference between moral and material progress rests on the different places that the sciences relative to each occupy in the hierarchy of the sciences. The fact that the science of morals is the last to fall under the positive method therefore brings ethics and the other sciences together in a way that suggests only that moral progress builds on the success of the material progress brought about by the application of the positive method to the other fields of study. The accomplishment of moral progress, for Comte, presents no special difficulties over and above those encountered in accomplishing material progress.

Secondly, following on from what has just been said, the 'problem of progress' is once and for all time solved. If one shares with Comte the belief that the positive method is uniquely suitable to all problems from those of astronomy to those of ethics, and that progress is achieved on realizing the method in its proper application to these problems, then moral progress presents *no* problems *methodologically* different from those of any other science in the hierarchy. There are obviously differences between sciences, but Comte's point is that these are *not* such that they require to be treated by different *methods*.

The problem of the relationship between material and moral progress is thus solved, for moral progress on this account follows necessarily from material progress, the progress in the sciences preceding it in the hierarchy.

Thirdly, Comte loosely takes progress to be synonymous with evolution. In the index to the *Positive Polity*, for example, the insertion for 'Evolution' reads 'see Progress'. Ginsberg points out that the terms 'progress', 'evolution', and 'development' have different though interconnected meanings. 'Development' he defines as 'a process whereby that which exists "potentially" becomes actual', and social 'evolution' as the process whereby 'new elements of culture can be shown to arise from the old by a process of diversification'. 'Progress' is 'development or evolution in a direction which satisfies rational criteria of value';[16] and so it is clear that these concepts can only be brought together with reference to some agreed standard, in Ginsberg's case the rational ethic. The logic of Comte's system gives him an agreed standard, namely that the positive method itself is a sufficient criterion of value, and so evolution and progress are identical. This is an inescapable conclusion for Comte—positive evolution, the only conceivable evolution, could hardly be unprogressive.

Each of these three consequences of Comte's positive idea of progress seems to me untenable. First, the Comtean case on progress, like the Marxist case on the inevitability of the proletarian revolution, is strictly non-empirical. Just as some Marxists claim that the revolution has not yet taken place because the objective conditions are not quite right, Comteans may argue that moral progress has not followed from material progress due to some betrayal of the positivist spirit.

These arguments are akin to that which states that 'x has not happened because y, defined or explained in terms of x, is not present'.

Secondly, the problems involved in accomplishing and/or measuring material and moral progress appear to have become more distinct as material-scientific progress has occurred. Some material-scientific progress obviously leads to moral good. The development of medicine is often a clear example of this. Some material-scientific progress appears to be irrelevant to moral progress. The programmes of space research seem to be in this category to a large extent. Nevertheless, some material-scientific progress either leads to moral regress or to situations that are, at least, morally questionable *on practically any theory of morals.* The development and use of technically sophisticated apparatus for genocide and torture will be regarded under this heading by those who accept the category of morality. Further, material-scientific progress can replace one evil by another, for example, where high rates of infant mortality are overcome and give rise to large, growing and starving populations. On the face of it, material-scientific progress necessarily leads to neither moral regress nor moral progress.

Thirdly, to equate progress with evolution is to deny that there is any real difference between them. Given Comte's definition of progress, only the term 'amelioration' creates difficulties. It is useful to distinguish between evaluative and non-evaluative terms in this context, for 'amelioration' suggests more than suitability to some environment, it is a judgment on this suitability to the environment. Comte is never happy when he has to distinguish the existential from the normative— one feels that Moral Science is meant to be a special science in a way that mathematics or even sociology is not. He never makes the clear distinction between science and morals that, for instance, Mill makes, though it is only fair to note that Acton suggests that Comte is on the whole more realistic than Mill on this matter.[17] So Comte lingers somewhere on the brink of the identity of fact and value in his analysis of the moral 'science', having returned, as it were, from over the brink in his social physic. Moral progress for Comte is something more than material progress, though his system hardly admits this, and progress is then bound to be something more than evolution.

Comte's theory of progress, and thus his whole system of sociology, may be severely criticized on all these counts, but as I have indicated, the great value of it lies in the complexity of the analysis of progress. Comte, perhaps more than any other theorist, indicates the necessity for new thinking on the distinction between material and moral progress.

Positivism and progress after Comte
The history of organized positivism after the death of Comte in

1857 revolved around personalities as much as ideas, for it was a religious sect rather than a philosophical school that remained to carry on the work of bringing about the Positivist society. Details of this story have been filled in for France,[18] England,[19] Germany,[20] the United States,[21] and South America,[22] and I shall content myself here with tracing out the particular effects that the Comtean idea of progress had for these later Positivists.

In the first place it is necessary to make some distinction between positivism and the scientism that seemed to be intimately bound up with it. Simon, in his meticulous study of nineteenth-century European positivism, restricts the latter term to the doctrines of Comte, and criticizes Charlton's wider definition or definitions of the term. The basic sense, 'philosophical positivism', Charlton defines as follows:

> It holds, in its simplest form, that, excepting knowledge of logical and mathematical systems—all of them without any necessary connexion with our observable world—science provides the model of the only kind of knowledge we can attain. All that we can know of reality is what we can observe or can legitimately deduce from what we observe.[23]

This is the root meaning of the positivism of Comte, and also of Mill, Charlton goes on to argue, and indeed his book is largely an account of the various defections from this 'ideal' which occurred in the work of the French philosophers of the Second Empire. This ideal then is positivism, and Charlton labels these defections from it, primarily in the lapses of Comte himself, Renan and Taine, as 'scientism'. This is most confusing, for 'scientism' is often used in precisely the same sense as Charlton uses 'philosophic positivism'. For example, Wellmuth, the Jesuit philosopher, defines scientism as

> the belief that science, in the modern sense of that term, and the scientific method as described by modern scientists, afford the only reliable natural means of acquiring such knowledge as may be available about whatever is real.[24]

Hayek speaks of scientism as a 'slavish imitation of the method and language of Science',[25] and lays the greater part of the blame for its currency on the heads of Saint-Simon and Comte, and he sees the twin daggers of scientism and positivism inseparably pointed at the heart of an understanding of society.

This is not simply a matter of words, for it was precisely this scientistic emphasis that gave the positivistic theory of progress of Comte and the Positivists its distinctive feature. Notwithstanding his theoretical debt to Turgot, Condorcet and Saint-Simon, Comte had actually set about doing what the others had only sketched or suggested. Comte, in fact, had set about constructing a science of society which was at the same time in all its essentials a theory of progress.

'When I speak of evolution and progress,' exclaimed Littré, who had broken with Comte over the Religion of Humanity but who still considered himself a 'true Positivist', 'I affirm a natural phenomenon; I am not merely spellbound by optimism . . . And since it is a natural phenomenon, chance must be excluded.'[26] Charlton's point is that the Comtean assimilation of 'la morale' as the seventh in the hierarchy of the sciences signifies a drift from positivism, as defined above, to scientism, which is nowhere strictly defined.* Therefore, any Positivist who accepts even the barest outline of the Comtean theory of progress, and this is surely a minimum requirement, must fall into scientism with the attempt to give a positivist answer to the problem of values. To avoid scientism then, the Positivist will have to keep his mouth shut or his pen dry or both!

From this tangle of ideas at least one thing is readily apparent. The idea of progress stands out most conspicuously in almost all French social philosophy of the nineteenth century, whether positivist or not, but more often than not it is the positivist-influenced theory that attracts special attention. Little is added to Comte's admittedly wide formulation, though it may be of some interest to select a few representative statements of post-Comtean theories of progress.

Littré's view has been referred to above; however, it is instructive to note that he considers man's progress as an 'actual ideal that requires knowledge (science and education), love (religion), beauty (fine arts), wealth (industry), and that in this manner contains all our individual, domestic and social existence, under its supreme guidance'[27] (my translation).

The case of Ernest Renan exemplifies better than most the metaphysical tendencies and implications of the positivist philosophy. Both Simon and Charlton as well as Flint and Bury point out the difference between Renan and Comte, and this hinges on Renan's ultimate rejection of science as a spiritually satisfying belief system. Renan's theories of progress slipped from the original Comtean position outlined above into an almost mystical and certainly religious conception, at once supernatural and superhuman, of progress embodied in a Christian-like God. However, for Charlton to characterize this as 'a turning-point in the history of the idea of progress',[28] on the fact that Renan places the end of progress outside man, seems an arbitrary judgment to say the least. What it does demonstrate is the instability of any theory of progress based on positivist-scientistic methodology in the broadest sense, for here pro-

---

* Discussing Claude Bernard, like Littré a true friend of positivism, Charlton comments on his rejection of 'the claim of scientism that science alone can offer a new ethic of life and reorder civilization'. Charlton (1959), op. cit., p. 81.

gress itself is always potentially the replacement for the God that this methodology sets out to banish.

The last Frenchman I shall mention in this context is the encyclopaedic Hippolyte Taine, not by any means a Comtean, but certainly a man whose later work might profitably be examined with relation to the positivist-scientistic tradition. Irving Babbitt has vividly recreated some of the tensions apparent in this enigmatic figure, showing how the vital impulse of his thought was to succumb finally to omnipotent mechanical law. In Taine's journey from disillusioned romanticism to scientific positivism we can almost see the life of Renan in reverse.[29] Both, however, meet similar difficulties because of their reluctance to give up either positivism or idealism, a choice that perhaps only Marx himself could carry through at this period (and, incidentally, Parsons at a later date).[30]

Taine nowhere elaborates a theory of progress as such, but he locates the sources of historical causation in race, epoch (*moment*), and surroundings (*milieu*). These are the causes, and the only possible causes, of what he terms 'moral motion', and moral no less than physical facts must be collected before one can start to look for causes. 'Given a literature, philosophy, society, art, group of arts,' Taine asks, 'what is the moral condition which produced it? What are the conditions of race, epoch, circumstance, the most fitted to produce this moral condition?'[31] It should be mentioned that Taine considered that these conditions operated as 'primordial' forces, and this alone raises grave doubts as to any theory of progress that might emanate from his work.

The surface impact of Comte and positivism in England, as is well known, was considerable. The principal figure in the dissemination of Comte's ideas in England was probably John Stuart Mill, who in the early 1840s could with some accuracy have been termed a Comtean. This uncritical phase in Mill's intellectual history was soon to pass, and though till the end of his days he retained a considerable amount of the lessons of the *Cours*, by 1848 he was writing to Littré that 'Most of his [Comte's] sociological opinions are diametrically opposed to mine'.[32] That it was Comte's theory of progress and the method by which he arrived at it that first attracted Mill and remained with him as an intellectual inspiration long after he had become totally repelled by the extraneous material of the 'Religion of Humanity', is strongly suggested by a passage from Mill's *Autobiography*. Referring to 'an early work of Auguste Comte, who, . . . announced himself as a pupil of Saint-Simon' (this is with little doubt Comte's *Plan des travaux scientifiques nécessaires pour réorganiser la société* of 1822), Mill asserts that:

This doctrine harmonized well with my existing notions, to

which it seemed to give a scientific shape. I already regarded the methods of physical science as the proper models for political. But the chief benefit which I derived at this time from the trains of thought suggested by the St. Simonians and by Comte, was, that I obtained a clearer conception than ever before of the peculiarities of an era of transition in opinion, and ceased to mistake the moral and intellectual characteristics of such an era, for the normal attributes of humanity. I looked forward . . . to a future which shall unite the best qualities of the critical with the best qualities of the organic periods; unchecked liberty of thought, unbounded freedom of individual action in all modes not hurtful to others; but also, convictions as to what is right and wrong, useful and pernicious, deeply engraven on the feelings by early education and general unanimity of sentiment, and so firmly grounded in reason and in the true exigencies of life, that they shall not, like all former and present creeds, religious, ethical, and political, require to be periodically thrown off and replaced by others.[33]

Mill's sensitive testament to the work of Comte, published in *The Westminster Review* in 1865, is both generous in its overall view and scathingly critical on Comte's 'later speculations'. Here too Mill points out the interconnections between the method of positivism and Comte's theory of progress, and the way in which 'empirical generalizations are raised into positive laws, and sociology becomes a science'.[34] The division of sociology into social statics and social dynamics allows us to separate out questions of social evolution and to ask about the nature of this evolution, and though critical of some of the detail of Comte's treatment of these problems, Mill leaves no doubt that he considers Comte's achievements in this area to have been of the very highest importance.

The official English Positivists, like the official French Positivists, were hamstrung by internal personality-doctrinal disputes. In England Richard Congreve became a disciple of the Religion of Humanity as early as 1854, and Frederic Harrison, John Henry Bridges and E. S. Beesly, former students of Congreve's at Oxford, joined him to a greater or lesser extent. Before long, however, Congreve's liturgical zeal began to wear down the others, and it became a matter of time and opportunity for the schism to occur. This it did in 1878 when Congreve broke with Laffitte, the leader of the French movement, and took his faction away to form a true Church of Humanity. This religion had a thinly spread vogue between 1880 and 1900 in several Northern cities and towns, but the movement as a physical and religious organization was never very strong. Curiously, the Positivist chapel in Liverpool hung on till 1945.

Meanwhile the 'loyalists', mainly under the leadership of Harrison, carried out an extremely diversified programme of an educational, social and socializing nature. It is only in this context that it becomes at all possible to speak about any influence the Comtean theory of progress might have had on the English positivist movement. In the words of the biographer of the movement, 'it was in the field of social reform, indeed, that the Positivists laid their stamp most distinctly upon English society'—its significance 'lay in its promotion of conciliation'.[35]

Better than they probably realized, these Positivists were carrying out Comte's prerequisites for progress in some detail. The call for progress on the basis of order that has been shown to be the core of Comte's theory of progress dictates just this, that gradual, what can be called evolutionary, change as opposed to drastic and revolutionary change was the correct road to progress in society. Thus, social reform, and not the full-scale social upheaval that some nineteenth-century working men and foreign intellectuals were advocating, was the mainstay of positivist activity.*

Significantly enough, the Positivists played a major part in advising the youthful trade unions on *legal* matters, and it was precisely in their role as conciliators that they were carrying out the Comtean doctrine on the avoidability of the class struggle. They were, both as 'liberals' and as 'Positivists', deeply concerned about the plight of the industrial classes: 'Are there not things in it [modern industry] which make feeble souls look on material progress as a curse?' asked Harrison.[36]

In his Hobhouse lecture for 1959 Annan, though discussing a sense of positivism which appears to have little or nothing to do with Comte, comments that it is its 'concern with morality which suggests the last reason why positivism maintained its strength for so long in this country'.[37] Given that Annan is speaking exclusively of positivist influence in British political thought, it is possible to extend his remarks as a more general characterization of what I have been discussing as positivism. It is indeed suffused with morality and often with moralizing. T. H. Huxley, the greatest proponent of scientific education of the nineteenth century, rejected Comte primarily for this reason. Although naturally in complete sympathy with the idea of bringing positive science to the people, he felt most strongly that Comte and the Religion of Humanity had betrayed the true spirit of science. It was, in his famous aphorism, Catholicism minus Christianity. English positivism in the main accepted the concern with morality and quietly rejected the excessive and authoritarian moraliz-

* The relations between Marx, the Positivists and the IWMA are discussed in an interesting article by Royden Harrison, 'E. S. Beesly and Karl Marx', *International Review of Social History* (Amsterdam), iv (1959), pp. 22-58 and 208-38.

ing of Comte as Priest and of the subsequent defenders of the Faith. However, what was essential, namely the conviction that progress in society could be 'scientifically' demonstrated and directed, and that this progress had a moral connotation, was not lost. In this way the theory of progress in the nineteenth century under the influence of Comte and the Positivists appeared not only less vague than that of the eighteenth century, but also as an intellectual achievement that was well in line with the ways in which Western societies were in fact developing.

And it was not only in Western Europe that this was happening. One commentator, speaking about the relatively backward Russia of the 1860s, describes how Comte's work 'brought the young rebels' emotional belief in progress into harmony with their intellectual attachment to scientific method', and draws a picture of the alliance of workers, peasants and intelligentsia which was for the adherents of a populist, positive and humanist religion, the true agent of progress.[38]

A brief comment on the lack of impact that either Comte personally or positivism in any organized form had in nineteenth-century Germany is in place. Perhaps, as Simon almost whimsically suggests, 'Hegel had immunized scientifically minded Germans against the appeal of historicizing metaphysics', and the reaction against Hegel (rather than a jump from the idealist frying-pan into the positivist fire*) tended to some variety of neo-Kantianism or British empiricism.[39]

Whatever the reasons, and the 'back-to-Kant' movement which filled the same type of intellectual need as Comte had done appears to be the most important, positivism did not catch on in Germany, and the positivism which did emerge in Germany and in Austria had nothing whatsoever to do with Auguste Comte.

In the Americas, too, Comte had varying fortunes. Although he did achieve some personal success in North America, particularly in New England, it was in South America that the movement made some quite astonishing conquests. Leopoldo Zea points out that Mexico, Argentina, Chile, Uruguay, Peru, Bolivia and Cuba all utilized the positive doctrine in one form or another from Comte, Mill and Spencer, 'as a means of at least catching up with progress'.[40]

It was in Brazil, supremely, that Comtean positivism and the Comtean theory of progress had its greatest actual triumph. Under the influence of Benjamin Constant and Pereira Barreto the Republic

---

* In fact, as Hayek reports (in *Counter-Revolution of Science*, p. 193), one of Comte's pupils, d'Eichthal, had given Hegel a copy of one of Comte's earliest tracts—no doubt the one to which Mill referred in the passage quoted above. The reported response led Comte to believe that Hegel was 'in Germany the man most capable to push the positive philosophy'.

of 1889 adopted positivism almost as its official ideology, and went so far as to put the Comtean motto of 'Order and Progress' on the flag of state! Cruz Costa, the Brazilian historian of ideas, devotes over a third of his recent book on Brazilian philosophy to the 'Advent of Positivism', and shows clearly the overwhelming importance of it in the history of ideas in Brazil. Primarily Cruz Costa argues that the movement attracted those who wanted a moral order 'deriving from a concept of intellectual progress, . . . that continued to be linked to traditional values'.[41]

Once again, therefore, no less in Brazil than in Paris, the new science and the old values are counterpoised, and the relations between material and moral progress cannot be ignored. Comte and the Positivists generally, as I have argued, saw this relation in terms of a necessary connection—that material or intellectual progress (that is the achievement of the positive stage by all the sciences in all respects) will inevitably lead to moral and social progress, the achievement of the positive stage by society and men themselves.

In the same way as I have criticized this position, so did several nineteenth-century Positivists see the fallacy of this necessary connection,[42] and indeed came up against much trouble within their systems of social philosophy because of it. Be this as it may, it appears to me to be undeniable that the Comtean theory of progress, in any of the characteristically positivist forms in which it appeared, had more than a local significance. As Simon has demonstrated in his *tour de force* on the general non-influence of Comte and his disciples, it is just as easy to find nothing in common among writers as it is to find everything in common. With full admiration for Simon's perseverance one can still agree with Ginsberg's assessment of Comte's work that 'its great importance in the development of sociology cannot be in doubt . . . he gave a new orientation to social investigation. The specialisms which have arisen since his time have been profoundly influenced by his outlook.'[43]

Basil Willey gives Comte the pre-eminent place among those who set the ideological tone for the whole of the nineteenth century, and suggests that it was in his irrepressible desire to reconcile the seemingly irreconcilable that Comte had his greatest direct and indirect influence. Discussing George Eliot in this context, Willey claims that

this 'conservative-reforming' impulse was the leading motif of her life: that her lifelong quest, as it was Comte's and the century's, was for a reconcilement between these opposites, a synthesis (as Comte would say) between the Static and Dynamic principles, between Order and Progress, Tradition and Enlightenment, the heart and the head.[44]

47

It was to such a synthesis that Marx was to apply himself around the time that the volumes of the *Cours de philosophie positive* were rolling off the presses in Paris, and I shall now examine the Marxist theory of progress.

Marx's theory of progress

Marxism is a theory of necessary and inevitable material and moral progress, although the extraordinary originality of Marx's synthesis led to a fairly widespread belief among Marxists in the first half of the twentieth century that the theory was a wholesale rejection of previous philosophies of progress. There is of course a grain of truth in this view.* Marx's strictures against the so-called 'Utopian Socialists'[45] were indeed a timely reminder that the unbridled optimism of the eighteenth- and early nineteenth-century social philosophers hovered dangerously near a fatalist albeit happy interpretation of history, whereas his 'dialectical materialism' paradoxically insisted that man was to play the vital role in making the inevitable history whose principal object he, as a species, was. As Lenin was later to suggest, Marxism was less of a theory and more of a guide to action!

Marx's theory of progress, in broad canvas, starts out by registering a most serious and undeniably sincere protest against the dreadful human suffering, in both its material and spiritually interdependent aspects, that the capitalist mode of production engenders. It moves on to an analysis of the historical necessity of this suffering, and concludes with a set of proposals designed to demonstrate how Mankind must aid the inexorable laws of social development to bring about an end to this suffering. It is tempting to draw out an analogy between the eighteenth-century *philosophes* and Marx in this connection. Just as the former appeared to have shaken themselves free of the 'heavenly city' and to have substituted posterity for providence, the latter appeared to have shaken free from the naïve optimism of his predecessors and to have successfully substituted a 'scientific socialism', complete with necessary laws, for vague notions about the growth of knowledge and the consequences of science. Let it suffice to say that the end-point of the Marxist theory of progress is no less optimistic than that of Turgot, Condorcet or Comte, and is generally somewhat more optimistic in its assessment of the possibilities of complete success than, for example, the theories of the Scottish historical school of the eighteenth century.

The astonishing originality of Marx's theory of progress and the whole social philosophy that rests on it, stems from the fact that it is

---

* The idea of 'progress' as a 'bourgeois ideology' is more accurately expressed as 'the bourgeois concept of progress is (pejoratively) ideological'. Thus stated, the Marxist theory of progress needs something like Mannheim's 'relationism' to escape the same predicament.

self-consciously revolutionary in the sense of total reversal of most of the things that nineteenth-century man, whether bourgeois or proletarian, held dear. The Communist Revolution is simply not to be compared with previous revolutions, and this is not only because the proletariat is the truly revolutionary class, but more so because the *scale* of the revolution is so much greater than anything that has ever taken place before. This is of course due to the tremendous potential of modern technology which makes the success of socialism a possibility. In this respect, Marx is nothing if not realistic, and in terms of the argument that I advanced at the end of the last chapter, his is the most representative progress theory of the nineteenth century in its recognition of the consequences of the institutionalization of science and technology, and the impact that modern industry was having on social life.

The French Socialists, principally Fourier, Proudhon and Blanc, were almost reactionary in their progressivism, for they tended to see the possibilities for improving society in the reversal of some of the modern industrial trends. This applies to Fourier in particular, and may be traced to his view of the immutability of human nature which contrasts violently with the views of practically every other Socialist, and especially with his contemporary forerunners of socialism like Godwin and Robert Owen.[46] The notion of progress as any kind of reversal indicates a curious strain of primitivism in nineteenth-century social thought which is illustrated by Saint-Simon.

Saint-Simon, equally a forerunner of Comte as of Marx, argued that progress occurred in 'organic' and 'critical' phases. Thus, the apparent regressions of the past were conceived of as organically progressive, whereas the present times of industrial-technological change were critically progressive. This oscillation was the basis of his philosophy of history, and Saint-Simon's followers developed it in strange ways. The fact, however, that Saint-Simon (as Comte after him) came to give religion a pre-eminent place in this scheme of things—as a Durkheimian mechanism of social cohesion—vividly suggests the primitivist strains in the thought of one of the most technologically-minded of nineteenth-century social thinkers.[47]

Let it suffice to say that practically nothing in the past held any nostalgia for Marx, and no traditional institution was safe from his revolutionary ardour; his 'communist society' was a dialectical extrapolation based on man's material conditions.

The Marxist theory of progress therefore displays originality over all the other theories so far examined on at least two interrelated counts. In the first place it is revolutionary, it eschews gradual material and moral amelioration; in the second place it is dialectical, it posits a development of contradictory states. Both of these conditions are considered necessary to the success of socialism and

E

inevitable within the historical process, so much so that it is perhaps a distortion to look at them even in analytical separation. Let me nevertheless take this risk in the hope that it might lend clarity to this brief exegesis.

'The Communist revolution is the most radical rupture with traditional property relations,' say Marx and Engels; 'no wonder that its development involves the most radical rupture with traditional ideas.'[48] This statement, then, expresses the scope of the proposed revolution; it covers the *total* existence of man in the material world, and as this material existence conditions man's consciousness, this too will inevitably change and with it will change 'traditional ideas', especially those of an ideological nature. Like the eighteenth- and many of the nineteenth-century theories of progress, Marxism links changes in the material conditions of man necessarily to changes in his moral condition, but as can be seen, in a rather special and novel fashion. Whereas these previous theories tended to suggest something like a straight-line relationship, or a near variation of one, between the development of knowledge and control over the material world and social and moral progress, Marxism claims that a 'radical rupture' in the one is a necessary condition for progress in the other.

One reason for this is to be found in Marx's discussion around the term 'alienation', both in its socio-economic and its philosophical senses, again extremely difficult to treat separately.* The root of man's alienation (which is both moral and a social concept) is held to lie in the socio-economic set of material relations considered by Marx to be empirically verified characteristics of the capitalist system. But what the Marxist theory of progress does, in effect, is to shift the emphasis from empirically observed characteristics to defining characteristics of the capitalist system of production, and thereby to legislate a set of necessary conditions for the attainment of total progress.

Moral progress thus depends on the dis-alienation of man which depends on the revolution in property relations and the end of the division of labour, which in turn depends on the 'expropriation of the expropriators'. This latter can only be successfully accomplished, so Marx thought, when the capitalist system has run its course. In a most vivid analogy Marx speaks of the embryo Communist society emerging from the womb of capitalism—and the dangers of premature birth are never far from his mind. Engels, in a newspaper

---

* Perhaps the clearest brief discussion of the uses of *Entäusserung*, roughly 'externalization', and *Entfremdung*, roughly 'estrangement', both of which have been translated as 'alienation', is to be found in the note by the translator, Martin Milligan, of the *Economic and Philosophic Manuscripts of 1844* by Marx (Moscow and London, 1961, pp. 11-12). I shall restrict myself to the term 'alienation' for simplicity here.

article published in 1875 concerning the prospects for revolution in Russia, states:

> The revolution which modern socialism strives to achieve . . . requires not only a proletariat that carries out this revolution, but also a bourgeoisie in whose hands the productive forces of society have developed so far that they allow of the final destruction of class distinctions. . . . Only at a certain level of development of the productive forces of society, an even very high level for our modern conditions, does it become possible to raise production to such an extent that the abolition of class distinctions can be a real progress . . . But the productive forces have reached this level of development only in the hands of the bourgeoisie. The bourgeoisie, therefore, in this respect also is just as necessary a precondition of the socialist revolution as the proletariat itself.*[49]

Revolution, it is plain to see, is a stage in the development of human history, but in contrast to gradual and evolutionary stages it represents a step or a plateau approach to human history. And just as gradual and evolutionary change appears to imply an effortless, almost automatic, working-out of autonomous forces, revolutionary change implies violence, effort and an active confrontation with historical forces. The Marxist theory of progress can therefore be considered as the first *fully activist* theory of progress, and, whether fruitful or not as a theory, it is this aspect more than any other that has fired the imagination of men for the last hundred years.

This is not to suggest that previous theories of progress were all passive or fatalist. From Francis Bacon's call to men of science that they should get out and experiment, to the reforming zeal of the English Positivists, progress had inevitably meant action in some area of life or another. It was Marx, however, who first saw the possibility and who first synthesized a justification for the complete upheaval of society, and who first dared to claim that this and no less was the necessary and sufficient guarantee of material and moral progress. It is to the concept of the 'dialectic' that we must turn to begin to understand why Marx could accept only total revolution, diametrically opposed to all that had gone before and yet inextricably linked to it in a historical sense, rather than the partial revolutions that had occurred in England, America and France, as the *sine qua non* of total progress.

The crucial figure in the history of the Marxist dialectic is, of

---

* It is interesting to compare this statement by Engels with the sympathetic but critical analysis of revolutionary paths by Barrington Moore, Jr., in his major work of historical sociology, *Social Origins of Dictatorship and Democracy* (London: Allen Lane, 1967).

course, Hegel, from whom Marx and Engels, most later Marxists and practically all commentators up till the last few years consider the *primary* inspiration for dialectical materialism to have come. The recent revolution in Hegelian scholarship effected (and perhaps successfully accomplished?) by the publication of Walter Kaufmann's reinterpretation of Hegel leads one to have very serious doubts on at least two points. Firstly, if, as Kaufmann and Lichtheim argue, there is no triad dialectic of thesis-antithesis-synthesis in Hegel at all, why has almost every writer on Hegel, and especially the Marxist writer, given the impression that this is the king-pin of the Hegelian system?* Secondly, and more important for my present concern with the Marxist theory of progress, if Marx did not derive his method of dialectic triads from Hegel, then from whom or where did he derive it?

Part of the answers to these questions may lie in understanding the Hegelian logic as 'oppositional' rather than one of dialectic triads. Hook, although he appears to interpret Hegelian logic in the way that Kaufmann has criticized, suggests as much when he argues that 'It is not so much the number of phases a situation has which makes it dialectical, but a *specific relation* of opposition between those phases which generates a succession of other phases'.[50]

There are many hints in Kaufmann's book that reinforce this view. For example, Hegel 'commends the German language for containing words that "have not only different meanings but even opposed meanings" '.[51] This notion of 'oppositional logic' is certainly of crucial importance for Marx. On the most elementary level it is clear that whatever difference 'turning the Hegelian dialectic the right way up' makes, it leaves the actual process of opposition exactly where it was—opposing 'material' to 'ideal' is the same as opposing 'ideal' to 'material' as far as *opposing* is concerned. This may sound like a trivial point, but it may be of some value in explaining the allegiance of a number of Marxists to Hegel, for if Marx has retained the oppositional logic, the core of the Hegelian system, and only amended him in detail, namely starting the opposition where Hegel was supposed to have left off, the methodological continuity between Marx and Hegel is not very difficult to maintain in its essentials.

'Alienation' could be fully overcome only by a revolution accomplished through the clash of opposites, and the Communist system

---

* If Kaufmann et al. are correct, then Popper's only compliment to Hegel vanishes, for he says (in *The Open Society and its Enemies*, London: Routledge & Kegan Paul, 1962, vol. 2, p. 39) in discussing 'the three-beat rhythm of progress which Hegel called the "dialectic triad" ' that he is 'quite prepared to admit that this is not a bad description of the way in which a critical discussion . . . may sometimes progress'.

was the opposite of the Capitalist system in all important respects. Marx uses the term 'antagonistic' to characterize this relationship, but whereas previous progress theorists might see the Church, or political absolutism, or climate, or scientific dilletantism, or any number of other factors, as 'antagonistic' (though historically necessary prerequisites) to material and moral progress, Marx and Marx alone took the giant and apocryphal step of indicting a whole system (a complete stage of civilization) as necessarily antagonistic to progress.* 'As we pursue our materialist thesis . . .' Engels exclaims, 'the most tremendous revolution of all time, therefore, immediately unfolds itself before us.' He continues, 'All traditional and customary outlooks on everything historical are negated by it.'[52] Comte simply does not use this language!

The class struggle is the outward, personalized manifestation of this antagonism, the bourgeoisie and the proletariat represent the groups of people, defined by their relationships to the means of production, that embody the oppositional logic. Nowhere is the metaphysical 'nature' of the real world more powerfully and persuasively expressed than in this notion of logic working itself out through the actions of men in their material existence. Private property, which *is* the division of labour, will be abolished, because its opposite will render it obsolete; the state will in time 'wither away' and will be replaced by 'the authority of the orchestra', or as Engels put it, 'the administration over things and not over people'. 'In place of the old bourgeois society,' Marx and Engels eloquently prophesy in *The Communist Manifesto*, 'with its classes and class antagonisms, we shall have an association, in which the free development of each is the condition for the free development of all'.[53]

In common with many other theories of progress Marxism tells us little about the actual details of the progressive future, though Communist society, by elimination, will inevitably be very different from, indeed opposite to, capitalist society. On the basis of famous passages in *The German Ideology*† and certain sections of the works of Lenin and Trotsky,[54] one can hardly draw a satisfying picture of life under Communism. There is, however, at least a pragmatic reason why this should be so on the basis of Marxist theory, for although Marx never himself commented on this point, there would seem to be every possibility that the oppositional logic would con-

---

* It is true that Kant and others developed theories of progress that contained elements of conflict before Marx, but though the notion may be similar, the scope and intensity of the Marxist use of conflict puts it in a category of its own. (See Chapter II above.)

† Gellner suggests that the closest approximation to the man described here is the English stockbroker (see *Thought and Change*, London: Weidenfeld & Nicolson, 1964, p. 93).

tinue to operate in human society, though not on the actual economic relations themselves.

This becomes rather a complex exegetical problem; nevertheless a few comments are in place. It is perhaps apposite to recall here that the advent of Communism was to herald the beginning of human history proper and not its end, and that one popular way of interpreting Marxism is to see its success as liberating mankind from economic slavery, the bourgeoisie no less than the proletariat, and as giving it its first real opportunity to develop in other than purely economic and industrial terms. On this reading, one of the major problems of Communist society would be that of the revolution in leisure. Marx's primary aim, after all, was the happiness of mankind and the abolition of human misery, and his theory of progress was his way of showing that this pre-eminently humanitarian ideal was both achievable and achievable only on his theoretical analysis of the material situation.[55]

Martin Nicolaus, in a very interesting paper which discusses some recent developments in Marxist scholarship and, more importantly, the rediscovery of an important piece by Marx (*The Grundrisse*), argues that, contrary to much modern critical opinion, Marx was quite aware of some of the problems that a developing capitalism might pose for his theory. It is perhaps too early to comment properly on the full impact of these developments on Marxism as a social theory or on the continuing impact that Marxism as a theory of progress will have on the developed world. Whatever the long-term impact in the short term, as Nicolaus puts it, apparently 'the *Grundrisse* blows the mind'.[56]

I shall return to some of the Marxists of the late nineteenth century in my exposition of the impact that the Darwinian theory of evolution had on the theory of progress.

A note on Hegel
Hegel himself presents a particularly acute problem for the history of the idea of progress. It is not altogether inaccurate to say, with Bury, that 'The spirit of Hegel's philosophy, in its bearing on social life, was thus antagonistic to Progress as a practical doctrine',[57] though the main reason that Bury adduces for this, namely that the system is a closed one and only admits of a past historical progression whose course had ended, is in itself misleading. We must look to Hegel's conception of philosophy to find the key to his complex notion of progress, for as we have seen, any full theory of progress must make some statement about the *future*; so it is with the predictive potential of philosophy that we are concerned. For Hegel, philosophy, like history, cannot be used for predictive purposes—in a sense (in the words of Wittgenstein) it 'leaves the world exactly as it is'. Kaufmann

makes this point clearly in the discussion of Hegel's philosophical method, which he terms, for the sake of the argument, 'dialectical' (that is what I have preferred to call 'oppositional'), as follows:

> But the fateful myth that this perspective is reducible to a rigorous method that even permits predictions deserves no quarter, though by now half the world believes it.
> The fact that Hegel himself never used the dialectic to predict anything, and actually spurned the very idea that it could be used that way, suggests plainly that ... Hegel's dialectic is at most a method of exposition; it is not a method of discovery.[58]

With reference to history itself, Kaufmann quotes Hegel's essentially similar judgment. 'What experience and history teach is this,' Hegel asserts, 'peoples and governments have never learned anything from history and acted according to what one might have learned from it.'[59] On account of this, it is fair to deny Hegel the theoretical possibility of any fully-fledged theory of progress.

On the other hand, Hegel appeared to believe in the infinite power of man to discover the secrets of the universe—in a particularly arresting phrase he speaks of 'the courage to know'. Thus, although Hegel sees historical progress which he identifies with the development of Freedom as having achieved its final goal, it would seem that the door is left open to intellectual progress.

Kaufmann has done much to dispel the widespread view of Hegel as a crudely conservative defender of the *status quo**, though the fact that Hegel was a conservative in spite of the radical implications of the method of the 'oppositional' logic is beyond doubt. Bury's view that Hegel's system is 'eminently inhuman' is a harsh judgment, though again not entirely without justification. It is fairer to say that Hegel was very conscious of human suffering in the past and wished to show that however irrelevant it was in itself to the grand historical process, it had not been entirely for nothing.

The matter rests in paradox. Condemned on the one side for fathering Fascism and social reaction, and on the other for providing the vital impetus to totalitarian Communism, and considered by many influential figures as the raving proponent of an absurd and nonsensical philosophy, Hegel cannot be ignored in an examination of the history of the idea of progress, though I have been able to consider him only in the most cursory fashion.

---

* This view is succinctly put by R. Haym, when he describes Hegel's *Philosophie des Rechts* as a 'scientifically formulated justification of the Carlsbad police system', *Hegel und seine Zeit*, Berlin, 1857. (Quoted in G. A. Wells, *Herder and After*, s' Gravenhage, 1959, p. 152).

IV Progress and evolution

Darwinism, the theory of natural selection, is a special case of the general theory of evolution, and neither the general theory nor the special case necessarily implies the idea of progress. Darwin's particular contribution to the history of the theory of evolution consisted largely in putting an end to the *scientific* opposition to evolution as such, though in his day (and even to this day) there was (and is) some opposition to Darwin's account.*

Evolution: new and old
In retrospect, there were only two really important versions of evolution that commanded any significant scientific support, and the issue between these was that of 'design', roughly whether or not evolution was a teleological process. Samuel Butler, who waged a frustrating and unreciprocated battle with Charles Darwin over this point for several years, characterized the latter's theory as 'new' evolution which rejected the necessity of design, and he opposed to it 'old' evolution which was considered to be necessarily teleological. Whatever the extraneous reasons for the Darwin–Butler controversy, and in spite of Dr Greenacre's interesting though ultimately unconvincing psycho-analytic interpretation,[1] Butler did have a great deal of justification and authoritative backing for his views. The celebrated names of Buffon, Erasmus Darwin, Lamarck and Spencer, plus those of Patrick Matthew (who, in a work on naval timber, had made some most illuminating remarks on the subject of evolution),

---

* 'The concept of organic evolution,' says a historian of biology, 'is not a theory but a fact ... proofs of evolution steadily arose out of studies in palaeontology, comparative anatomy, embryology, taxonomy, physiology and geographic distribution.' (Ben Dawes, *A Hundred Years of Biology*, London, 1952, p. 264.) Induction, it appears, is not quite dead in science.

56

Etienne and Isidore Geoffroy St Hilaire, are brought together by Butler to endorse collectively the thesis that 'the design which has designed organisms, has resided within, and been embodied in, the organisms themselves'.[2] Butler might have added the name of Friedrich Engels to his list, as I shall presently argue.

Part of the difficulty lay in the expression 'natural selection' itself, for as even Darwin admits, 'in the literal sense of the word, no doubt, natural selection is a misnomer', and it has been open to the objection (wrongly of course) 'that the term selection implies conscious choice in the animals which become modified'.[3] Two simple examples, one from the animal world and one from the development of man, will illuminate the different types of evolution theory, or more accurately, the different mechanisms that have been suggested to account for evolution.

(1) How did the giraffe come by its long neck? The 'old' evolutionists argued that over a long period of time the giraffe evolved a long neck through its striving to reach the leaves on the high branches of the trees in order to survive. Design, therefore, plays a major part in this process for the long neck was the result of some purposive action on the part of giraffes. Darwin and the 'new' evolutionists, on the other hand, explained this phenomenon by arguing that long necks had 'survival value' for giraffes, and so those giraffes with the longer necks were naturally selected. From this it followed that because of differential rates of breeding over time all the short-necked giraffes would eventually disappear. Design, therefore, had no place in Darwin's explanation and the giraffes' purposes, if they had any, were quite irrelevant to the process.

(2) How did the organs of speech evolve? Engels, in his essay, 'Labour in the Transition from Ape to Man', written in 1876, answers this question in terms of the freeing of the human hand for labour. Not only did this start men on the road to the mastery over nature, but

> the development of labour necessarily helped to bring the members of society closer together by multiplying cases of mutual support, joint activity, and by making clear the advantage of this joint activity to each individual. In short, men in the making arrived at the point where *they had something to say* to one another. The urge created its organ; the undeveloped larynx of the ape was slowly but surely transformed by means of modulation in order to produce constantly more developed modulation, and the organs of the mouth gradually learned to pronounce one articulate sound after another.[4]

This explanation obviously would have been quite unacceptable to Darwin. As far as he was concerned no 'urge' could ever have created any 'organ'; given that communication had survival value, and both accounts agree on this, Darwin would explain the evolution of the organs of speech by natural selection. Those men whose speech organs were developing would be selected in the struggle for survival (a phrase that Spencer supplied), and so in time man would have the physiological means for speech as a naturally selected characteristic.

Therefore, in place of purpose and design, Darwin substituted the notion of random variation, but random in the sense of 'cause not adequately known (or knowable)' rather than chaotic or haphazard. Both the small variations in the length of the neck in some giraffes and the small variations in rudimentary speech organs of man in transition were picked up by the evolutionary process because they meant more fitness of the organism to its environment. In his *The Descent of Man* (1871), published twelve years after *Origin of Species*, Darwin further elaborated his theory of natural selection, and claimed to have demonstrated that 'of all the causes which have led to the differences in external appearance between the races of men, and to a certain extent between man and the lower animals, sexual selection has been by far the most efficient'.[5]

Again it was the series of chance variations and not any kind of design or purpose that provided the raw material on which the evolutionary process worked. It is interesting to note that in his very infrequent references to the theological implications of his theory (which I shall examine below) Darwin always appeared to leave the possibility that the Creator and evolution could be reconciled. 'I see no good reason,' he states at the end of *Origin of Species*, 'why the views given in this volume should shock the religious feelings of any one.'[6] Rather, he suggested, man becomes more noble on the evolutionary theory, and certainly the idea of the most magnificently exalted primate would appeal to many over that of the fallen angel!

In its broadest aspect modern biological science has accepted Darwin and rejected Butler and Lamarck, although for a time in the first quarter of the twentieth century the development of Mendel's and Weismann's genetic theories presented problems for the Darwinian account, and schools of neo-Darwinism and neo-Lamarckism appeared. Nordenskiöld, writing in the early 1920s, comments that 'the history of biology might really close with the establishing of the dissolution of Darwinism'.[7] This statement must be taken in its proper context, and it is here that the ideas of evolution and the idea of progress meet and interact with mutually important consequences.

I have tried to show that of the ideas of progress present in the theories and reflections of men who had written about history and society from the times of antiquity, a certain type had taken a firm grip at the time of the institutionalization of science which had occurred around 1800. Part of this institutionalization process involved what might be termed the popularization of various sciences, and there is some good evidence that geology was a science that had caught the imagination of the public, at least in England, in the first decades of the nineteenth century. It was therefore no accident that of the two men generally recognized as having sparked Darwin's theory of evolution one was Charles Lyell, who in 1830 published *The Principles of Geology, Being an Attempt to Explain the Former Changes of the Earth's Surface, by Reference to Causes now in Operation.*

Lyell, like most of his contemporaries before Darwin, just missed the theory of evolution by natural selection. Irvine, in his joint biography of Darwin and Huxley, truly suggests that 'in those days a biologist could hardly make a discovery without staring evolution in the face'. With reference to the Galapagos Islands for Darwin in particular and probably any biological or geological researcher in general, he states that '[they] not only suggested evolution, the facts demanded it. Here distribution reduced the creation theory to an absurdity.'[8] Indeed, Lyell's *Principles* was the pillar on which the anti-catastrophist or anti-diluvialist case was to rest till Darwin's *Origin of Species* appeared to argue the case against him, which, to his credit, Lyell accepted and supported at once.

It is hardly claiming too much to assert that the crux of the matter, the element that tipped the scales in the surprisingly rapid public victory that Darwinism achieved in spite of powerful scientific and non-scientific opposition, was the idea of progress that was current in mid-nineteenth century England (and the rest of Europe).*

Like the idea of progress, the notion of evolution has cropped up time and time again in the history of thought. There is a portrait by Leonardo da Vinci of a woman holding a stoat in which the girl's skull is a copy of the stoat's, her hand matches its paw, as if Leonardo were signalling to the centuries following that he knew of evolution. There is no doubt that the concept of evolution as opposed to that of the separate creation of species was in the air long before the mechanisms of evolution were elaborated. Not all prominent scientists, however, even in the age of science, could successfully transcend the Scriptural accounts of these matters which were more difficult to reconcile with current ideas of progress of mankind than some evolutionary theory. However, as I have shown to be the case with the Anglican progress theorists around 1800, the Scriptural account

* I have argued this case with respect to geology in an unpublished paper, 'Geology, Positivism and Progress: A Case-Study in the Sociology of Science'.

in at least one of its versions was not entirely incompatible with some theory of progress.

In Catholic Europe the situation was otherwise. Linnaeus, perhaps the most inspired taxonomist who has ever lived, had by the middle of the eighteenth century classified well over four thousand species of animals on the basis of six main groups of sexual characteristics, but he still claimed that each species had been created separately and was to all intents and purposes immutable. Buffon questioned this view, but in deference to the clerics who surrounded him, or more charitably, because the idea never fully struck him, he failed to draw the evolutionary consequences from the rejection of the invariability of species. In any case, as one historian of science has observed, Buffon's ideas seem 'to look back to Empedocles much more surely than they look forward to Darwin'.[9]

By one of the coincidences with which history suspiciously abounds, it was in 1809, the year of Charles Darwin's birth, that Lamarck's *Philosophie Zoologique*, the first really scientific treatise on evolution, appeared. But even Lamarck resisted the final conclusion and excluded humanity from his reflections, though it was plain to see that this was something of a Galilean strategy. As has been noted above, Lamarck and many of his French followers explained evolution by purpose and design. This, however, was only part of his theory, and the part that in the opinion of at least one present-day commentator, Professor Darlington, was dependent on a more important and influential Lamarckian hypothesis that Darwin himself came to accept. This was the continuously and still controversial hypothesis of the inheritance of acquired characteristics, which is of great significance for any theory of progress.* Darlington presents

* This is a topic that demands extended, technical discussion, neither of which, unfortunately, I am able to give it. Several more historical points should nevertheless be made. 'The inheritance of acquired characteristics,' as Simpson, Maynard Smith and many others have pointed out, is a misleading expression for Lamarck's (and Darwin's) view that it is more accurate to speak of inheritance due to use and misuse of characteristics. The former position figured prominently in the 'Michurin science' and the Marxist biology of Lysenko and his colleagues in the Soviet Union until quite recently. These movements have been rather sensationally exposed in an unhappily partisan manner in the works of Professor Zirkle (see particularly *Evolution, Marxian Biology, and the Social Scene*, Philadelphia, 1959). H. Graham Cannon, in his *The Evolution of Living Things* (Manchester, 1958), puts forward an almost universally rejected vitalist interpretation of evolution in company with grave doubts about the 'selectionist' thesis. The words of one reviewer illuminate Cannon's position: 'the difficulties he finds in accepting a theory of evolution by natural selection in which small variations are inherited according to Mendelian laws will find echoes in many quarters' (T. H. Hawkins, in *Nature*, 181 (1958), p. 1365). Finally, a recent paper by the animal psychologist, Broadhurst, 'The Inheritance of Behaviour' (in *Science Journal*, 1 (June 1965), pp. 39-43), reports some interesting experiments on the inheritance of emotional characteristics in rats. The issue, at any rate, is not closed.

the issue in an instructive fashion. Lamarck, he argues, saw evolution as *directed*, principally by the influence of the parents' environment on the heredity process, while the selectionist view was that the essential factor lay in the *selection* of the environment on the offspring. These two positions are characterized as 'soft' and 'hard' heredity respectively, and Darlington claims that it was the English physicians, Wells, Lawrence and Prichard, who were responsible for the 'hard' heredity view, and that Darwin vacillated between the two and notwithstanding his theory of instincts based on 'hard' heredity, he concludes *The Descent of Man* in a largely Lamarckian fashion.[10]

Leaving aside the direction versus selection conflict among the proponents of evolution, and turning to the public reception of the theories of evolution, Darwin's status and the importance of his achievement is denied by none. Darlington, a very harsh critic of Darwin's originality, who goes so far as to impugn his very integrity as a scientist, admits that it was he more than any other man who convinced the *world* of the historical fact of evolution. No more striking confirmation of this view exists than the remarkable variety of positions that were considered to have been strengthened as a result of Darwin's work, and I shall attempt to show that this is a consequence of the fact that Darwin's arguments were quickly seen as generally favourable to the idea of progress. Indeed they were the scientific justification for the idea of progress.

Darwin's grandfather, Dr Erasmus Darwin, played a part in this story around the turn of the century, especially with regard to his extraordinary brand of evolutionary poetry. 'It was the application of the idea of progress to the great chain of being that produced the temporalized chain,' says Primer in a fascinating paper. 'Dr Darwin is the prophet of progress and more significantly of evolution.'[11]

The reason why Darwinism was employed by the proponents of widely differing theories of society and history, therefore, is bound up with the fact that there were also widely differing theories of progress behind these, and no one at this time was fully prepared to give up the idea of progress. In all of this, what Darwin had actually said was to be of secondary importance.

The abortive and dogmatic theological opposition to Darwin was almost immediately routed. The famous confrontation between Bishop Wilberforce, prompted by the eminent anatomist Richard Owen*, and T. H. Huxley, the undisputed champion of Darwinism, ended in humiliating defeat for the independent Creationists before the shocked meeting of the British Association gathered in Oxford.

---

* Owen, whom Darwin quotes several times in the *Origin of Species*, might reasonably have been expected to support the new theory, for he had made several similar suggestions in the course of his own work. However, he proved to be a most bitter adversary, much to Darwin's chagrin.

It was clear that the Church would have to come to terms with Darwin, for to fight him meant to reject 'progressivism' by implication, and this was too high a price to pay in nineteenth-century England (and America also, as we shall see) for the majority.

With what might now be seen as undignified haste, the Church took Darwinism, albeit its own versions, to its very heart. 'From being a detestable scientific truth,' it has been remarked, 'Darwinism had emerged as an agreeable religious myth' in the 1870s.[12] The greatest theoretical difficulty to the acceptance of 'raw' Darwinism by Christians lay in its rejection of design and a Designer. Darwin, as I have already indicated (see note 6 above), tried to soften this blow as much as possible, though his correspondence suggests that he had given up the idea of God at a fairly early stage of his life and that he paid whatever lip-service to religion as he did in order not to offend the sensibilities of his friends and especially of his devout wife. Perhaps he need not have bothered, for not only theologians but also working scientists were soon using his theory of natural selection as an argument for Divine purpose.

Asa Gray, Darwin's most important exponent and supporter in the United States, described himself as 'one who is scientifically, and in his own fashion, a Darwinian, philosophically a convinced theist, and religiously an acceptor of the "creed commonly called the Nicene", as the exponent of the Christian faith'.[13] Essays in Gray's *Darwiniana* include those entitled 'Natural Selection not inconsistent with Natural Theology', and 'Evolutionary Teleology'.

The story of Darwin's reception in American theological and scientific circles is both fascinating and apposite. Schneider, in his excellent article on this subject, distinguishes between the dogmatic and the philosophical theologians. The former, like the dogmatic scientists or laymen, would simply deny that science had any relevance for theology, whereas the latter, mainly of the Presbyterian or the Unitarian persuasions at the time, worked hard to reconcile their own particular brand of Darwinism with their own particular denominational convictions. All in all, the Darwinian revolution succeeded well in American philosophical theology, for it was not long before the establishment of professorships of the Harmony of Science and Revealed Religion (at Princeton) and the Harmony of Science and Revelation (at Oberlin College) were set up. G. F. Wright, holder of the latter, described Darwinism as 'the Calvinistic interpretation of nature'. Matters reached such a pitch in the 1880s that John Dewey was moved to protest against such a 'flood of evangelical appropriation of evolutionary language and enthusiasm'.[14]

Dillenberger, writing in 1961, gives more weight to the opinion that theological reception was 'mixed' and calls attention to some of the very important men who could bring themselves to accept no version of Darwinism, the most prominent of whom was Hodge, the extremely influential theologian of the Princeton Theological Seminary.[15] However, the impression remains that in spite of the opposition, Darwinism had won a substantial victory in America as T. H. Huxley's stupendously successful tour in the 1880s was to show.

The man who brought the most methodological clarity into the Darwinian controversy was probably Chauncey Wright, the American scientist. He pointedly made the distinction between Darwinism, a scientific theory that attempted to answer questions about the natural world, and what he termed 'German Darwinism', a metaphysical system which purported to explain everything in the natural and any other world. What the French *philosophes* had done to Newton, Wright complained, the German metaphysicians had done to Darwin. An Anglo-Saxon *cri de coeur* if ever there was one! But Wright's strictures that Darwinism should be treated solely as a scientific hypothesis and not indiscriminately applied on a cosmic and all-pervading scale fell for the most part on deaf ears, and it was not until T. H. Huxley so dramatically upset the apple-cart in his Romanes lecture of 1893 that Darwinism began to be seen as the double-edged sword that it was.

The apple-cart contained the simple and supposedly self-evident truth that evolution meant progress; what Darwin had described was on the whole a process that worked to the advantage of mankind.

Darwinisticism and social evolution

The three interlinked and often confused terms, progress, development and evolution, may either be identified or distinguished from each other, or any one may be treated with reference to the other two. Whichever the combination, we find that it more or less implies the vital elements of a theory of progress. If the three terms are used interchangeably to signify the same thing, and this thing has evaluative content, then one is logically obliged to hold that, if evolution take place at all, inevitable and necessary progress is simply another way of speaking of this evolution. Comte, who rarely used the term 'evolution', and who rejected it in biology,* identified the verbs 'progresser' and 'développer',† and, as I mentioned above, in the index to the *Positive Polity* the reference to evolution refers the reader to progress.

At the other extreme, T. H. Huxley opposed this optimistic view that Herbert Spencer had made into one of the most powerful social

---

* In fact, it was not until 1909 that Emile Corra officially repudiated the positivist opposition to evolution. (See Simon, op. cit., p. 67.)

† This is most clearly evident in his *Cours de philosophie positive* (Paris, tome iv, pp. 192-9).

and political philosophies of the age, by arguing almost prophetically that ethical progress, far from following as a necessary consequence of biological or cosmic evolution, was more a matter of combating it. Huxley had seen the danger of erecting a metaphysic around Darwin's work, for he knew that this could only serve to stifle proper understanding of it and indeed to support positions against which he and Darwin were diametrically opposed. He had joined battle with Spencer in the 1860s, at first on the basis of a warm personal friendship, and waged it continuously in such publications as his essays, 'Administrative Nihilism' of 1871 and 'Struggle for Existence in Society' of 1888. 'Evolution and Ethics', Huxley's Romanes lecture, was the culmination of this battle, but the victory was surely Spencer's.

Simply, it was too much of a temptation for the nineteenth-century mind, and even the most subtle nineteenth-century minds, to pass up this golden and scientific opportunity of demonstrating social evolution within any of a variety of theories of progress by means of Darwinian evolution and the mechanism of natural selection that seemed to establish it.[16]

Morse Peckham makes the important distinction between Darwinism and Darwinisticism, where the former refers to what Darwin actually said* whilst the latter refers to all those statements that were improperly imputed to him. Echoing Chauncey Wright, Peckham characterizes Darwinisticism as a form of metaphysical evolutionism in whose development Hegel had played a prominent part. Though the grand thesis of metaphysical evolutionism, 'from simple to complex means from good to better, infinitely or finitely, as your metaphysical taste determines',[17] was in theory demolished by Darwin, this made little practical difference to those who sought scientific justification for their cosmologies.

The key figure in the controversy around social Darwinism or Darwinisticism in one form or another is Herbert Spencer, and the matter is not simplified by recognizing that Spencer created social Darwinism some years before the publication of *Origin of Species*. In an essay written in 1852 he had hypothesized that 'any existing species—animal or vegetable—when placed under conditions different from its previous ones, *immediately begins to undergo certain changes fitting it for the new conditions*',[18] and he combined this with an unequivocal rejection of Special Creation. Spencer's evolutionism was Lamarckian in so far as he accepted the inheritance of acquired characteristics, but as Darwin was later to do the same this presents

* Peckham, who edited the variorum edition of *Origin of Species* in 1959 for the centenary of its publication, points out that there are more than seven thousand sentence variants throughout the editions. Finding the 'real' Darwin is obviously a difficult and specialist task.

no insurmountable objection to the case for Darwin's cognitive relationship to social Darwinism as represented by Spencer.

Spencer, like Darwin, had been impressed and stimulated so much by the work of Malthus[19] that in his early essay on 'Progress: Its Law and Causes', of 1857, he extended the brief argument of the 1852 paper that progress (and evolution, for there was no firm distinction between them in Spencer's work at this time) was largely due to the pressure of population. And, more importantly, this had vital consequences on the survival and extinction of various groups in society.

Before examining this social Darwinism, it is of some interest to look at the form of Spencer's theory of progress or social evolution, which he took from the biological researches of Wolff, Goethe and von Baer who had characterized the development of seeds as a process of increasing complexity.

> From the earliest traceable cosmical changes down to the latest results of civilization, [Spencer asserts] we shall find that the transformation of the homogeneous into the heterogeneous, is that in which progress essentially consists.[20]

This is intended to be an argument that is supported on the one hand by empirical observation—the Nebular hypothesis on the genesis of the solar system was to be a confirmation of the general principle—and on the other hand an *a priori* deduction from the nature of cause and effect. Every cause produces more than one effect, Spencer argued, and effects are more complex than their causes; so it follows that the law of increasing heterogeneity, the law of progress, holds good for the social as well as for the physical world.* Both of these lines of argument are for obvious reasons very poor, and it is not surprising that in his later works of the late 1870s and 1880s he modified the first, especially with respect to the claim that all change is good, that is that all evolution is progress. The *a priori* argument on cause and effect was not taken up again in this very problematic manner.

Spencer's social Darwinism was a specific application of his theory of progress to the laissez-faire industrial economic individualism of Victorian England, and it demonstrated his thesis of historical pro-

---

* Spencer reported that in the mid-1860s he had realized that his First Principles had been wrongly organized in an important respect, which he rectified in subsequent editions of the work. In the amended versions he argued 'that the formation of an aggregate necessarily precedes any changes in structure which occur in the aggregate; and that therefore integration is the primary process and differentiation the secondary process'. (*An Autobiography*, London: Williams and Norgate, 1904, vol. 2, p. 154.) This apparently inocuous insight was taken up by Durkheim and Parsons with meagre reference to Spencer, and has had a very major effect on the development of sociology in the twentieth century.

F

gression from the militaristic to the industrial state, this latter being a prelude to the ethical state in which the human character would be truly perfected. He has been chastised justly for some of the excesses of his often extreme individualism, though it should be pointed out that, as his extreme sociological organicism is complemented by an unmistakable mechanicism on the matter of social aggregates, his views on state action and the individual were not in all cases critical of the former.

This and his whole attitude to laissez-faire is nowhere more carefully presented than in *The Study of Sociology*, which was first published in 1873, and was going into its twenty-first edition by the time of his death in 1903.* It is significant that these topics are most fully discussed in the chapter on the preparation in biology that the sociologist requires. After stating the thesis of the 'survival of the fittest' in society and 'the way in which a far-reaching biological truth underlies rational conclusions in Sociology', he says:

> ... I do not mean the conclusions above indicated to be taken without qualification. Manifestly, up to a certain point, the removal of destructive causes leaves a balance of benefit. ...
> All I wish to show is, that there are limits to the good gained by such a policy.[21]

Like Spencer I do not wish to be taken without qualification. It is only fair, however, to point out that there were many occasions when he did implicitly distinguish state action from state interference, and he was not sparing in his attacks on the more obvious iniquities (or inefficiencies) of the laissez-faire system.

His general position, nevertheless, is crudely individualistic and antagonistic to any interference, especially by public or private philanthropy, in the inexorable working out of the jungle law of social and economic existence. In a crucial footnote, Spencer remarks that most readers probably think that he is simply 'carrying out the views of Mr Darwin in their applications to the human race'. But, in *Social Statics* of 1850 and in his essay 'The Development Hypothesis' of 1852, to which I have already referred, he had already begun to work out the implications of natural selection without, he admits, any recognition of 'spontaneous variation' nor 'divergence of type' which were Darwin's own discoveries.[22]

Problems of priority aside, and there is a great deal of evidence for yet another case of independent discovery here (as with Wallace and Darwin), how far can Spencer be said to be 'carrying out the views of Mr. Darwin', when he tells us of 'the fact that the quality of a society

---

* Spencer's popularity, as measured by the sale of his books, was quite phenomenal. Hofstadter reports that between 1860 and 1903 he had sold 363,755 volumes of his work in America alone.

is lowered morally and intellectually, by the artificial preservation of those who are least able to take care of themselves'; or that 'Fostering the good-for-nothing at the expense of the good, is an extreme cruelty'; or finally, when Spencer sees the primary requirement of social life in the principle 'that each shall so live as neither to burden others nor to injure others'?[23]

Let us examine Darwin's *The Descent of Man* in order to evaluate the relationship between Spencer's social Darwinism and the original item. This book is an investigation of the process of evolution with special reference to the workings of sexual selection in man and the higher primates. On the whole it is an optimistic tract, and like *Origin of Species* it tries to underplay the notion of 'nature red in tooth and claw' that was to characterize much social Darwinism. As one commentator puts it, Darwin had discovered 'that the charnel house was a factory of progress'.[24] Society appeared to have some mechanisms which ensured that only the most attractive animals were able to propagate themselves fully while the less attractive, through failing to obtain sufficient sexual partners, died out. In mankind too similar mechanisms appeared to operate. Darwin here quotes evidence to show that the intemperate have a high mortality and a low reproductive rate, and further that the unmarried (by implication the unfit) had a greater mortality rate than the married. A note of caution is sounded here and it gives Darwin an opportunity, one of a very few, to make some remarks on the idea of progress. It is thus worth quoting him at this point:

> If the various checks specified . . . and perhaps others as yet
> unknown, do not prevent the reckless, the vicious and otherwise
> inferior members of society from increasing at a quicker rate
> than the better class of men, the nation will retrograde, as has
> occurred too often in the history of the world. We must
> remember that progress is no invariable rule. It is most difficult
> to say why one civilized nation rises, becomes more powerful,
> and spreads more widely than another, or why the same nation
> progresses more at one time than another. We can only say
> that it depends on an increase in the actual number of the
> population, on the number of men endowed with high
> intellectual and moral faculties, as well as on their standard
> of excellence. Corporeal structure, except so far as vigour of
> body leads to vigour of mind, appears to have little influence.[25]

Lest the wrong impression is given, Darwin shortly after asserts that 'progress has been much more general than retrogression', and at the very end of his two volumes, in a passage that seems at once to sum up his paradoxical metaphysics and to deny that he has one, he says:

Man may be excused for feeling some pride at having risen, though not through his own exertions, to the very summit of the organic scale; and the fact of his having thus risen, instead of having been aboriginally placed there, may give him hopes for a still higher destiny in the distant future. But we are not here concerned with hopes or fears, only with the truth as far as our reason allows us to discover it.[26]

In each of these quotations, the views of Darwin are in general accord with those of Spencer. True enough, Spencer elaborated in detail many points (or probably more accurately attitudes) that may have offended Darwin's sensitivities, but then Spencer was a social philosopher and the leading sociologist in England at the time, whereas Darwin was a biological scientist and only marginally and certainly not professionally interested in social problems or social theory. The core of Spencer's social Darwinism, therefore, was not Darwinisticism in the sense that it distorted what Darwin had actually written out of all proportions, though whether it was German metaphysical Darwinism, in Chauncey Wright's sense, is another matter, and one that bears consideration.[27]

My limited defence of Spencer cannot be applied to many other so-called social Darwinists, or those who applied Darwinism to social phenomena, or those who used it to justify their preconceived social theories. The following, one of many such judgments, is not an exaggeration nor even an attempt at philosophical satire:

Darwinism as an expression of a fundamental law of nature became a new orthodoxy to which appeal was made to justify diverse opinions in many spheres. It was invoked to explain social evolution in general and to support individualism and socialism, competition and cooperation, aristocracy and democracy, brute force and kindliness, militarism and pacifism, ethical pessimism and optimism, creative emergent evolutionism and evolutionary naturalism.[28]

Perhaps the single most abused notion was that of the 'survival of the fittest' which Spencer had picked up from Malthus and handed on to Darwin, and which was used by writers from Carlyle to Nietzsche, from Bagehot to Maine, Haeckel, Pearson, Renan and many others, each in his own particular way and to serve his own particular purpose.

One of these, Ernst Haeckel, the great German evolutionist and the virtual creator of scientific monism, stimulated considerable controversy when, in an attempt to save his form of social Darwinism, he claimed that socialism and Darwinism were incompatible. A host of Socialists leapt immediately into battle with Haeckel and one of them, the Italian Enrico Ferri, a renowned criminologist, presented a particularly interesting case against Haeckel.

The main burden of the attack, as Ferri understands it, is that whereas Darwinism proves the natural inequality of men, operates through the struggle for survival, and leads eventually to inevitable social aristocracy, socialism is supposed to reject all three of these positions. But no, Ferri objects, socialism rests on the basis of these Darwinian premises, and it *solves* the unsavoury problems of man in the competitive society.* Socialism was certainly incompatible with crude social Darwinism, as Marx and Engels had said all along, but was quite compatible with the true, undistorted Darwin. Even more than this, 'As Virchow† justly remarked, socialism is nothing else than the logical and vital outcome partly of Darwinism and partly of Spencerian evolution'.[29]

Ferri takes each of the three supposed propositions of Darwinism and shows that socialism is really a sophisticated treatment of them rather than a rejection of them. Socialism recognizes the differences in men, he says, but it holds in spite of this that they are all men and believes in the dignity of men. The struggle for survival may be the rule in nature, but socialism, by showing that a more equitable and at the same time a more efficient social organization is possible, demonstrates that this 'natural' law may be overcome by socialist man in a socialist society. Thirdly, laissez-faire individualism does not even permit an aristocracy, the best, to be selected simply because in terms of social talent and worth it is so inefficient. Socialism at least, by providing equality of opportunity, would ensure that everyone was properly rewarded for his contribution to the social good.

Therefore, the most revolutionary theory of progress of the nineteenth century and the formidable evolutionary theory of progress were linked.

As happens not infrequently in intellectual history, as I have implied, many writers appeared to have been quite content to espouse one part of Darwin's theory, and simply to ignore and often contradict other parts, and these by no means always the least significant aspects of the theory. In a most interesting study of the reception of Darwinism in the British periodical press between the publication of *Origin of Species* and the year after the publication of *The Descent of Man*, Professor Ellegard documents this point well. 'It is clear that Darwin's contemporaries were, in a way, prepared for an evolution

---

* Marx had previously commented apropos the crude social Darwinists of the extreme laissez-faire school that they had rightly described the economic jungle of Victorian England.

† Virchow, who discovered that all cells come from preceding cells, was an anti-evolutionist *and* an anti-socialist.

theory,' he says. 'But they were not at all prepared for the sort of evolution theory that Darwin actually propounded.'[30]

To many, what Darwin 'actually propounded' made little difference. For example, as we have seen, both the Christians* and the Marxists took what they liked from Darwin and simply pretended that the rest did not exist.[31] The history of social Darwinism is replete with such curios, but it becomes deadly serious when one realizes that from them Gumplowicz developed his sociology of war as a necessary prerequisite to social progress. Bismarck, Chamberlain and Roosevelt all thought that imperialism was justified by the subtitle of the *Origin of Species*, and racists from Bernhardi to Hitler have claimed scientific validity from Darwinian sources.[32]

Hofstadter, in his review of these phenomena in America (an account that demonstrates convincingly the main thesis of the sociology of knowledge), shows clearly how the history of social Darwinism as a theory followed the history of America as an emerging power. The individualism of the age of competition slowly gave way to the age of imperialism, and the social Darwinists adjusted their theories, and what they chose to ignore from Darwin, to suit their interests of the times. Sumner, the leading social Darwinist in America and a leading sociologist, did not allow theoretical complications to blur the clarity of his vision. 'The progress of civilization, according to Sumner [says Hofstadter], depends upon the selection process; and that in turn depends upon the workings of unrestricted competition.'[33] It is true to say that Sumner was really Spencer's American representative,† for he followed Spencer's line in every issue of importance.

The social Darwinists, therefore, were an extremely varied and in most cases quite unconnected group of social theorists. Lumping them all together under the title 'social Darwinism' appears to me to have at least two important justifications. In the first place, they were all anxious to appropriate some cognitively acceptable scientific backing for their assorted social and political theories. Cowles, in his remarks on the history of the concept 'the struggle for existence', shows clearly the tremendous persuasive power of one idea that could solve problems in economics and politics, in biology, and in

---

* An extraordinary instance is supplied by the indefatigible and skilful apologist, C. E. Raven, when he argues that the idea of salvation through suffering, the Christian image of Christ on the Cross, coheres well with the Darwinian notion of the struggle for survival (in 'The Struggle for Existence', *London Quarterly and Holborn Review* (October 1959), pp. 280-309).

† The chapter on Sumner in Barnes' *Introduction to the History of Sociology* is entitled 'Spencerianism in American Dress'. It is significant that Sumner, like Spencer and in opposition to many of the social Darwinists, opposed imperialism in the strongest possible terms.

the area of social change.[34] Bagehot was merely expressing the spirit of the age when he entitled his major work *Physics and Politics*, and the spirit of the age was precisely the scientism that Comte had worked so hard to establish. The model of the sciences that the social Darwinists 'aped' was that of the author of *Origin of Species*!

The second justification is that, whatever brand of social Darwinism we examine, whether socialist or laissez-faire individualist, whether Christian-teleological or atheist-materialist, whether vitalist or mechanist, each variety espoused some unmistakable notion of progress. The idea of progress had become an assumption without which it seemed impossible to construct a social theory in the latter part of the nineteenth century. Material progress had won such an astounding victory over the pessimists, of whom there were very few remaining,[35] that moral progress was almost literally being dragged along with it.

The warnings of Huxley[36] against the dangerous identification of evolution with progress had been partially heeded (had not both Spencer and Darwin acquiesced to the possibility and actuality of regression?), but it was like trying to stop a runaway train on a downward slope. The crash had to come, for progress had now been proclaimed as near to necessary and inevitable from so many different sources that it was widely believed to be necessary and inevitable. In the never-ending dialectic of ideas and actions, the process had come almost full circle. The idea of intellectual progress which had been instrumental in the development of science and technology had now been sanctified by that very same science and technology. Theories of progress gained enormous prestige in the nineteenth century precisely because they were presented as having been derived from or related to the great discoveries of science. The institutionalization of science, in short, had made the metaphysics of progress respectable. But by the very canons of science this brief honeymoon could not last, for just as the methods of science had in one age set up the theories of progress, in the next age they would be tested; if found wanting the methods of science would reject them. Such is the price of scientism.

In the next chapter I shall examine the ways in which the theories of progress of the nineteenth century fared in the tests to which the twentieth century submitted them.

V The decline of optimism

It is grossly inaccurate to claim that on the day the First World War broke out, the idea of progress died a most unnatural death. What does bear consideration, however, is the view that the war was a crushing blow to the idea of progress at a time when it was undergoing a serious revaluation, both directly and indirectly. Accordingly, this chapter will distinguish between the pre-war reflections of Durkheim and Weber, and the post-war prophesies of Spengler and Toynbee. The sociologist Sorokin, who does not fit in exactly with either pair, is dealt with in the company of Spengler and Toynbee for reasons given in the appropriate section of the text.

Durkheim and Weber
Durkheim and Weber, for all their differences, can be seen as the first men to carry out sociological work, both in theory and in practice, in an acceptably modern sense; from their efforts most contemporary sociology derives. This is not to deny the importance of Simmel and Pareto, Westermarck or Hobhouse, Tönnies or Ward, but simply to claim that Durkheim and Weber were the greatest of the early sociologists and that their interests and approaches set the tone of twentieth-century sociology to an appreciable extent. They are not to be compared with Comte or Spencer, for they were attempting quite different things, both theoretically and methodologically. In the first place, neither Durkheim nor Weber felt the need to construct explicit philosophies of history to deal with the development of a determined world. No Law of the Three Stages or evolutionary hypothesis was necessary or indeed desirable, though this is somewhat less true of Durkheim than of Weber. Secondly, there is a real attempt in their works—its success is in this context irrelevant—to seek empirical evidence for hypotheses, and these problems of scientific justification in their work remained ones to be solved by

argument rather than by fiat. Again Durkheim, significantly influenced as he was by Comte, demonstrates these traits somewhat differently from Weber.

How then did they treat the idea of progress—the mainstay of the pre-scientific sociology? For both Durkheim and Weber the question was not so much the general one of explaining the whole history of humanity and thereby leaving out the mass of historical detail that would, if properly considered, render this an impossible task, but the more specific one of investigating the causes of the technological industrial society of the twentieth-century Western world.

For Durkheim the essential variable in this process of industrialization appears at first to be the division of labour, but it is soon clear that this factor is something in the nature of an intervening variable between population pressure and a form of social organization characterized by the relationship of organic solidarity. This latter replaces mechanical solidarity as the main type of bond that holds men together in society. As far as material progress is concerned, there is really no doubt that the division of labour, in the sense of functional specialization in which Durkheim uses the expression, is necessary for the industrial society to develop. But here Durkheim is very careful to point out that this necessity is a consequence of the density of population and *not* a manifestation of any teleological law of progress. The cause of the division of labour, and also thereby of civilization, appears, he argues:

> not as an end which moves people by its attraction for them, not as a good foreseen and desired in advance, of which they seek to ensure themselves the largest possible part, but as the effect of a cause, as the necessary resultant of a given state.[1]

The details of Durkheim's argument in *The Division of Labour in Society*, one of the great classics of sociology, are too well known to require extended discussion here for the purposes of mere exegesis. His science of ethics, however, as it directly entails a theory of moral progress, must be considered at this juncture.

The basic premiss of the science of ethics is that man in society, and not simply man as such, is a moral being, for 'man is a moral being only because he lives in society, since morality consists in being solidary with a group and varying with this solidarity'.[2] This position is most persuasively argued in *The Elementary Forms of the Religious Life*, published in 1912, nineteen years after the first edition of *The Division of Labour*. Organic solidarity, far more intensive and powerful a form of social cohesion than mechanical solidarity, is, as has been noted, the consequence of the division of labour, and therefore the latter becomes the foundation of the moral order.

73

To the objections of Marx and others that it is precisely the division of labour that dehumanizes rather than makes man moral, Durkheim counters a rather oblique argument that, if nothing else, leaves us in no doubt as to his penchant for attributing positive moral worth to the division of labour as it progresses. Indeed, on his argument that I have briefly reconstructed above, he could do little else. The matter, nevertheless, does not stop here, for Durkheim makes a special point of dismissing any necessary or indeed special link between the progress of the division of labour and of happiness, and his reason for rejecting any utilitarian principle of progress is an important pointer to his attitude to the moral progress that we are considering. Durkheim rejects the search for happiness as a criterion for progress because pleasure and pain, he considers, are essentially relative. More importantly, he goes on to say that as happiness cannot be considered causally relevant in explaining why different peoples progress in different ways and at different rates, then *no* individual factor can possibly be held to account for social change. Further, as the changes in the physical environment are infrequent, we are forced to accept the conclusion that 'it is in the social environment we must seek the original conditions'[3] of progress.

This and other brief statements throughout the book preview the work published two years later in 1895, *The Rules of Sociological Method*, one of the most powerful and influential methodological treatises in the history of sociology. There Durkheim elaborated the approach that has come to be known as 'sociologism',[4] which, within the long tradition of methodological collectivism, has played its part in withstanding the onslaughts of the methodological individualists and the psychological reductionists. Morality for Durkheim is not simplistically a matter of the individual making his moral choice in a sociological vacuum but, in its most significant sense, is a function of the social structure whose obvious vehicle is man in society, related to his fellows in a more or less solidary fashion. It follows from Durkheim's line of argument that the more solidary the social relations in a particular society, that is one characterized by a high level of organic solidarity and thus a more developed division of labour, the more highly developed will be the moral order.

For the success of the division of labour depends on each fulfilling his function properly, and when the body social is viewed seriously as an organism then it is plain that the smallest upset in any one part of the society could have unintended consequences on any or all of the other parts. Successful progress in the division of labour taken in this sense leads to moral quietism and to the conception of moral worth outlined not long before in Bradley's stern essay on 'My Station and its Duties'.

It is not surprising that Durkheim was known for his general conservatism, and from arguments such as these, modern sociological functionalism, though it has travelled a long way from Durkheim and by many diverse paths, has yet entirely to divorce itself.[5]

In the conclusion to *The Division of Labour* Durkheim gives some further indications of the possibilities of moral progress, not only over the condition of societies typified by organic solidarity. There is every chance, he argues, that the peaceful fraternity of mankind, especially of an intra-group nature, will take place with the progress of the division of labour. Inter-group harmony on an international scale and the abolition of wars is also likely, but he suggests that this will most probably occur due to the dominance of those peoples who have progressed furthest.

The record is not as optimistic as my account suggests. In his study of *Suicide* of 1897 Durkheim highlighted, by means of extensive statistical analysis, some of the problems that faced a society in its transformation from the traditional to the modern-industrial form of social organization. A key concept developed from the first chapter of the third book of *The Division of Labour* is that of anomie, variously interpreted as rootlessness, normlessness or the state that occurs in a society when the solidary organs are out of touch for any length of time. This is of course an abnormal form of social solidarity produced by a 'pathological' division of labour. Anomic suicide 'results from man's activity's lacking regulation and his consequent sufferings',[6] and with egoistic and altruistic suicide comprises the three types of suicide that Durkheim's sociological analysis reveals. I cannot here go into the details of his insightful discussion, though it is interesting to note that when Durkheim cites 'overweening ambition' as one condition leading to anomic suicide he further exposes himself to criticisms that his sociology is a justification of the *status quo*.

It is gratuitous to speculate, however, that Durkheim realized that all the various parts of the body social might not always fit into place, and important to remember that he is the source of insights into both the functional theory of religion and the study of social dislocation and criminality.

Durkheim never resolved the paradoxes inherent in his theory of moral and material progress. Starting from the well-worn fact of the pressure of population density, he endeavoured to identify and explain the mechanisms whereby this structural fact about a society might be causally linked to the forms of social organization observed in a world in the midst of industrial and perhaps moral progress. Synthesizing the division of labour, the forms of social solidarity, types of legal sanctions, and other sociological variables, he provides the first sociological theory of progress, with the possible and partial exception of Marx's, that the modern student can take at all seriously.

In turning to Weber we are struck immediately by two facts. First, his work is somewhat more pessimistic than that of Durkheim; and second, it seems to focus on different *types* of problems. Max Weber, by his own declaration, might be sceptical about the present study, for he concludes a short analysis of the term 'progress' with the words:

> After all has been said, I still regard the use of the term 'progress', even in the limited sphere of its empirically unobjectionable application, as very unfortunate. But the use of words is not subject to censorship; one can, in the end, avoid the possible misunderstandings. [7]

We can only begin to appreciate this attitude by examining his views on the place of values in the cultural sciences, and particularly sociology. Weber steered the dangerous but, as he saw it, necessary path between ethical relativism and the objective verification of moral codes. Weber's running battle with the use of value-judgments in sociology defines his attitude to the latter position—that there can be no possible scientific justification for preferring one ultimate value over any other. 'An empirical science cannot tell anyone what he *should* do—but rather what he *can* do,' Weber argues, and he goes on to state emphatically that '*scientifically the "middle course" is not truer even by a hair's breadth*, than the most extreme party ideals of the right or left'. [8] There is no question, then (to put it in its most uncompromising form), that he is forced into an acceptance of the 'anarchy of ends'.

But this is precisely what he does not or is psychologically unable to accept, for to do so would be to sink, with little hope of rescue, into the quicksands of ethical relativism. Weber's solution to this dramatic and crucial problem is to deny that scientific objectivity in the face of questions of value suggests moral relativity or worse, moral indifference, in the way that his predecessors and many subsequent social theorists, it may be added, had thought. Value-judgments have no place in science, and one of Weber's primary concerns, especially as an editor of and contributor to the *Archiv für Sozialwissenschaft und Socialpolitik*, was to expose instances where writers under the guise of scientific analysis had permitted their own values to prevail. Ostensibly, he betrayed no self-righteous hypocrisy on this issue, for he called on all those engaged in the cultural sciences to ask themselves, and to continually make clear to their readers, '(and—again we say it—above all to one's self!) exactly at which point the scientific investigator becomes silent and the evaluating and acting person begins to speak'. [9] This point is the thread that runs through his twin essays of 1918, 'Politics as a Vocation' and 'Science as a Vocation', holding together what one commentator has described as 'his familiar distinction between value-spheres and his ethic of responsible choice'.[10]

This 'ethic of responsible choice' may be seen as the reflection in morality of Weber's central substantive sociological pursuit, in common with Durkheim, to explain the rise of the Western industrial world. Where Durkheim had constructed his views on material progress around the division of labour, Weber constructed his around the process of rationalization in society, best seen in the form of bureaucratic capitalist organization. The strength of the analysis gains much from the use of the ideal-type, a heuristic device that Weber considered to be an essential first step towards the possible explanation of sociological phenomena. The ideal-type is formed by the 'one-sided *accentuation* of one or more points of view and by the synthesis of a great many . . . *concrete individual* phenomena . . . [it] cannot be found empirically anywhere in reality . . . It is a *utopia*'.[11] Bureaucracy, perhaps his most elaborate example of the ideal-type in action, is linked with the rational-legal form of the legitimization of authority to characterize capitalism. This was taken to be far more than a mode of production, in much the same way as Durkheim took the division of labour to be far more than an economic relation. It was, in fact, a total form of social organization, and indeed the form to which Western civilization most closely approximated.

Now Weber logically (but not chronologically) was faced with the problem of finding some mechanism through which the whole process of rationalization could get started, and further, he took it upon himself to explain why rational bureaucratic capitalism had occurred only in the West. The economic interpretation of Marxist materialism was never strictly ruled out by Weber; on the contrary he held that Marxism was a useful though in the last resort a one-sided theory. Bearing this in mind, the argument of *The Protestant Ethic and the Spirit of Capitalism* may be understood far less as a polemic against Marx and far more as a serious attempt to balance the Marxist interpretation with one that started from the opposite philosophical if not sociological assumptions about the nature of change in society. Roughly, as I mentioned in the previous chapter, Marx had worked from the material base of society, particularly the relations of production, and had argued that ideas and values, occupying some 'unreal' superstructural realm, could be causally explained only with reference to this real material world.[12] Weber, on the other hand, attempted to show that there could be and indeed had been at least some interaction, with causal significance, between the material and the ideal. Therefore, Weber argued, it is important to examine the belief systems of various historical periods in order to obtain some clue to this possible interaction. His thesis of the relationship between religious systems and economic change, specifically the protestant ethic and the spirit of capitalism, was the first tentative result of this line of thought, and was supported by the great comparative studies of the religions of India and China and Ancient Judaism.

The protestant ethic, or rather the ideal-type of religious ideas and aspirations that Weber was to characterize, provided the crucial mechanism in which Weber saw both the key to the rise of capitalism and the distinguishing feature of Western civilization. His painstaking researches, which have withstood remarkably the criticisms of specialists in several areas*, reinforced the general thesis by pointing out again and again that the economically relevant characteristics of protestantism were missing from the other religious systems that he studied. By means of the 'thought experiment', that is the thinking away of certain variables in a situation and 'observing' how the resulting situation would differ from the original, Weber was led to assert his major propositions as to the ways in which religion and economic action were connected. This was done with some vigour and a confidence, though academically restrained as was the man himself, which leaves little real doubt as to his view of the significance of the general process of rationalization for social organization.

To complete this bare sketch of what may be loosely termed Weber's philosophy of history it is imperative to mention the concept of charisma, 'the specific and exceptional sanctity, heroism or exemplary character of an individual person... "the gift of grace" '.[13] Bendix, in his book on Weber, emphasizes the unstable aspect of this type of leadership when he describes it in terms of 'magic power as a unique and hence transient attribute of an individual'.[14] Due to the nature of the situation, charismatic authority, to last, has paradoxically to transform itself or to be transformed into one or a mixture of the other two analytical types of the legitimization of authority, namely traditional- and rational-legal forms. Weber's term for this transformation is 'the routinization of charisma', and from this account it is possible to derive the suggestion of a cyclic theory of history. In a discussion of the great Arab philosopher of history, Ibn Khaldun, Gellner asserts that 'at the core of his pessimistic theory is a belief that there is a sociological antinomy between civilization and social cohesion',[15] and he goes on to argue that this pessimism of

* Weber has of course been attacked by some specialists and praised by others. See, for example, Gabriel Kolko, 'Max Weber on America: Theory and Evidence', *History and Theory*, 1 (1961), pp. 243-60, for a slashing critique, and Otto B. van der Sprenkel, 'Max Weber on China', *History and Theory*, 3 (1964), pp. 348-70, for a generous defence of the Weber thesis.

Ibn Khaldun is paralleled by Weber's antinomy between bureaucracy in its rational-legal form and charismatic leadership, by nature anti-economic and revolutionary. Weber was not at all certain that this movement between charismatic and bureaucratic authority was entirely one-way, for he left open the possibility that rational bureaucracies could succumb, as in fact they have frequently done, to charismatic and arbitrary leadership. This being so, it is justifiable to attribute to Weber the semblance of a theory of historical cycles.

Gerth and Mills, in their interesting introduction to a collection of Weber's essays, modify this conclusion somewhat. They correctly point out that his views on value-judgment in the cultural sciences preclude Weber from having a philosophy of history in the usual sense, either of cycles or progress. However, on the basis of his general leaning on the process of rationalization in all spheres and the albeit often hesitant suggestions of moral worth that subsist in his enlightenment-style conception of reason, Gerth and Mills 'nevertheless feel justified in holding that a unilinear construction is clearly implied in Weber's idea of the bureaucratic trend'. They go on to argue, on the other hand, that 'charismatic movements' and 'rational routinization' are in 'antinomic balance',[16] and this seems to provide the lever that will open the issue precisely where Gerth and Mills wish to close it. H. Stuart Hughes sums up the matter with reference to Weber's clear recognition of the dangers inherent in both bureaucracy and charisma. 'In Weber's thought,' Hughes exclaims with much justice, 'the whole vast ambiguity of our century was held for one brief moment in a desperate synthesis.'[17]

The most accurate conclusion, then, is that Weber did hold a unilinear theory of material progress, in his role as a descendant of the enlightenment and an optimistic believer in the success of the protestant ethic. But as a twentieth-century man, and one whose political and historical acumen was not blinded by superficialities and novelty, Weber suspected that a 'sociological antinomy between civilization and social cohesion' might truly be the case. It is significant that he considered that bureaucracy might present a greater threat to democracy than charisma itself, for it 'accompanies modern *mass democracy* in contrast to the democratic self-government of small homogeneous units'.[18] The anti-economic, anti-scientific and profoundly anti-rational character of charismatic authority is of course entirely opposed to material progress, and if the possibility of this interruption of 'the bureaucratic trend' is always present, then a cyclic rather than a unilinear progress theory of history emerges. The paradox was unresolved by Weber, and this in itself is evidence of the increasing maturity of sociology and the great achievement of Weber in avoiding any dogmatic answer to the problem. Like the concept of anomie in Durkheim, charisma in Weber stands as a reminder that there were problems that could not easily be solved and that these problems often split sociological theories down the middle. Whereas Hegel and Marx had taught that the way to resolve the contradictions in the world was to contradict these in turn, Durkheim and, to an even greater extent, Weber broke through to the insight that perhaps verbal manipulation could only resolve contradictions on paper, and that man had to live with some contradictions. Weber, when asked what learning meant to him, replied: 'I want to see how much I can endure.'[19]

It is fitting that this short discussion of Weber should end with reference to the remarks on progress in his essay 'The Meaning of Ethical Neutrality' in *The Methodology of the Social Sciences*. Weber distinguishes three meanings of progress which are in 'widespread confusion'. These are progressive differentiation, progress of technical rationality in the utilization of means and increase in value. He further distinguishes between a 'subjective rational action' and a 'rationally correct action' (this derives from his general sociology), where the latter is simply technical progress. His position here on the relationship between material and moral progress is quite unambiguous.

> An increase in the subjective rationality and in the objective-technical 'correctness' of an individual's conduct can, beyond a certain limit—or even quite generally from a certain standpoint —threaten goods of the greatest (ethical or religious) importance in his value-system. . . . The use of the term 'progress' is legitimate in our disciplines when it refers to 'technical' problems, i.e., to the 'means' of attaining an unambiguously given end. It can never elevate itself into the sphere of ultimate evaluations.[20]

Whether Weber would have held firmly to this position had it been *reason itself*, and by implication the whole process of rationalization and all its sociological correlates whose moral worth was under attack, is a subject for speculation. Logically, reason is no more or less morally reprehensible than unreason, but Weber himself held that reason and science are not irrelevant in the struggle among values. Science teaches both clarity and consistency, and the importance of these is not to be underestimated*. In the conflict between the ethics of faith and the ethics of responsibility, it is a special type of value-judgment—if it is a value-judgment at all—to prefer the latter.[21]

It is a testament to Weber's greatness as a social scientist and to his dignity as a man that he grappled with the dilemma of moral pro-

* There is an interesting parallel between Weber and, for example, Ginsberg here.

gress and scientific objectivity and did not, like so many before and since, attempt to resolve it in a dogmatic manner.[22]

Spengler, Toynbee and Sorokin

As the difference in the theories of history of Spengler, Toynbee and Sorokin are no more illuminating than their very considerable similarities, it is both convenient and helpful to consider them *en bloc* in contrast to the work of Weber and Durkheim. It is perhaps permissible to comment at the start that in many ways it is as if Durkheim and Weber had never written and social philosophy was still in the age of Comte, Spencer and Hegel! In recognition of the fact that these remarks are less true with reference to Sorokin, I shall deal first with Spengler and Toynbee.

The point of origin of these two world historians is that of the problems of the rise and decline of civilizations. Each is a cultural relativist to the extent that all of these units—Spengler isolates eight cultures (for him a civilization is the senile phase of a culture) and Toynbee twenty-one—are rather self-contained entities and have criteria of truth, value, etc., of their own.[23] At this level, noting how they trace the birth, maturity and decline of these world-historical units, it appears that they are men who reject the ideas of material and moral progress and who espouse cyclical theories of history. Spengler more than Toynbee was a prophet of doom and mystery, for he did not deign to give any real explanation as to why all vital cultures should slide into the inevitable darkness of civilization. Like the death of the organism, the death of civilizations is inexplicable in the sense that the causal principle does not apply to World History at large.

Toynbee at first sight* is not so mysterious, for he more or less rests his case on the ability to explain those very processes of rise and decline of civilizations that Spengler found so mysterious. Although wishing to attribute a certain amount of autonomy to his civilizations, he introduces the categories of affiliation and apparentation to maintain some continuity between those societies that seem linked. Civilizations emerge from primitive societies when they respond successfully to challenges, and civilizations lapse back to the primitive state when they do not respond successfully to challenges, specified by Toynbee as 'times of troubles or interregnum'. An astonishing array of historical detail is amassed to support these rather obvious theoretical statements, and it is notable that most of

---

* There is a problem of interpretation here for Toynbee's monumental *A Study of History*, in twelve volumes, not only took twenty-seven years to appear, from 1934 to 1961, but also underwent a quite radical change in principle about half-way through. In addition, many recent works of his further complicate the picture.

Toynbee's critics pay homage to this empirical richness usually before and after tearing his organizing principles and the 'scientific hypotheses' to pieces.

Let me examine the implications of these impressive historical documents for the problems of progress. Spengler could not be any more unambiguous on this issue than he in fact is. In example after example he argues that the machine age, characterized as 'Faustian', that the twentieth-century engineer-civilization holds so dear, is bound to crumble to dust like every other culture that has been misled by the mystic forces of fate into the form of civilization. In every field this decadence is evident, in art forms, in sciences of materialism, in economics, in politics, in religion. The death of style in culture and its replacement by 'exoticism, eclecticism, and emphasis on size'[24] are the signs that alert the executioner of civilizations, and Spengler was in no doubt that Western civilization was truly exhibiting these dreaded signs. This particular cataclysm would be fought out between Money and Blood, acquisitive capitalism and violent Caesarism, liberal democracy and the despotism that it inevitably spawns. Barbarism would slowly gain the upper hand and the life-cycle of Western civilization would run its course, in the thousand or so years that are allotted to each unit in history. The fulfilment of this plan, Spengler claims, does not depend on human action, 'we have not the freedom to reach to this or to that,' he says, 'but the freedom to do the necessary or to do nothing. And a task that historic necessity has set *will* be accomplished with the individual or against him.'[25] In the face of Spengler's antiseptic terror, we have no chance, therefore, even to follow T. H. Huxley and to combat the cosmic forces.

Moral progress has even less opportunity in this scheme of things than material progress, for at least there is no objection to limited progress in technique within the life-span of any culture. Spengler's relativism is of an extraordinarily unrestricted variety, for it includes not only moral values as we should expect, but also mathematics and science, philosophy and religion, and all aspects of life and works. This radical and uncompromising sociology of knowledge (perhaps the only internally consistent sociology of knowledge?) derives from the notion that each High Culture has a prime symbol, valid only in reference to its own culture, which suffuses all the productions of the culture. No single concept of number, to take a famous example, is correct or incorrect. Truth is relative in *all* its manifestations to the culture that produces the particular brand under consideration, and as all will eventually succumb as civilizations to their cosmic fate, all truths have the same status in the harsh and relentless eye of world history.

Toynbee's thesis is milder and perhaps more comforting to some than Spengler's. In the first place, it is clear that Toynbee is unwilling to foster a completely determinist case, and that he leans, especially in the later volumes of *A Study of History*, towards an interpretation that will permit mankind to derive some *human* meaning from the whole affair, something that could never be done on the basis of Spengler's work. The difference is that Toynbee is a profoundly theological theorist, and as his volumes came rolling off the presses it became increasingly apparent that his interpretation of 'empirical history' was permeated through and through with Christian metaphysics. As a result a theory of progress can be extracted from his work. It is, however, both a religious theory of progress and a theory of religious progress. The former is seen in his explanation of the growth of civilizations through 'creative' individuals or minorities. These, when they are not religious figures or groups as they very often are, turn out to be theologically relevant in the first instance. The setting up of a universal church by breakaway dissidents is another instance of the theological factor in the dynamics of social change. But the most important step that Toynbee takes in his religious theory of progress lies in his explanation of how civilizations actually grow. Material progress or progress in techniques is not the answer, for

> Growth means that the growing personality or civilization
> tends to become its own environment and its own challenger
> and its own field of action. In other words, the criterion of
> growth is progress towards self-determination; and progress
> towards self-determination is a prosaic formula for describing
> the miracle by which Life enters into its Kingdom.[26]

In the context, there is no doubt as to the meaning of these cryptic words. Salvation works as an inner dynamic towards the twin goals of freedom for man and freedom for his spirit.

The theory of religious progress is expressed most clearly in Toynbee's book of 1948, *Civilization on Trial*, in which he radically modifies the earlier cyclic theory of *A Study of History*. The rise and fall of civilizations, he argues, has one very positive result in that it brings about a gradual evolution of religion, so that though we cannot speak of progress from one civilization to another in meaningful terms we can speak of religious progress. The highest religion is naturally the Christian one, and civilization is engaged in 'Heavenwardly progress'; as Sorokin says, for Toynbee 'human history or the total civilization process thus turns into a creative theodicy'.[27] Therefore, where Spengler concludes in pessimism and the emptiness of meaningless cycles, Toynbee rescues his whole philosophy of history by this theological sleight of hand. Given religious progress, he can now work back over secular history and construct a spiral in place of a cyclic theory (a theory of progressive cycles), and this appears to be a special type of progress theory more than a special type of cyclic theory.

The paradox emerges, therefore, that Spengler, viewing from around the time of the First World War, could give no crumb of comfort to an anxious world, whereas Toynbee, writing after the European holocaust and the beginning of the age of possible total nuclear destruction, actually wrote a probable happy ending into an account not greatly different in theory and in fact from that of Spengler.

Sorokin's integralist synthesis shows that Toynbee was not alone of the post-Spengler generation to eschew the latter's too radical conclusions, and likewise that the influence of Spengler on all subsequent philosophies of history was to be considerable. The work of the three men is, in the words of an expositor of Sorokin, 'a gigantic re-examination of the theory of progress',[28] and the Russian-born American, like the German and the Englishman, boldly paints a canvas of spectacular historical-social dimensions. The study of history of Sorokin, entitled *Social and Cultural Dynamics*, published in four volumes from 1937 to 1941, is certainly the most comprehensive study of its kind ever carried out by a professional sociologist.*

The organizing principles of Sorokin's scheme are the three basic values that determine the modes of cognition in societies, viz. the ideational, the idealistic and the sensate. Throughout the volumes of brilliant and often original historical-social interpretation, it becomes plain that for Sorokin the sensate mode of truth and cognition, characteristic of Western technological society, is in some sense morally reprehensible. The formal similarities to Spengler here are notable. Each culture is traced through the stages of the ideational and the idealistic, and thence to the period of decline and decadence, the sensate, with its bankrupt system of values. As with Spengler, this sorry stage is the one in which Western civilization presently finds itself. Sorokin illustrates this three-stage birth and decay cycle with reference to all of the important areas of culture, the fine arts, science and philosophy, religion, the law and ethics, and the forms of social relations and their organization.

The dynamic of change in society and culture is not some mystery which confounds the patient researcher, but is contained in the actual study of the empirical detail of all the civilizations under review. This dynamic Sorokin entitles 'The Principle of Immanent Change', and he summarizes it as follows:

1. The reason or cause of a change in any socio-cultural

---

* The work of A. Kroeber, the American anthropologist, *Configurations of Culture Growth* (Berkeley, 1944), deserves mention here. Kroeber, however, does not impress a theoretical scheme on his material to anything like the same extent as Sorokin.

system is in the system itself, and need not be looked for any-where else.

2. Additional reason for change of a system is its milieu, which is again composed mostly of the immanently changing systems.

. . .

4. Bearing the seeds of change in itself, any sociocultural system bears also in itself the power of moulding its own destiny or life career. . . . each sociocultural system is the main factor of its own destiny.[29]

The dilemma of freedom and determinism confronts Sorokin as it does all theorists of history. In as far as the system once it emerges must follow a predetermined career, then, Sorokin admits, history and his theory are determinate. On the other hand, so 'far as the future of the system is determined mainly not by external agents, but by the system itself, such a determinism is indeterministic or free';[30] thus internal developmental variations are permitted for all civiliza-tions, and history once again has a meaning and hope once again is salvaged.

Sorokin is at once much more convincing and much less mystical than Toynbee as to the bases of this hope and this meaning. Many commentators (and Sorokin himself) have claimed that his theory of change is essentially dialectical.[31] Seen in this light, his attempted synthesis of the three main supersystems of culture into one that maintains the best features of each and expels the worst becomes more easily understandable. The dialectical triad consists of 'fluctua-tions' (rather than cycles) between the ideational and the sensate, with the idealistic system holding the middle ground. The great synthesis, introduced a little suddenly in the fourth volume of *Dynamics*, sets up what Sorokin terms 'integral truth' which embraces the three former types characterized by intuition, reason and the senses. This compromise or combination of the best of all cultures is intended as something of a 'super-truth'.* The social system in which this new concept of truth and cognition will flourish, however, will more nearly approximate the ideational or the idealistic rather than the sensate type, one feels. In his Centre for Creative Altruism, attached to Harvard University, Sorokin was till his recent death engaged in scientific study towards the blueprint for a utopia based on 'the ways and power of love'.

Sorokin has paid little attention to the issue of material progress; he appears to take it as comparatively unproblematic and obviously linked to the sensate phase of culture and the growth of science and

---

* It is instructive to contrast this type of argument with Weber's explicit denial that the 'middle course' in politics makes any value-judgment more scientific than the extremes.

technology. Moral progress, on the other hand, poses important questions for him. Sensate ethics, which first became dominant in the West in the sixteenth century, is identified by its hedonism, its sensualism and its general utilitarianism, and it, along with the 'weakness' of sensate law, presents a great threat to the moral fibre and indeed the historical persistence of Western civilization. It is here that Sorokin most definitely parts company from Spengler and travels the same road as Toynbee. For there is a possibility of reprieve; our sensate culture need not necessarily crash around our ears and we need not consider inevitable the utter destruction of Western civilization. It can be saved by our good efforts, especially those like Sorokin's own work in creative altruism, and that means only as much as a redirection on to the path of idealistic and ideational culture systems.

The outcome of Sorokin's work is not unduly pessimistic. The danger, to be sure, is ever-present, and the two world wars, along with the almost permanent rupture of peace in recent times, the rate and nature of crime and vice, and the sometimes hopeless efforts of the world organizations, all go to prove that the only solution lies in deposing the ego and substituting in its place the value of altruism as the component of man's supraconscious. That this is seen as possible is indeed a valiant theory of moral progress, even more courageous because it is maintained to be so against the present immoral sensate culture. More realistic than Toynbee, Sorokin does not grant religion a special exemption from the general decadence of the time, though it must be added that Sorokin's answer is no less theological in essence, notwithstanding the fact that Toynbee puts his faith in a particular institutionalized religion whereas Sorokin opts for a vaguer 'spiritual regeneration'.

More generally, both Sorokin and Toynbee, again in contradistinction to Spengler, espouse an attitude that suggests in the long run a spiral or progressive cyclical theory of history. This stems from their moderate relativism as opposed to Spengler's extreme relativism, for they see that some cultures build on their predecessors in a variety of ways, though in neither of them is this very closely specified.

One final remark needs to be made. Sorokin, though he has changed or developed his theory over the years, cannot be accused of the same *volte face* as Toynbee. The latter, it seems to me, came to approximately the same final conclusions as Spengler, and they shared the same historical intent though they certainly differed in the mechanisms they abstracted from the record of historical change. Spengler was a prophet of doom and decided on his interpretation accordingly; Toynbee was a prophet of Christian millenarianism. The change in Sorokin's system comes from within the system: the intent is sociological rather than historic. The change in Toynbee's system comes from outside, from a need to salvage meaning and particularly Christian theological meaning from history, almost in spite of history. Sorokin has claimed that he never intended to set up any inevitable scheme in which a dying sensate order would necessarily be followed by a new ideational order. 'I do not have any sufficient logical ground,' he says, 'on which to contend that the observed order is invariable.'[32]

In intention if not in actual practice, the sociologist Sorokin may be distinguished from the philosophers of history Spengler and Toynbee, but I maintain that all three engaged upon a qualitatively different enterprise from Durkheim and Weber. What does bring them all together, however, is the sceptical attitude towards the by now old-fashioned nineteenth-century view of progress which they accepted as more or less inevitable, and their opposition to the implicit and often explicit value-judgment that was made in linking material and moral progress.

For Spengler this relationship was entirely reversed—the machine age signified moral decline. For Weber the rational bureaucracy that had to support the technological-industrial society contained its own very real perils. Durkheim, Toynbee and Sorokin are at one in their attribution to religion of a crucial significance in social life, though of course in the case of Durkheim religion was not to supply an answer to the problem of moral progress.

The task of the next chapter will be to follow up this opposition to the ideas of progress that the nineteenth (and for that matter the eighteenth) century bequeathed to the twentieth century.

VI Progress as a contemporary problem

In 1920 one of the most important events in the history of the idea of progress occurred with the publication of the first edition of J. B. Bury's inquiry into its origin and growth. This was and probably still is the single most influential work in the field, covering the history and suggesting a forceful interpretation of progressive thought in the West*.

In this chapter I shall attempt two things. Firstly, I shall discuss the controversy around the modernity of the idea of progress, and I shall suggest that this controversy is the result of a confusion of two concepts of progress—the innovational and the non-innovational—and that the non-innovational concepts of progress of writers who lived before the institutionalization of science were often mistaken for non-progress views. Secondly, I shall draw attention to a group of writers who are united, often in very different ways, by a common fear of the dangers of science and technology.

The modernity of progress
The Bury thesis, that the idea of progress was a distinctively modern achievement, quickly became an historical orthodoxy. As with all orthodoxies, opposition if not reaction appeared swiftly. It came from disparate sources such as the disillusioned liberalism of Carl Becker and the rather irate theological protestantism of Baillie, Dawson and

---

* Bury's work ends in the late 1800s. Ginsberg takes the story further but too briefly. Professor W. Warren Wagar of the University of New Mexico is currently engaged in a full-scale study of the history of the idea of progress from where Bury left off to the present day (personal communication, 1968). Charles Van Doren's large volume, *The Idea of Progress* (New York, 1967), is almost entirely analytical and ahistorical, and though it does present many recent views on progress its organization and methodology make it an unhelpful if not thoroughly confusing contribution to the field.

PROGRESS AS A CONTEMPORARY PROBLEM

others. Mixed into this was the sometimes blatant anti-modernism of all those who were appalled at the sort of civilization emerging from the progress of science and technology.

Becker, whose book *The Heavenly City of the Eighteenth Century Philosophers* I have discussed above, argued that the *philosophe* notion of progress was more or less a rehash of previous notions of providence, and that the metaphysical content was similar.[1] In a recent study the American historian D. W. Noble places Becker's thought in the perspective of an emerging American notion of progress, and what he has to say is relevant to my theme of the ambivalence towards progress in the twentieth century.

The key figure in the genesis of the problem of progress, Noble suggests, is Rousseau, for he pointed out most powerfully the disjunction between material and moral progress. The *philosophes*, or the majority of them, 'refused to find such an absolute conflict between their belief in the progress of civilization and their belief in a purified and primitive state of nature. They continued to believe in both progress and primitivism.'[2] This ambivalence, Noble argues, reappears throughout American history, especially in relation to the 'Frontier thesis' and the 'American Covenant' of Thomas Jefferson, in the struggle between history and nature in the development of America and American historical thought, and in the specific concepts of progress of men such as Becker, Beard and Turner.[3]

Becker and Beard, for example, changed their attitudes to progress quite dramatically. After the First World War both men seemed somewhat disenchanted with the optimistic premises of material progress. Beard, retracking on an earlier embryo-technocracy, found progress only in American isolationism and a restoration of the covenant with nature in which Turner had located the greatness of the country. The machine, he claimed, led only to misery. Becker had at an early stage given up the search for a science of history and seemed to be content with postulating, at most, the progress of the mind. Further than that at this stage he would not or could not go.

By the 1930s all had changed. In his introduction to Bury's *The Idea of Progress*, a new edition of which had been issued on the occasion of the 'Century of Progress Exposition' in Chicago, Beard clearly set out a most optimistic theory of progress based on the

dynamic character of technology. . . . there is nothing final about it . . . the passionate quest of mankind for physical comfort, security, health, and well-being generally is behind the exploratory organs of technology. . . . Curiosity would have to die out in human nature before technology could become stagnant, stopping the progress of science and industry.

Beard does not overlard the ethical correlates of technology as crudely as those in the previous century had done with evolution, though the same ultimate suggestion is present when he asserts that 'defenders of progress must assume that on the whole it is in a desirable direction'.[4] This statement could only come from one who confused material and moral progress, and is a common weakness in the technocratic argument.

By the middle of the 1930s Becker, too, had come round to the more pragmatic view of progress, and in the course of this conversion had radically altered his original thesis on the enlightenment concept of progress. He now considered that the latter was a more mundane and physical affair, and not really a simple derivative of the spiritual concept of the medieval philosophers. In line with this, Becker now defined progress in terms of the power that man had over nature and the world in general, and he saw the obstacles to progress in an improper distribution of this power and a lack of responsibility for it. Both Beard and Becker, therefore, chose progress over primitivism, but not without a deep struggle.* America, if one can generalize about such a phenomenon, opted for the reality and continuity of material progress and its positive moral associations.[5]

In America the most obvious blow to the progressive faith, the First World War, was less serious than in Europe, and even the Great Depression of the 1930s seemed to have had a less traumatic effect. Becker's eventual accommodation to Bury's interpretation of the modernity of the idea of progress and its internal links with science and technology, and even more so Beard's actual technocratic theory, are significant pointers to the American attitude at the time when the European scourging of the idea of progress was in full swing.

Sociology in America, like that in Europe in the previous century, thrived on the idea of progress as much as the idea of progress thrived on it. Sumner and Ward, the fathers of American sociology, were late nineteenth-century style evolutionists, the former in fact is called the 'American Herbert Spencer' by Barnes in his history of sociology. Ward, taking a belief in progress to great extremes, formulated the concept of 'telesis' which referred to the conscious improvement of society.[6] This was a recurrent theme in American sociology in the first half of the twentieth century—that social science could, by discovering the mechanisms of society, direct social progress. The Chicago school, under the leadership of Albion Small, pioneered in the important fields of deviant studies and urban

---

* It should be mentioned that Beard's isolationism versus Becker's cultural internationalism divides them, and perhaps America as much as their similar views of progress unites them.

sociology. The *raison d'être* for the work was precisely the moral progressivism for all to fill the gap left by material progress for the few. The sociologists felt a real need to augment the scientific nature of the discipline with a measure of responsibility and involvement. Barnes, in summing up Small's contribution, asserts:

> Small was exceeded only by Lester F. Ward in the persistence and ardor of his contention that sociology is to be justified, if at all, through its potential contributions to the triumph of scientifically guided social betterment. In other words, he always insisted that, in its fundamental goal, sociology is social ethics. [7]

There is no doubt, however, that the progressive training of the teachers (to say nothing of their actual progress theories) set American sociology off on the path clearly marked with signposts of material and technological progress leading to social justice and moral progress. And if this road was not inevitable, then sociology in America was committed to easing and encouraging the difficult journey. Meliorism and social reform, more than any other labels, characterized the growth of the profession and the disposition of its practitioners.

The relationship between this story of American intellectual life and the work of Bury may at first seem a little remote. In the sense of tracing out the climate of opinion, the general and perhaps often ill-digested diet of ideas current during a particular stage in history, the connection appears more clearly. On one level, it is nonsense to speak of the collapse of the idea of progress, for as I shall argue below some notion of progress is necessary to the continued existence of man as man on earth and specifically in society. There has been, of course, a very significant reaction, especially in Europe, against the idea of progress in the last half century, part of which I have already outlined above and the rest of which I shall attempt to sketch in below in the remainder of this chapter. What I want to make clear at this juncture, and why I thought it necessary to emphasize the generally progressive tendency of American sociology (British sociology might have served the same purpose), is that a great deal of the work, if not the majority of it, done in this period in social and related studies was of a generally progressive and optimistic character. This will, I hope, put the gloom and pessimism, the warnings of approaching disaster and the signals of a bankrupt civilization that we have seen and are to see, in a proper socio-historical perspective.

Becker, relatively speaking, had no particular axe to grind when he attacked Bury's account of the genesis of the idea of progress in *The Heavenly City*. Indeed, the careful comments on the idea of progress that the Cambridge historian made on his own account probably struck a sympathetic note with Becker. This was not so for an important group of writers of a theological bent who provided an opposition to Bury, and continue to do so, with the weapons that make for the most exciting disputes, namely polemic combined with brilliant scholarship. Professor Wagar has begun to describe the work of this group in a recent paper which, though brief, is to the point. [8] The leading members of this group (they are not formally affiliated) are Dawson, Lowith, Niebuhr, Baillie, Voegelin and Brunner. The relevant works were published around 1950, with the exception of Christopher Dawson's *Progress and Religion* which was published in 1929, pre-dating even *The Heavenly City*. In his paper, Wagar is more concerned with the arguments that these writers use in countering Bury's account of the modernity of the idea of progress, and he spends rather less time on their actual criticisms of the idea. As I am concerned with the latter as well as the former I should at this stage mention Dean Inge, one of the first Christian critics of the idea of progress whose Romanes lecture, published in 1920 (the same year as Bury's book), charges progress with being a 'superstition' that 'had the singular good fortune to enslave at least three philosophies—those of Hegel, of Comte, and of Darwin'. [9]

Inge's attack on the idea of progress is a well-argued and in places a finely-pointed performance. He shows with no little skill that the three philosophies which the idea enslaved are hardly favourable to the theory of progress, and he quotes T. H. Huxley and Bertrand Russell in support of the view that even 'naturalism has severed its alliance with optimism and belief in progress'. [10] He does not, however, align himself with those who, like Rousseau, Whitman, Thoreau, Ruskin, Morris and Carpenter, have criticized civilization *per se*, for he acknowledges that advances in some spheres have certainly come about. These advances, wonderful as they are, 'do not constitute real progress in human nature itself', [11] and without this (largely unexplained notion of) real progress these gains may at any time rebound back on man with terrible consequences.

Inge is fully conscious of the problem of values that any theory of progress faces, and his insistence on a fixed and absolute standard of values based on the Christian hierarchy was at least a recognition of a difficulty that many had simply ignored. He does not, therefore, commit the fallacy of lumping together all forms of progress in one composite concept, though it must be said that he himself never appears to think through to the constructive from the destructive level in his analysis, for his rather primitivist critique of some aspects of industrial society, his almost Christian-naturism, is in all essentials what I shall later characterize more fully as a form of non-innovational progress.

This view is not merely reactionary theology, but one that has echoes in some very distinguished chambers. In his essay, 'The

Dilemma of Civilisation', Inge states the problem in terms that Tönnies, Weber and Durkheim would have appreciated:

> Increasing complexity of organization is not necessarily progress, if by progress is meant the passage from a less desirable state of life to a more desirable. The more complex structure of society may impose itself because it has a greater survival value; it is not certain that any measures of social reform can make life in a highly industrialized community satisfying to the individual without impairing the efficiency on which the existence of such a community depends. This is the great problem of sociology . . .[12]

This was indeed a central theme in the attacks on the idea of progress mounted by the other Christian theologians I referred to above, but not the only one. Dawson, for example, argues that the great need is for 'a religion which will be an incentive to action and a justification of the material and social progress which has been the peculiar achievement of the last two centuries'.[13] This religion must itself be progressive, and this means that only one that contains Revelation and thus an historical sense would be suitable to the requirements of science, industrialism and the modern state. Christianity, which fulfils these conditions by dint of its eminently thisworldly attitude, seems to be the only serious contender, and Dawson concludes in a manner not unlike the later Toynbee on a note of optimism. The spiritual progress involved in modern Christianity represents for him a new form of life in the cosmic process.

This, as can be seen, is hardly an attack on the idea of progress, being more in the nature of a gentle rebuke and a reminder that progress of the spirit is the hard core of progress itself. Nevertheless, Dawson does strike a rather curious note when he warns that the fate of the Hellenic world, namely the flourishing of the intellect while the 'life-force' of the people withers, could mean that 'the higher and the more intellectually advanced civilizations of the West may be inferior in point of survival value to the more rudimentary Oriental cultures'.[14]

The main offensive comes from Baillie, Niebuhr, et al., and Wagar distinguishes four steps in their critique of Bury:

> . . . an insistence upon the radically ahistorical world-view of classical civilization.
> . . . Against this conception of time and history early Christianity . . . offered the pagans a hopeful and meaningful conception of history. . . . the modern idea of progress . . . is only a rendering in secular concepts of the Christian epic . . .

> The results are illegitimate, since they pervert the meaning of the original Christian teaching and spring from the unholy union of Christian doctrine with modern Western *hubris*.
> ... Finally ... certain medieval heresies and movements in the Protestant Reformation [acted] as agencies for the transmission of Christian doctrine to the apostles of the idea of progress during and after the Enlightenment.[15]

Emil Brunner puts the matter even more bluntly when he says that progressivism 'is the bastard offspring of an optimistic anthropology and Christian eschatology'.[16] That civilization has somewhere taken the wrong turning and that this mistake is ideologically signified by the development of the idea of progress are the underlying assumptions of this school of thought. But any heresy, however extreme, can always be corrected, and the continuing corpus of work of theologians and theologically-oriented historians and social scientists on the origins and the legitimacy of the idea of progress may be seen as part of a massive attempt, from varying sources, to redirect our civilization.

In the terms of this study it is helpful to look a little more closely at the *concepts* of progress around which this battle is being fought. As Wagar correctly comments, there 'is not one true, monolithic, goldplated Idea of Progress',[17] but as yet he has not gone beyond this. In introducing the concepts of innovational and non-innovational progress I shall try to impress some order on this more than usually complex field.[18] It is, I maintain, a theoretical gain to deal with the Judeo-Christian concept of progress as principally a non-innovational one, as I suggested in the first chapter. That is to say, this idea of progress consisted in sponsoring the maintenance and spread of ideas and institutions that were considered morally good. This is not at all incompatible with material progress, in a limited sense it encourages it, but it is incompatible with the view that progress as such is to be *measured* and/or *judged* by the spread of *new* things and ideas—the innovational concept of progress that is caught by the notion of the 'institutionalization of invention and discovery'.

This latter, the innovational concept of progress, is the one that characterizes modern industrial and technological society. It is of course related to the non-innovational concept of progress but, as an intellectual or actual historical development, it does not necessarily follow from the non-innovational concept of progress.*

The proponents of the non-innovational concept of progress are

---

* It should be quite clear that, for example, the modern sociology of development is centred largely round the problem of how in practice the transition from a non-innovational concept of progress to an innovational concept of progress is achieved.

not necessarily Primitivists or Luddites in the recognized sense of these terms, for it is quite meaningful to argue that industrialization has at time t gone far enough, and that a stop should be called. The vital point in this connection is that in the history of the world the intervening variable between the non-innovational and the innovational concepts of progress, and the societies of which they are characteristic, is the institutionalization of science and technology.*

The views of the Christian thinkers, while not usually wildly optimistic, rarely sunk to the depths of despair. Some important social theorists of this period, however, tended to a greater pessimism and this was very much linked to their analyses of what they hypothesized to lurk beneath the surface of man and society.

It is convenient and by now almost traditional to distinguish between those thinkers broadly termed the 'irrationalists' (which has come to mean not only those who used reason to attack reason but also those who used some form of unreason to attack reason) and those who made a minimum of judgment on the issue and simply pointed out that the forces of irrationality were important and demanded attention in any social theory, and the rest who implicitly or explicitly defended reason.

The work of Pareto represents one of the most important attempts to bring the irrational under the scrutiny of scientific sociology. Hughes, in his intellectual history of European thought from 1890 to 1930, considers this concern with the irrational as *the* major focus of social thought of this generation. Pareto's category of the 'residues', the constant underlying elements in human sentiments, is contrasted with his 'derivations', the variable aspects that serve to differentiate one society from another, particularly 'ideologies'. The two most important residues, namely (1) 'instinct for combinations' and (2) 'persistence of aggregates', lead us to Pareto's theory of speculators and rentiers, which has links with the political sociology of Machiavelli, the cyclic theory of the foxes and the lions.[19]

This theory saw history as a constant circulation of élites, manned now by foxes and now by lions (on the principles of the first and second residues respectively), and, needless to say, allowed little progress. This is clearly the case on Pareto's theory of the residues, the non-logical springs of action.† If man in society was subject to this force and had only very limited control in his own action, then to speak of progress was a delusion, and Pareto gives substantial

---

* Although my examination of progress has been exclusively of the West, by the twentieth century the impact of science and technology was being felt around the world, and theories of progress based on science abounded. For a particularly interesting case, see D. W. Y. Kwok, *Scientism in Chinese Thought, 1900-50*, New Haven, 1965, esp. ch. 6.

† The distinction between 'irrational' and 'non-logical' is ignored here.

evidence that man indeed has been deluded. He speaks of 'the holy name of Progress'; 'the Progress-lust' as pathological; 'the Olympus of Progress'; 'the theology of Progress'; and so on.[20] In a mood of chagrin he complains, in tones that would no doubt gladden the hearts of latter-day pedestrians, that 'if in our day of triumphant democracy the automobile did not enjoy the protection of the god Progress, it would be proscribed'.[21]

This wholesale rejection of progress as a workable doctrine, linked to the emphasis on irrationality in human action, is also characteristic of the Freudian critique of civilization, but there is one vital difference and this lies in the attitudes to Reason writ large. Whereas for Pareto, 'the worship of "Reason", "Truth", "Progress", and other similar entities is, like all cults, to be classed with non-logical actions',[22] for Freud the only hope for humanity lay in the successful defence of Reason against the dark forces of Unreason, and it was his achievement to make clear just how difficult a task this is.

In 'Civilization and its Discontents' of 1930, Freud expressed most clearly the social-psychological problems that any theory of progress must face. That he was in little doubt as to the reality of material progress is plain from a slightly earlier essay, 'The Future of an Illusion', which sums up moderately and unsensationally the misgivings that his generation felt about the idea of progress.

> While mankind has made continual advances in its control over nature and may expect to make still greater ones, it is not possible to establish with certainty that a similar advance has been made in the management of human affairs; and probably at all periods, just as now once again, many people have asked themselves whether what little civilization has thus acquired is indeed worth defending at all.[23]

The basis for this attitude, not many steps from despair, is that the sense of guilt parallels the rise of civilization, and that 'the price we pay for our advance in civilization is a loss of happiness through the heightening of the sense of guilt'.[24] Very briefly, this sense of guilt is the outcome of the traumatic foundation of the social order when the sons murdered the father, and have been so doing symbolically or have been desiring to do so in each generation since the original horde was thus transformed into the necessarily coercive society. The fear and envy of the sons for the father, the possessor of the authority and the women, turned to remorse once the patricide had been committed, and civilization has borne this burden of ambivalence ever since. The incest taboo and the other repressive norms of civilized society were the constant reminders to men of the dreadful origin and possible demise of their civilization.

The correctness or incorrectness of this theory is not at issue here, what I am concerned with is how Freud uses it in relation to the idea of progress. 'The fateful question for the human species,' he asserts, 'seems to me to be whether and to what extent their cultural development will succeed in mastering the disturbance of their communal life by the human instinct of aggression and self-destruction.'[25] Freud is neither utopian nor a prophet of utter gloom, and that he was ultimately a meliorist, believing that improvement in man's inner and outer lot were possible, is apparent from the mass of his scientific work devoted as it was to the ways in which these improvements could take place. The great oppositions in his work between Eros and Thanatos, love and self-punishment, and the reality-principle and the pleasure-principle, are analogous to the great opposition in Weber between bureaucracy and charisma, and in both the ambivalence testifies to the views of the nature of reality and their courage in resisting the temptation to falsify what they understood in the name of neat theory. After all, the phenomenon of light may be regarded in terms of waves or particles or both or neither—and how much more complex is social reality and the collective minds that organize it?

Philip Rieff, in his important study of Freud, argues a very convincing case on the moral significance of psycho-analytic theory. He shows that Freud tended to link what was good for the individual with what was anti-social, and because this dilemma could never be entirely resolved, truth and knowledge rather than goodness and happiness became the more realistic goals. Rieff concludes that normality was not used by Freud as a statistical concept but as an ethical ideal, the hospital and the couch would replace the church and the parliament in their normative functions. 'The Ethic of Honesty' would prevail, for man would come to understand the transience of pleasure in itself, and the reality-principle, the vehicle of reason and the source of true freedom due to its acceptance of the limitations of choice in the social and psychological world, would come into its own. Thus Freud perceived psychology as a moral science, and history as the story of what men did with their opportunities.[26] Freud was a critic of the idea of progress because he saw only too well that moral and social progress had not reached the stage at which he could consider that his deep suspicion of modern civilization was misplaced.

It is true to say that Continental philosophy in the twentieth century has not generally paid much attention to the idea of progress. The reasons for this are interesting and important, but this is not the place to deal with them. The 'self' and not 'society' or 'history' has been at the core of Continental philosophical thought in the first half of this century.

H   97

The reaction against technology

I now come to a group of writers linked together by only one thing, their opposition to industrial society, either as a form of social organization in its entirety or to the extent to which it has developed. These writers share no common philosophical standpoint; they have neither the Christian theodicy of Dawson or Baillie nor the all-encompassing theory of history of a Spengler. What binds them together and what makes them significant for this study is their active and in some cases their almost pathological dislike of the machine and the excesses of science.

The issue is clearly set out in the Hibbert lectures of 1934 by L. P. Jacks, significantly entitled *The Revolt against Mechanism*. The mechanical bias, oriented towards problem-solving, Jacks argues, is too simplistic and tends to inhibit creativity. Therefore, 'the more conscious our age becomes of its mechanical mindedness the more inclined it is to revolt against mechanism.'[27] The centres of this revolt are both philosophical and scientific. In the work of Bergson, the French mystical philosopher, the dominance of mechanism and of the machine in society is condemned and a vitalistic and almost teleological universe, summed up in the concept of 'creative evolution', is portrayed. In natural science, Jacks cites the opposition of Einstein, Eddington and Jeans to the idea of a machine-made science and an 'observatory-made universe'. As a modern Christian Jacks cannot entirely reject the machine, but he does construe the task of religion as holding mechanism in firm check. In the last resort, however, in the choice between an intelligible but uninteresting or an unintelligible but interesting universe, Jacks, together with Bergson and Lloyd Morgan (an American exponent of 'Emergent Evolution'), takes the latter choice, the romantic option.*

Approaching the problem from a different angle—concern at the rate of scientific advance rather than an intrinsic dislike for the machine as such—Sir Josiah Stamp asks the question: Must science ruin economic progress? In Stamp's hands the argument appears moderate and in accord with common-sense, at the very least.

> If changes in social forms and human nature or behaviour cannot possibly be made rapidly enough for the task, then in that sense science may 'ruin' economic progress, and the world might be better served in the end if scientific innovation were retarded to the maximum rate of social and economic change.[28]

---

* It is not surprising to read in the preface to Dean Inge's essays of the mutual friendship and ideological co-operation between himself and Dr Jacks, considering that one essay in Inge's book 'raises the great question whether the over-mechanisation of life has not impaired the intrinsic qualities of the human race, so that what we usually call progress may have to be paid for by racial retrogression'. (Inge, op. cit., p. vi.)

In a formal sense this view has similarities to the theory of cultural lag, popularized by the American sociologist Ogburn, in the early 1920s. Ogburn's theory stated that changes in material culture often outstripped those in non-material culture (that ideas lagged behind things), and this analysis illuminated the disharmony in modern societies. Stamp's thesis is not as simple as this, for it is not clear whether he means science as a system of knowledge or physical processes or both, and whether he means social and economic progress as progress in beliefs and attitudes or material things or both. The impression is that scientific innovation refers more to material culture and social and economic progress to non-material culture. If this is the case, and Stamp's warning that too rapid scientific progress might through its disturbance effect be deleterious to society suggests that it is, then we may see how easily the apparently mild thesis on possible restrictions to science can easily turn into a threat on the very nature of the activity of science itself.[29] A recent Soviet view of the cultural lag theory sees the work of Ogburn (and Lewis Mumford) as sociologizing the chasm between moral and material progress that had been noted by Bergson and Heidegger.[30]

Marxism by and large accepts the existence of a cultural lag, but has its own explanations of how it occurred and of how it can be remedied, and these are diametrically opposed to the views of Stamp. Whereas Stamp sees the causes in the world market and world politics, and the cure in a cut-back if not a complete moratorium on scientific research, the Marxist sees the cause in the relations of production and the cure in total social revolution which will advance society rather than hold back science. Seen in this light, the reaction against the machine, in its many and various forms, is the non-innovational solution to the perceived gap between material and moral progress—where Marxism is the totally innovational solution.

Just how far back this reaction was capable of looking is illustrated in the remarkable book of the Italian feminist, Gina Lombroso, translated into French as *La Rançon du Machinisme* (*The Costs of Mechanism*). In a sustained attack on mechanism, the industrial society and 'that religion of Progress which still raises so much hope',*[31] she enunciates a variation on the cyclical theory of history, linking decline in one aspect of a civilization with progress in another. For large-scale industry and its concentration she reserves special and almost violent abuse; she sees in it a 'perilous monstrosity', it is the harbinger of 'wretchedness', and it brings to all classes 'momentary and superficial distractions, to the detriment of the hardy intellectual and moral gratifications which may stem from idealism'.[32]

---

* All the quotations from Lombroso are translated by myself, as are those from Friedmann following.

Lombroso is rather less pessimistic about the possible future than about the present she portrays so gloomily. She does not concede that the situation is irreversible, for she sees a real opportunity for man to alter his position before it is too late. Having diagnosed that modern evils and injustices come from the concentration and enormity of industry, she calls on all mankind to fight against these tendencies with the encouraging (though in the circumstances surprising if not contradictory) statement that:

> This will be all the more easy as neither the injustices nor the enormity, nor the concentration are tied up—in any way—with the moral, social, scientific, or intellectual progress of the society in which we live. . . . It is therefore small-scale industry and small-scale individual cultivation towards which the world must travel in order to find again its equilibrium.[33]

Lombroso was by no means alone in her views, and indeed others went even further in the direction of advocating the restoration of feudalism around this time. Georges Friedmann's study of the crisis of the bourgeois idea of progress in the years between 1895 and 1935 describes such reactions within a context particularly relevant for the present work. Friedmann speaks of the 'artisan utopias' which were increasingly advocated during the economic depressions as part of the general disillusionment with technological progress. Political expression to this ideology of the artisan was manifest in the form of Artisan Associations, created in the 1920s and 1930s in most of the major European industrial countries, including France, Italy and Germany. 'Artisan ideology,' says Friedmann, 'is found again in the work of most of those in whom we have seen suspicion of technology,' and he cites Duhamel and Caillaux, both obsessed with 'quality'; Adam Müller, an economist who is devoted to feudalism; the fascist proponents of the corporate state; and Gina Lombroso herself; all of whom look backward and not forward for the solution to the problems faced by their civilization.[34]

All of these protests come under the heading of the philosophies of '*la civilisation restreinte*' (the restricted civilization), and this is a direct attempt to hold back or even eliminate material progress, in order to further some conception of moral and social progress. There could be few better models for this enterprise than the ideal-type of feudal medieval civilization.

This whole attitude is summed up by M. Tailledet, the president of the *Confédération générale de l'Artisanat français*, in an address to a Congress of Artisans. He speaks of the 'material and moral anxiety of the soulless world' and the 'inhuman philosophy of the machine'. Tailledet is apparently more perturbed than Lombroso over the effects of the machine and the industrial system on those who labour under them, for he claims that:

> The large-scale enterprise, which ties man to the machine, levels his sentimental longings, regiments him for greater efficiency, bends him under automation, diminishes his intellectual faculties only to develop the swiftness of his reflexes, leads us to say that modern mechanism, seen from the point of view of the worker, entails (especially for an individualistic people like the French) a certain deficiency of intellectual and moral values.[35]

Friedmann, in his commentary, makes an important point here. He correctly distinguishes between the 'automatic machine which entails the abdication of the personality . . . and the individual machine, which the worker operates alone or with a few mates'.[36] This protest, then, is more in the nature of a plea to 'humanize the machine' (as Bergson had put it) than to abolish all machines for all time. Indeed, the artisan in some cases needs machines, and there is a strong argument to suggest that the development of craftsmanship and art depend on the development of tools and the materials to be worked, and for this certain types of machines are necessary. This is of course an entirely different thing from full-scale technological and industrial society, but there is little evidence that the proponents of the artisan utopias had given any serious thought to the cut-off point, the stage at which the machine *civilization* is considered to have changed from an individual to an automatic and potentially dangerous one. Enormous difficulties would also arise from the sociological question of the relationship between the level of mechanization and the social structure, for it is widely accepted that the difference between feudal and industrial social structure is one of kind rather than of degree. This reaction to the machine, therefore, like that of Jacks, is the 'romantic option' and Friedmann's hope that Marxism will in its own way solve the problem can be characterized as the 'forward-looking romantic option'.

A more recent and more sophisticated version of this latter view is that of Alfred Sauvy, who makes the critical distinction between recessive and processive progress in an essay on 'Technical Progress, Employment and Unemployment'.[37] Recessive progress reduces the number of workers and causes unemployment if there is no similar reduction in the working day. Processive progress, on the other hand, tends to increase employment. The ills of recessive progress are serious for it reinforces monopolies, aggravates chronic over-population, and is generally anti-social; it is the 'push-button economy'.

On Sauvy's account, therefore, some types of technological advance lead to social progress, whereas other types do not. The message of Sauvy, as with others, is that technological progress cannot be dogmatically assumed to lead inevitably in all cases to social or even economic progress.[38]

Most of these writers that I have discussed were writing before the Second World War, and it was increasingly obvious that this was a period in which the machinery of the modern industrial state was to be put to its most horrible and efficient uses. The interest of the Nazis in the artisan solution, and their hankering after the old values of 'blood and soil', did not prevent them from building up a massive state machine to carry out their policies. Further, though a reminder is gratuitous, in 1945 the Americans exploded the first nuclear bomb on civilians and a new age in the history of man dawned. In the face of these enormous abuses of the machine we would not be surprised to find that the last twenty years has borne a plethora of anti-technological thought. This has not generally happened, and because of this the pieces that continue the pre-war protest are especially noteworthy.

Of these the most intemperate and least liable to convince is the diatribe against the modern world delivered by F. G. Juenger: mechanization actually produces more manual labour; it spreads not only poverty but also the delusion of wealth; it pillages the earth; it rapes nature; it ruins education; in sum, 'technology may reach perfection, but never maturity'; it is perfection without purpose. Juenger gives little detail in his short and sketchy account of the rise and potential collapse of civilization, but he is adamant that 'no human invention could possibly abolish the reciprocity between mechanical progression and elemental regression'.[39] This is little more than a cryptic restatement of Rousseau's suggestion that material progress necessarily leads to social and moral decline, with nothing approaching the subtlety of the latter's argument.

A mild criticism of machine-civilization is contained in the work of the Christian existentialist, Marcel. He notes, rather regretfully, that the technical is opposed to the natural environment and in a mystical way speaks of what can only be referred to as the 'autonomy' of the machine. Technology, in his view, appears to have some inner dynamic; terrible things have been done with machines but 'man has not "decided" to use the lifeless machine wrongly'.[40] With the destruction by the machine of the relation between man and his natural environment, depersonalization inevitably results. Marcel concludes with the hope that love will succeed in exorcising this daemonic world.

The most sustained and powerful attack on technology in the modern world is that mounted by the French writer, Jacques Ellul, and if the murmurings of the backward-looking mechanophobes have seemed a little amusing or pathetic, Ellul's thesis seems to me to be deadly serious. If the technological society cannot answer it, then it is doomed.

Ellul's thesis was first presented in *La Technique* (1954), restated and developed in a contribution to a volume on the technological society (1963), and further specified in another and longer paper on 'Western Man in 1970', also published in 1963. In his restatement, Ellul summarizes his position, and I shall briefly give an account of this, using his own words as far as possible. The technological society has supplanted nature; it is artificial, autonomous with respect to values and ideas; it is self-determining in a closed circle; it grows according to a causal but not a goal-directed process, means 'have primacy over ends', and all parts are mutually implicated to the greatest possible degree; individual techniques develop 'ambivalently' (that is for every problem solved another arises); all social phenomena are not so much influenced by it, as situated *in* it; 'Psycho-sociological techniques result in the *modification* of men in order to render them happily subordinate to their new environment, and by no means imply any kind of human domination over Technique'; ideas, judgments, beliefs and myths have already been essentially modified by the technological society, and the traditional state of freedom with respect to choice and judgment no longer exists.[41]

The thesis, thus, is quite uncompromising. Technology has *already* permeated all areas of life; it is not a power to which we succumb or to which we resist; it is a medium, the medium in which we live; man is 'a natural secretion of technical progress'.[42] The documentation that Ellul musters to support his extreme view is most impressive, and he particularly singles out the economy, the state and human technique for special attention. In a given civilization, technical progress is irreversible but it was not an inevitability of history, rather a conjunction of favourable circumstances that led to the technological society. The Greeks, Ellul claims, actually rejected it, and this rejection 'was a deliberate, positive activity involving self-mastery, recognition of destiny, and the application of a given conception of life'.*[43]

Although Western industrial civilization is now and for ever will be burdened with technological society, it is possible by bringing about a new civilization to escape from technique. It has to be admitted that Ellul is profoundly pessimistic as to our chances of

---

* This statement suggests that in fact the Greeks operated under a non-innovational concept of progress. The presence of a slave population, obviating the necessity to make labour more tolerable, lends further credence to this view. See the discussion in the first section of Chapter I.

ever achieving this, and if his position is not overstated, then he is right to be pessimistic.

Technological progress is thus condemned by Ellul but, and this may seem strange, he often insists that technology is amoral, in itself it is neither good nor bad. However, and this must be of great significance if his thesis is to have any *moral* implication whatsoever, he does assert that:

> the further technical progress advances, the more the social problem of mastering this progress becomes one of an ethical and spiritual kind. . . . [for] *If* we desire to preserve man's freedom, dignity, and responsibility, it is precluded to act upon him by technical means, like psychology, and so forth. To transform a man into a reasonable being and a good exploiter of techniques *through* certain psychological procedures is precisely to destroy him as a spiritual and ethical subject.*[44]

Technological progress, therefore, does eventually have very crucial moral implications, though the technological society precisely attempts, by its incessant drive towards consensus and the integration of man in society, to obviate the necessity for any moral decisions. The decisions in a society of technique are all technical decisions, and as the power of and in the society increases, the criteria of value cease to be of a moral nature and become more and more of a technological nature. The totalitarian state, the epitomy of the alliance between the state and technique, is captured by the élite which benefits most by the apparatus of technology. Morality itself gives way at last, and the channels of protest and revolt are institutionalized and thereby emasculated.

What, if any, solution is open? Ellul suggests five necessary conditions on which a solution depends. Firstly, the problem must be diagnosed and men must wake up to the dangers. The 'happiness' of the technological society must be exposed if men are to liberate themselves. Second, the myth of Technique must be ruthlessly destroyed; it must be seen to be what it is—a commonplace. Next, technical objects must be put in their proper perspective; things can be exploited without man becoming attached to them. Four, a live philosophy is necessary to combat the technique on an ideological level. And last, a dialogue with the *technicians*, an almost superhuman task, is absolutely essential. These are 'the five conditions necessary that an opening on the technical problem can even become a possibility'.[45]

---

* This is very near the Laing and Cooper school of psycho-analysis (or anti-psychiatry), though no doubt Ellul would give them no special dispensation for *their* technique. Michel Foucault, in his *Madness and Civilization* (London, 1967), has many interesting things to say in this connection.

The political aspect of Ellul's thesis is further developed in his book *The Political Illusion*, where he argues that there is some contradiction between the technological order and the proper operation of politics. The technicians, and techniques, are taking over, though it is important to point out that there are many more notes of hope in this later work than in the earlier, desperate writings.[46]

Another Frenchman, Jean Meynaud, has in a recent work provided the dire warnings about the technocrat or expert take-over of political power that we might have expected from Ellul. Meynaud analyses the ideology of the technocrat and sees in technocracy the great 'peril' against which modern society must struggle. 'This fight,' he concludes, 'can only have meaning if we reject completely the theory that progress and technique alone have the ultimate ability to settle the latent tensions and open conflicts which its development has caused.'[47] It is clear that Meynaud is here speaking of what I have termed 'innovational progress'.

Two aspects of the problem Ellul raises are discussed in different and illuminating ways by Herbert Marcuse and Ernest Gellner. Marcuse is concerned with the deleterious effects of technological progress on man's humanity in capitalist society. Though technology and science change in contemporary society, institutions and the productive process and the modes of human existence do not. 'This containment of social change is perhaps the most singular achievement of advanced industrial society,' he claims.[48]

This is not an uncommon criticism: E. M. Zhukov, a Soviet commentator, argues that 'the capitalist system has now become a brake on social progress';[49] but Marcuse goes on to criticize the nature of technological society as such and not only its capitalist form, though the latter is the target of most of his specific remarks. 'Pacified existence' is the term Marcuse uses for the probable end of technology in the advanced industrial society, and it is notable that he does not anticipate the *horrors* that Ellul fears. This society is or will be a society of paradox that is only too real, for it 'turns everything it touches into a potential source of progress *and* of exploitation, of drudgery *and* satisfaction, of freedom *and* of oppression'. A similar paradox pertains to sociology, and psychology, for as they help improve human conditions 'they also testify to the ambivalent rationality of progress, which is satisfying in its repressive power, and repressive in its satisfaction'.[50]

In an essay published in German over thirty years ago, Marcuse clarifies the voluntaristic dialectic of man's relation to technology in a way that is quite different to Ellul's virtually necessitarian gloom. Marcuse speaks of his social theory confronted with the order of established relations of domination in capitalist society:

the critical theory of society presupposes the disengagement of science from this order. Thus the fateful fetishism of science is avoided here in principle. . . . Even the development of the productive forces and the evolution of technology know no uninterrupted progression from the old to the new society. For here, too, man himself is to determine progress: not 'socialist' man . . . but the association of those men who bring about the transformation. Since what is to become of science and technology depends on them, science and technology cannot serve *a priori* as a conceptual model for critical theory.[51]

Where Marcuse sees this 'transformation' in the interrelated spheres of political change and the free development of human capacities, Gellner is more specifically concerned with 'the transition from a relatively stable society . . . to a period of radical change, [which] is something fundamentally different from *continued* change, in a society which has learned to take change for granted'.[52] This '*continued* change' state is achieved when the hump of industrialization has been overcome, and the institutionalization of science and technology as the crucial factor appears to be implicit in his argument.

Indeed, he makes the important point that the transition is largely a question of the social role and organization of knowledge, and in a striking phrase comments that 'science is the mode of cognition of industrial society, and industry is the ecology of science'. Science, however, 'offers no guarantee of stability, it is morally meaningless, and it respects no hierarchies',[53] and yet Gellner sees little of the threat in technology that is apparent to both Ellul and Marcuse. On the contrary, for Gellner, 'industrialism is good, and industrialism must happen', and this *must* is a hypothetical imperative predicated on the wish of men to improve their standard of living.[54] Though modern society has not yet properly digested science, Gellner leaves no doubt that he considers it to be noble fare.

Thus Gellner sees only one revolution, the great transition that will change man and his world, that will alter the balance between being and knowing, and that will for once and all sever the great chain of being with tribal-customary societies on one side of the pale and scientific-industrial societies on the other. Where Ellul, Marcuse and Meynaud see transition, in some or all of its features, as giving cause for great alarm, Gellner welcomes it paradoxically on humanitarian grounds.

Although he devotes the early part of *Thought and Change* to a telling criticism of earlier theories of progress and social evolution, and he especially rejects that theory of history that he terms 'the world growth story', his own theory of progress which links nationalism with the great transition to industrialization is notable for its optimism. The great leap forward theory, as we may characterize Gellner's contribution, is clearly a theory of innovational progress.

Where Gellner suggests that man has not properly digested science, Marcuse suggests that science is an inadequate diet, and Ellul documents the spectacle of man choking on it.[55]

The critiques of progress that I have discussed in this chapter have not on the whole been directed to a logical analysis of the old theories of progress, but rather to an historical analysis. In the words of one commentator, writing in 1949, 'the idea of progress promised to mankind an ever-improving secular future as a necessity of nature itself. Human affairs in recent times have not borne out that expectation'.[56] The shock of this reverse, or to be more accurate, this persistence of evils amongst the new and wonderful things of our scientific civilization, allied with the 'God is dead' philosophy of Nietzsche and its dispassionate development by Sartre and others into a moral philosophy, provided important pessimistic currents of thought in twentieth-century Europe. This century can best be characterized as the one in which the 'quest for meaning' in history and in moral conduct became pressing, when the old explanations from authority became inadequate and when men, unable to detach themselves from the world, were faced with the occasional problem of situating themselves in it.

This was, and is, also a particularly trying time for the men of ideas—the men whose task it has always been to interpret and to explain the world to each other, if not to mankind. The progress of the sciences, and especially physics and biology, has been astonishing and highly paradoxical. Older ideas of the possibilities of knowledge and its certainty have broken down since man's first encounters with the make-believe land of the small particle, and the inroads made into genetic codes, the chemistry of history, only serve to further cement the conviction that there is something more to man than the mechanisms and processes of his body. But 'What?' asks the scientific sceptic. And 'So what?' asks the critic of the idea of progress. There is a great gulf between civilization on the one hand and the individual in his life groups on the other, and though the former and its history may appear to lack meaning and value, the latter must have some meaning and value, for, to repeat Durkheim's aphorism, life is preferable to death in the vast number of cases. Could it be, then, that temporary setbacks are being mistaken for utter disasters, that the critics of progress are picking out the exceptions and ignoring the rule that would support the progressive view? Can it be that the intellectuals in their well-worn role as prophets of doom and despair are so divorced from life as it is daily lived that they do not recognize material and moral progress when they see it? Is Ellul, when he claims that man is losing his distinctive feature and that technology obscures the search for the meaning of life,[57] merely betraying a personal defeat?

These are the questions that must be answered by any viable theory of progress. In the next part of my study I shall attempt to demonstrate that however ideologically unfashionable and scorned theoretically the idea of progress may be, it is essential to modern social thought, and that a sociological theory of progress is not only possible but necessary.

part two

A sociological theory of progress

VII   Two concepts of progress

All theories of progress have failed the test of time. Apart from the remaining Marxists, social evolutionists, and the plainly old-fashioned, no one nowadays holds a theory of progress of any consequence. The theory is dead as much from neglect as from actual opposition. The reasons for this are not difficult to find, for in the passing comment that progress usually elicits in the standard works of sociology, philosophy, politics or the history of thought in general, it receives neither experiential nor logical support. This is not because the concept of progress is intrinsically useless, but because it has been insufficiently specified, empirically utilized in a crude fashion, and disastrously oversimplified in its theoretical applications.

History, theory and aspiration
An analysis of progress must operate on at least three levels of reality. These may be illustrated by posing three questions which are quite distinct analytically, though they are empirically very much interdependent. The questions are (1) What has actually happened in history? (2) How have men attempted to explain this? (3) What do men want from life? I shall attempt to deal with these three questions in turn.

The first question is mainly about events, although even to say this much is to start to prejudge the nature of history. I shall, however, assume the existence of a real world in which things happen, have happened, and will continue to happen, and I shall treat as unproblematical the view that although we can have no definite and absolute knowledge about anything, we can nevertheless be almost certain of some historically documented events. This is not to say of course that our historical knowledge may not improve all the time, as is the case and possibility with most knowledge.

And indeed, this is the very point that I would wish to make in this context, namely that if history shows us anything then it shows us that at least knowledge accumulates and that progress in the pursuit of knowledge seems assured. The progress in man's control of his environment as a result of the progress in certain forms of knowledge is accepted by most, if not all, social thinkers as a self-evident fact. This much history and especially recent history tells us. But scientific progress turns out to be a two-edged sword, as has been made abundantly clear, for it is constantly being used to smite anyone foolish enough to argue further for social or moral or any other form of progress.

The historical record therefore (and I am here only repeating what is part of the common conception of the vast majority of those who concern themselves with the past) leads us to the following type of answer to the first question. What has actually happened in history is the obvious occurrence of progress in all those branches of knowledge that have to do with man's control of his natural environment and some other branches besides.* Social progress has probably taken place, if we can in fact say anything at all on the subject. As for moral progress (though it is probably of no little therapeutic value to speak of it), we can say nothing of much significance about it. Alternatively, it can be said that progress in knowledge has taken place, while progress in virtue has not.

In a sense, theories about battles are as much a part of history as the battles that they try to explain. In this way the first and the second of my three questions are, as I suggested, not empirically distinct, though I should like to argue that they are analytically distinct, and very usefully so. There have been in the main three types of theories of history, felicitously referred to by Frank Manuel as 'the shapes of philosophical history'.†1 These three possibilities are, broadly, regress theories, cyclic theories and theories of progress.

Regress theories usually suggest that history has shown not a general forward movement but rather that things are becoming worse. This, of course, presupposes that things were at one time better than they are now, and that the previous desirable state of man and society appears to have vanished either for ever or for the foreseeable future. Thus, progress on this view would consist in a return to the past state of affairs, selected as the peak from one of the possible peaks gone by from which the decline occurred. This type of regress theory must be distinguished from its close neighbour, conservatism,

---

* There have of course been periods in history when knowledge has stood still or has even been lost, but the general trend has been cumulative and progressive. I am speaking, of course, about the Western world.

† I do not adhere closely to Manuel's account in the following. Theories which treat history as a completely arbitrary flux I do not consider at all in this context.

whose peak tends to rest in the recent past and tends to be realistically attainable if only the 'rot can be stopped'. As a theory about what has actually happened in history, regression has had not an insignificant vogue, especially in the more pessimistic periods of the twentieth century, and is only now being overtaken in the main by more optimistic views.

A second variety or shape of history is that illustrated by the analogy of the wheel. These theories are often known as cyclic theories, and they may be optimistic (progressive) or pessimistic (regressive) in nature, depending on which phase of the cycle one happens to be on at the particular time in question. A very frequent version of this thesis accepts that science and technology might progress for exceedingly long periods of time, but that the state of man's social and moral activity would demonstrate a more cyclic pattern—now progressing, now regressing. Recent history, on some popular interpretations, gives credence to this view.

In its most important form, the cyclic theory of history operates with specific, autonomous units such as civilizations, cultures or societies, and suggests that, on an organic analogy, these have lives of their own, that they are born, mature and decline and die. The differences in civilizations can be understood only with reference to the working out of unique patterns within the units and the eventual and inexorable fate of each and every one.

The third type of theory of history is, of course, the theory of progress, and for convenience I shall distinguish three categories, namely the unilinear, the spiral and the 'quantum' theory.

The unilinear theory of progress, characterized by Gellner as the 'world-growth story',[2] is basically the sociological version of the theory of evolution. As I have dealt with this at length in Chapter IV, I shall only pause to repeat that, despite the defects so ruthlessly exposed by Gellner and others, it is by no means as dead as purely rational appraisal might imply.*

The spiral theory of progress is properly a hybrid of the cyclic and progressive varieties. It suggests that history can be seen as a series of progressive cycles, and that the past does come around again but in an ever-improving form. This is well caught in the apparently paradoxical expression that 'nothing ever really changes, but don't forget the bad old days'. Spiral theories are more akin to theories of decelerated progress or problematic advance than to genuine theories of cycles, for the end-point of history on these spiral accounts always shows some measure of total progress over any time in the past.

The quantum or episodic theory of progress differs from the

* Gellner himself fully realizes that this is so and has, in *Thought and Change*, given one explanation of the phenomenon.

unilinear theory in replacing gradual improvement with one leap or a series of leaps. Gellner's example of the Social Contract and his own theory concerning the hump of industrialization are cases of the quantum theory, where almost cataclysmic transformation of the world is the necessary prerequisite to progress. Revolutionary theories, and Marxism springs immediately to mind, are of this type. The post-revolutionary quantum can only be brought about, that is progress within the context of the theory, when some definite break with the past occurs and the pre-revolutionary quantum is thereby transmogrified into the new and good society, usually by some imaginative leap.

I should find it difficult to cite examples of actual theories that illustrated one and only one of these types of progress—a pure theory is perhaps more of a gleam in the eye of the historian of ideas than an actual identifiable entity. The fact remains, however, that different as they are they all revolve round the issue of progress, and although this statement is obvious enough, I shall now go on to argue that *all* theories of history likewise revolve round the idea of progress. To do this I shall have to face the third question that I set myself at the beginning of this chapter, namely: What do men want from life?

Like the other two questions I have been examining, this question is a matter of fact, an empirical question the answer to which can only be achieved by looking at what we know about what has actually happened in the world, what has been written about it and what men have said. The three questions are, however, directed towards three areas of facts: facts about events, facts about theories and facts about aspirations. On my definition of progress which focuses on the satisfactory solution of problems that man confronts in society, there is only one realistic answer to the question of what men want. Men want progress, they have always wanted progress, and if the nature of the world is to remain comprehensible, then men *will* always want progress. That is to say, there is something intrinsic to the terms 'progress' and 'aspiration', on my account of the matter, that links them in some sort of sociological necessity not entirely independent from the very ways in which we use the terms in discussing the problems they raise.

This can be shown by posing the question: Could men ever wish that *their* problems were not satisfactorily solved? If an affirmative answer is given, that men might sometimes wish *their* problems, or a particular problem, might not be solved, then we should be led to examine the case very carefully, for though it does not seem to involve a logical contradiction it appears to offend against good sense. Empirical investigation might expose to us the fact that one particular problem is dependent for its solution on the prior solution of another problem, and in this case reference to some time sequence and a restatement of the position would clear up the difficulty. The problem then would be seen in context, and a series in which the particular problem in question is a subsidiary member would obviously have to be solved.

A more threatening case to my argument would be that where the solution of one problem would seem to entail the production of other and perhaps more serious problems. There are many examples of this state of affairs. In the natural and biological sciences it is very often said that each answer brings an indefinite number of questions about the universe. But to see this as a difficulty for the view that all men always want to solve all their problems is to confuse the production or acknowledgement of problems with their solution. It is precisely this distinction that Popper has built into his philosophy of science, for example, to show that science is a pre-eminently progressive activity. The better a scientific hypothesis, Popper argues, the greater the possibilities of falsification and the more problems to be solved.[3] The production of problems, recognized or (more usually) unrecognized, in no way implies that men do not aspire to solve them. The matter of the unintended and unrecognized consequences of action in society has been subtly analysed by R. K. Merton,[4] and in Kingsley Davis's controversial article it is argued that unintended consequences are the unique concern of sociologists.[5] So I may claim that the line of argument that I am following here is nearer one core of modern sociology than might at first sight be apparent.

Taking this train of thought to one extreme it is now necessary to deal with a complex point concerning the assumptions that I have had to make about history and society in order to be in a position to maintain the proposition that men always do want progress and that they really aspire to the solution of all their problems. This would seem to imply that this is a possible aspiration and that men have never been confronted with the great dilemma that renders the solution of one problem in society incompatible with the solution of some other problem. To crystallize this issue into a concrete example (that has been met several times in the foregoing history of the idea of progress), what of those who argue and believe that scientific progress can lead only to moral regress and that we must choose between knowledge and virtue, for we cannot have them both? How do we answer Rousseau and how do we reassure Ellul? It is this point that must be satisfactorily met before a sociological theory of progress, realistic in terms of the world in which we live, is possible.

When a problem is to be solved, then the way in which the problem is put, the possible solutions allowed, the means which are considered legitimate to achieve the desired end, and even the persons who may or may not solve it, are factors that may well differ from one society to another. Problem-solving, therefore, may be relative to different groups, to different cultures and to different periods. It is clear that the interests of one group or one culture might conflict with those of another, but what is also clear is that one group or one culture may espouse truly conflicting ends. Men may wish for two general states of affairs; they may wish to solve two problem complexes; and they may find that the solution to one cannot be reconciled with the solution to the other.

One way out of this dilemma is to posit a hierarchy of values and settle for the hope that men will consider one problem complex to be more important than another. This is quite adequate for dealing with situations like times of war, for example, when funds for national recreation are subordinated to funds for waging war. In this case solutions are postponed. But in the case of a hypothesized opposition between scientific progress and moral progress, this solution is inadequate. Men want knowledge and virtue, and they want them both now—and there is rarely any firm guarantee that a postponement of one will make the attainment of the other more certain.

A satisfactory theory of progress must allow for the solutions to both these problem complexes. Such a theory would obviously founder on the traditional distinctions between material and moral progress, between scientific and social progress, or between any that referred solely to the area in which progress was to be made. As I tried to show in the first six chapters these types of distinction were often made, and the more critical thinkers to a greater or lesser extent realized the possible and indeed frequently occurring difficulties to which they led. A theory of progress, if it was to answer the questions set at the levels of events, theories and aspirations (especially the latter), had to break away from the old distinctions; and the sometimes apparent discomfort with the old distinctions, shown by some of the most convinced proponents of the idea of progress,[6] serves to reinforce this view most strongly.

Therefore, an examination of the literature on progress, a particular and fairly conventional account of what has happened in history, and an intuitive idea of the aspirations of social humanity lead in my opinion to a general sociological theory of progress based on the criterion of innovation. In the simplest possible terms, my theory suggests that the most satisfactory idea of progress, one that will answer the fundamental questions on the levels of events, theories and aspirations, or at least point in the direction of answers to these questions in a consistent fashion, must be based on the radical distinction between innovational and non-innovational progress.

As a first approximation, to set the scene for a deeper analysis of the nature of innovation, I will reiterate the distinction between progress that requires the introduction of new things for the solution of problems and progress that requires the maintenance and spread of familiar things for the solution of problems. These are innovational and non-innovational types of progress respectively.* Indeed, one of the consequences of the change in the idea of progress with reference to the institutionalization of science, to which I have often referred in the preceding pages, was precisely that innovational progress came to be seen as the *only* type of progress and that some societies tended to reserve the label 'progressive' for themselves.

It is, accordingly, one of the polemical tasks of this book to suggest the reasons why certain societies are labelled 'unprogressive', and to find the sociological and political significance of the pejorative use of this label.

The first of my initial questions concerned the events of history—what has actually happened. It is clear that of all the problems that have ever faced men some have been solved to the general satisfaction, some remain unsolved and some are in the process of solution. It is equally clear that the solutions to some of the problems satisfactorily solved have come from innovations, and that some have not done so. Irrespective of whether all men would agree that a particular problem fitted into a particular category of the classification that I use, there is no doubt that some problems would; this is a fair start, for it suggests that the distinction on which I intend to build a theory of progress is obvious and that to some extent it reflects reality in its broad outline.

The second question was about theories of history. As I mentioned in my discussion of the shapes of philosophical history, my account of progress leads towards the view that all theories of history are to a greater or lesser extent theories of progress. Some theories of history are blatantly progress theories, others are different only in that their creators exhibit more care and recognize difficulties as real rather than apparent, and yet others, the remaining theories of history, are progress theories in disguise. There are in my opinion several good reasons for this seemingly fantastic claim. In the first place, all theories of history may be considered as descriptions of how and explanations of why progress has or has not happened. Thus, cyclic theories hold that the mechanisms of progress wind down (or some such thing) before they can be wound up again. Regress theories hold that men, in any or all aspects of their lives, continually meet increasingly insuperable problems, and so progress

* The term 'non-innovational', although somewhat clumsy, expresses the intended meaning better than any other at present available.

and even stability is deemed impossible. This line of reasoning is by itself quite inadequate, for it could be countered by the claim that all theories of history were really about 'successful' or 'unsuccessful' regression, or more or less proper cycles. But one fact sways the balance; that is the fact that there is no significant tradition of total hell as one might expect if all theories of history were variants of the regress theme,* and there is not much of a tradition of regular ups-and-downs as one might expect if all theories of history were variations on the cycle theme. There is, however, a large and great tradition of utopian thought which has been well documented[7] and which, in spite (perhaps because) of its critics, lives on. Lastly and further, even the most pessimistic and hopeless exponents of regression theories, for example Jacques Ellul, make some recommendations for last-ditch survival. Very often their work is framed in the form of 'a warning' or 'a plea for humanity', or some such alarm, and this in itself is tantamount to saying that here we have a theory pointing out all that is wrong, the erroneous or 'false-consciousness' solutions to the problems of men, and *this* is the correct answer to these problems. Take heed, they exclaim, or progress will be lost! And this is a theory of progress and not a theory of regress— sceptical, but a theory of progress none the less.

The distinction between innovational and non-innovational progress appears to be useful in so far as there is an arguable case that all theories of history are theories of progress, not in logic but in sociology, on the basis of what is generally understood about historical events, theories and the aspirations of men in society. Briefly, the distinction helps to explain the reason why certain societies, that seem to be coping satisfactorily with what they define as their problems, are termed 'unprogressive' or 'backward', or some such thinly-veiled pejorative, on the basis of some traditional and even modern theories of progress which are disguised as theories of regress or stagnation. Where a society is characterized on my theory as operating on a non-innovational concept of progress, someone who conceives only the one concept of progress, namely innovational, will tend to regard the society in question as totally or partially unprogressive or backward. This judgment will be made irrespective of whether or not the problems of that society, their problems, are being satisfactorily solved. The situation can thus arise, and I have no doubt that it does arise, that a self-entitled progressive society can perceive another as unprogressive where in fact the former (on the basis of an innovational concept of progress)

* D. P. Walker, in *The Decline of Hell* (London, 1964), argues that even in Christian circles the idea of hell had declined largely by the seventeenth century. The negative utopias of Aldous Huxley and Orwell and other science fiction writers are significant exceptions rather than the rule.

is less successful in solving its problems than the latter (on its basis of non-innovational progress).*

Theories of history may be about innovational and non-innovational concepts of progress, and many theories of regress and cycles can be usefully studied as a matter of the preference that one theorist has for one of these concepts of progress, and whether or not he believes that the movement of history is exemplifying his choice.

The third question dealing with men's aspirations is not so much clarified by as intrinsic to the distinction between innovational and non-innovational progress. To attempt to answer in detail the question 'What do men want out of life?' would be both rash and pretentious. It is, however, important to state that whatever we want we can get through innovational or non-innovational means or through both. Certain problems in certain societies call for certain types of solutions, and it is only another way of framing the thesis that primitive and advanced industrial societies are structured differently in many complex ways to say that some societies, to progress, will tend to favour the innovational and others the non-innovational approach to problem-solving. That men aspire to progress is self-evident, and there are obvious reasons why this self-evident truth (like others) is vehemently opposed by some, especially those who deal with societies utterly foreign to their own.

The nature of non-innovational progress differs in important respects from the nature of innovational progress, and not the least important aspect in which they differ is that of minimum possibility. Roughly, the minimum level of non-innovational progress is nearer quiescence than the minimum level of innovational progress. One analogy is that of the difference between a man thrashing around in the water as against a man making extremely lazy and slow strokes. They may move the same or no distance, but the former would appear to be active, the latter passive. So it can appear with the two concepts of progress.

Innovation

It is now essential to analyse the concept 'innovation', to discuss how it has been used in the literature of sociology and philosophy particularly, and to explain how I intend to use it to further my theory of progress. Three terms, innovation, invention and discovery, are often grouped together to describe the same cluster of phenomena. Indeed, in the major full-scale systematic work on innovation in the bibliography of the contemporary social sciences, the anthropologist H. G. Barnett claims that 'communication is facilitated by conforming to ordinary usage. Beyond this purpose no significance

* This, *in extremis*, may be analogous to Tom Lehrer's (and others') definition of a psychiatrist as 'someone trying to help people who are happier than he is'.

should be attached to the differential employment of "invention" and "discovery". Both are names for innovations'.[8]

It is profitable to examine the very sophisticated case made for the reappraisal of the common-sense distinction between invention and discovery in a lecture delivered to the British Academy by the logician W. C. Kneale, and I should like to devote some attention to this as it illuminates the basic point that Barnett obscures.

Kneale begins by pointing to the dispute that arose in the philosophy of mathematics between the Formalists such as Hilbert and the Conventionalists such as Frege. The essential difference between these schools was that the former conceived the truths of mathematics as the creations or inventions of mathematicians and the latter conceived them as discoveries, in the sense in which the geographers make discoveries and name them. Kneale ingeniously shows this dispute to be ill-formed and 'due to mistaken notions of freedom which have been introduced by talk of creation'.[9] In the first place, he argues, in English, Greek, German and Russian, and no doubt in many other languages, the words for invention and for finding, or discovery, have been historically connected. This alone rouses suspicion, and an analysis of invention in different aspects of life activity does little to allay this suspicion. In the case of the useful arts, 'invention of things is only a special case of the invention of processes',[10] and we may equally well speak of the discovery of processes or the finding of methods. Invention in the fine arts suggests another nuance, that of *finding* possibilities that will interest us when once our attention has been directed towards them'.[11] In addition to this 'fictive imagination', the use of invention in the non-fiction arts like music and painting clearly implies the *finding* and selection of patterns from sets of large possibilities. In these two areas, therefore (and who would deny that they collectively encompass a great slice of life?), the distinction between discovery and invention is anything but clear-cut—on the contrary the confusion is almost systematic.

Kneale now goes on to examine the case of morality, and the proposition that 'morality is a human invention', and he demonstrates 'that those who talk of the making of the moral law by men usually give such an account of the making that it is possible also to call it a finding . . . the word "discovery" might suggest a source external to ourselves'.[12] Returning to his original concern, the dispute between the Formalists and the Conventionalists in mathematics, Kneale concludes that this kind of invention 'is after all only the finding and selection of an interesting possibility'.[13] Generally, then, the contrast between invention and discovery very often does not bear very close scrutiny, for inventions may be systematically comprehended in terms of discovery, and especially in terms of finding methods and processes. Therefore, the conclusion is reached that 'the fact that the calculus of logic can be described as an invention does not justify us in saying that the principles of logic are man-made. . . . I have no idea of invention wide enough to cover . . . this latter thesis'.[14]

Kneale is right to stop where he does, for this is the point at which one must consider the likelihood of certain metaphysical entities, for mountains are one thing and methods are another, and the extension of the concept of invention that Kneale avoids will necessitate a direct confrontation with such entities. I shall consider this issue only in so far as it concerns the use to which I put the term 'innovation'.

As was mentioned above, non-innovational progress is intrinsically more quiescent than innovational progress. This is not to be taken in a literal sense, for the activities characteristic of tribal societies, for example, the ritual dance and the exchange of goods, may of course be as activistic as those characteristic of modern societies, the football match and the supermarket. It is intended in a socio-historic sense, for the society that is characterized by innovational progress will be subject to different types of change and these changes on different levels to the societies whose progress is non-innovational. One good indicator of this is the span of recognizability of a society. We hear stories of men released after years of imprisonment in this country who quite literally do not recognize the society into which they have re-emerged. This is the essence of the innovational society, for there is not simply quantitative change (more or less of things) but qualititative change (different things and different patterns), and the variable in which I am interested here is that of novelty. From this aspect Kneale's analysis of the idea of invention suggests some useful clarifications of this notion.

In the first place, it is clear if we are to escape the problem of inevitably confusing invention with discovery, and if we are to avoid the almost inexhaustible task of spelling out different relations for these two concepts in every sphere of life activity, then we must be prepared to specify clearly the way in which innovation is to be distinguished from invention and discovery. To follow Barnett is to relinquish responsibility for this sort of decision and, as I shall show below, to drain all specific meaning from the process of innovation, thus prohibiting in all but the most meagre sense the possibility of non-innovational action.

Next, Kneale's analysis implicitly suggests that novelty is not in question in the apparent contrast between invention and discovery. In his remarks about the selection of patterns from among the total possibilities, he gives the impression that invention or discovery is a form of shuffling around of reality and latching on to certain emergents, selecting almost on the principle of interest alone. This view of novelty is a truly philosophical one, and it might be interpreted crudely to mean that real novelty is impossible and that the distinction that I am trying to set up between innovational and non-innovational progress is bound to fail if it is based on such an uncertain criterion. This point has been elaborated by Popper in his attack on that variety of historicism, if it exists, that claims to be able to predict and explain rationally 'intrinsically new' social situations. Popper, working on the same notion as Barnett, allows novelty 'of arrangement', but precludes the possibility of rational analysis and prediction of 'intrinsically new events'.[15] This distinction between arrangement and intrinsic novelty corresponds in Popper's scheme to that between the standpoint of causal explanation and the appreciation of the unique, and seems to me to be a confusion that is relevant to the questions around novelty and innovation that I am considering.

Such a distinction ignores the category of recognizability. In order to recognize either novelty of arrangement or intrinsic novelty one must neglect certain aspects of a phenomenon and be prepared to emphasize others. The very act of recognizing 'intrinsic novelty' precludes the manner in which Popper phrases his distinction, for if it were impossible to analyse it rationally, and perhaps even to predict it in some very general way, then it is most difficult to see what could be meant by recognizing it. Barnett, in one sense, goes to the opposite extreme when he gives the impression that because each response differs from all others and each stimulus differs from all others, in that they are not identical, then innovation is basic to the human condition.[16] Here we could recognize nothing but novelty.

The American philosopher M. R. Cohen sums up the most reasonable rebuttal of those two rough extremes when he remarks simply that 'as new truth like new beauty cannot be totally unlike the old—we could not recognize it as truth or beauty if it were—it follows that the proper use of old knowledge is an indispensable aid in the discovery of the new'.[17] Where Popper speaks of 'novelty of arrangement' and Barnett speaks of the recombination of the elements in some configuration, I should like to leave this rather specific, and for my purposes misguided, aspect of the analysis of innovations open. The advantages in this are substantial, for it permits both extreme unfamiliarity with elements and extreme familiarity with elements to be classed as possibly innovational situations. This leads to the notion that phenomena might be innovational not so much 'in themselves' but more importantly, in terms of some social context. This in turn leads to a conception of innovation and non-innovation as ends of a continuum rather than as twins in a dichotomy. And this is how I should like to consider the difference between innovational and non-innovational progress: they are at different ends of a continuum and although the extremes, like black and white, are almost always easily distinguishable there is a vast grey area in the middle. The complexity of social life dictates that the criteria of difference cannot be determined entirely from outside this continuum, but must be always sensitive to the ways in which innovational and non-innovational progress act upon one another.

Therefore, the thoroughly psychologistic nature of Barnett's account of innovation seems to me to be entirely misconceived. When he claims that 'the conception of something new is independent of the consequences of its conception',[18] and when he opines that 'group complexity is meaningless as far as innovation is concerned; the complexity of individual knowledge is the pertinent consideration',[19] he is treating innovation as if it was something individuals do in thought, and only this. He is suggesting that the criteria for innovation rest with the individual, his knowledge and his experience, as if (like his notion of innovation) these were somehow isolated from a social context for the duration of the innovational process. All this, with the exception of the isolation of the individual and his understanding, is true enough and trivial enough. The interesting point is that, within certain social situations, the relevant phenomena *become* innovational under certain circumstances, and that the explanation and understanding of these processes of innovation or indeed non-innovation do not rely solely, if at all, on the method of psychological reductionism or on an appeal to individual motives, which comes very much to the same thing.

It is this process of an event or an action *becoming* innovational, necessarily within the grey area between unmistakable innovation and obvious non-innovation, which is especially interesting. An event or action does not become innovational because an individual, or a group for that matter, feels that a certain novelty has arisen, but because the event or action is having a certain effect on the society, the social structure in which it occurs. Thus, on my account, innovation and non-innovation are structural matters; they attain significance in so far as they can be seen to have consequences for the forms of social organization that characterize the society in which they occur.* Novelty, then, is never something either intrinsic to a state of affairs or the rearrangement of elements, for these are very individual matters and it is difficult to see how they are indepen-

---

* R. P. Dore, in an essay 'On the Possibility and Desirability of a Theory of Modernization' (in Asiatic Research Center, International Conference on the Problems of Modernisation in Asia: *Report*, Korea University, 1966, pp. 157-66), draws a distinction between 'transitive' and 'intransitive' uses of the term 'modernization', which is germane to my point.

dently relevant to non-individual entities such as those we must deal with in sociology. Popper as a methodological Individualist and Barnett as a psychological Reductionist thereby fail to appreciate that innovation in society and novelty in this context are processes that can only be explained and understood on non-individual, structural levels of abstraction, inaccessible by their methods.

In a rough-and-ready fashion this point is made by S. C. Gilfillan (with reference to invention rather than innovation) in his strange work, *The Sociology of Invention* of 1935. He states thirty-eight rather uneven social principles of invention which include:

> *Inevitability.* With the progress of the craft of invention, apparently a device can no longer remain unfound when the time for it is ripe. . . . There is no indication that any individual's genius has been necessary to any invention that has had any importance. To the historian and social scientist the progress of invention appears *impersonal*.

However, Gilfillan goes on to say that 'invention can only come at the hand of some sort of inventors'.[20]

It should be quite clear by now that my own personal methodological bias is anti-individualist and, what I consider to be much the same thing, anti-reductionist. It is difficult to imagine how a sociologist working with concepts of society, institutional change, progress, innovation, and a host of other tools, could approach his subject otherwise. Issues such as this are of course not matters for final demonstration in one way or another, but good arguments for one view and against the other will naturally sway the balance.[21] In the present case the question may be specified with relation to the processes of invention, discovery or innovation as follows: Can we satisfactorily explain and understand these phenomena through an examination of individual motives, or must we investigate the role of social factors as they bear on the phenomena independent of the particular individual motives concerned? Is there any sense, therefore, in which the sociologist may conceive of invention, discovery or innovation impersonally? The mere fact that I can characterize societies as operating on an innovational or a non-innovational conception of progress, and make some sort of meaningful statement thereby, suggests that one can indeed conceive of the phenomena impersonally, and without reference to particular individual motivations.

As far as invention and discovery in science are concerned, there is a good deal of evidence to suggest that there exists a social system of science and that individualistic accounts of what happens in science must miss out a vital dimension. But this is an empirical question to some extent,* whereas I wish to use the term *innovation* with a built-in sociological meaning.

Each innovation, as opposed to a more common-sense usage of the terms 'invention' or 'discovery', must be judged on social as well as scientific and technological grounds. There is little point in ritualistically straining towards a trouble-free distinction between these three terms, for up to now, this has not been necessary. But, as I pointed out above, although the invention-discovery distinction may be left unsettled, the general task of setting up the concept 'innovation' as a useful tool in my particular analysis cannot be left problematic to this degree. To do this would be to relinquish the specifically sociological responsibility, so does Barnett, and to opt out of the matter of explaining what happens to inventions when they have been invented and what happens to discoveries when they have been discovered. *Innovation, then, is what I term the impact of inventions and discoveries on society,* and this event is analysable, as are all events, in terms of the characteristics of the elements involved and the relationships between the elements involved.†

In what I term innovational societies, or societies that illustrate the innovational approach to problem solution to progress, the impact of inventions and discoveries will be great; in non-innovational societies the impact will be small or perhaps nil. Therefore, I do not claim that non-innovational societies are necessarily societies in which there is never any invention or discovery, although this is obviously the limiting case, but rather that non-innovational societies are those societies in which invention and discovery have a minimal social impact. Similarly, I am not claiming that innovational societies are those with the highest possible incidence of invention and discovery, though again this would be the limiting case, but rather that in innovational societies invention and discovery have the maximal social impact. I cannot stress the point too strongly that I consider innovation and non-innovation, as characterizations of modes of progress, to be at opposite ends of a very long continuum.

I am here trying to distinguish between the very different phenomena of inventiveness and propensity for discovery on the one hand, as against innovativeness on the other hand. These are phenomena which, in my opinion, are all too often confused. It is not my intention

---

* I present some empirical evidence in a short *Appendix* at the end of this chapter.

† All students of innovation are indebted to the careful and interesting work of E. M. Rogers, particularly his *Diffusion of Innovations* (New York: Free Press, 1962). His recent book, *Modernisation Among Peasants* (New York: Holt, Reinhart & Winston, 1969), is particularly interesting in terms of its application to the sociology of development. However, as can be seen, my analysis proceeds along different—though probably compatible—lines.

to elaborate a full-scale typology of social organization, but I shall not allow the fact that this enterprise, once the spring of sociological theory, is so unfashionable today to prevent me from making some suggestions in this direction.

An interesting classification of societies has been obscured by the conflation of inventiveness and potential for discovery with innovativeness, in most if not all the literature on social change. On the one hand there are those societies that show a very high level of inventiveness and a great potential for discovery in certain fields, and on the other hand there are those that show little or no inventiveness and appear to have no potential for discovery in those fields. This is certainly one dimension along which societies can be and have been classified. To carry out such an exercise properly one would be obliged to examine the history of all branches of culture and social life, and it would not be altogether surprising if it were established that high inventiveness and potential for discovery in some aspects of social life co-existed with low inventiveness and potential for discovery in other aspects of the social life of the same society. Further, we should positively expect such variations over time, and between different societies, both synchronically and diachronically.

A second dimension is that of innovativeness, understood as I set it out above in terms of the impact of inventions and discoveries on society. We can therefore classify societies from the most highly innovational, those in which inventions and discoveries have the greatest impact on society, to the most minimally innovational, those in which inventions and discoveries have little or no impact on society. Again, we should not be surprised to find that the level of innovativeness varied within societies according to the aspects of social life under consideration, that it varied between societies, and that it varied both synchronically and diachronically. I do not know of anyone who has taken the trouble to classify societies on their levels of innovativeness as distinguished from their levels of inventiveness and discovery, and indeed there would seem to be a good reason, on the surface at least, for this neglect. It is somewhat pointless to classify, for example, nuns by sex or bachelors by marital state, and naturally when invention and discovery are taken to be kinds of innovations, the same holds for inventiveness and potential for discovery and innovativeness. However, it is clearly possible that those societies that demonstrate a high level of inventiveness and a high potential for discovery might demonstrate a low level of innovativeness *in the same respect*. And similarly, a low level of inventiveness and a minimal potential for discovery might accompany a high level of innovativeness *in the same respect*.

On the other hand, I do not for a moment deny that in any

aspect of culture and social life, high inventiveness and discovery are more likely to occur with high innovativeness, and that low inventiveness and discovery are more likely to occur with low innovativeness. These are the congruent cases, for it is obvious that where nothing is ever invented or discovered anywhere there can be no innovation at all, and that where there is a very high level of invention and discovery a very low level of innovation would be most difficult to maintain in practice. In another sense, however, they are not the congruent cases, for A. Etzioni's suggestion in his theory of complex organizations[22] that the other types strain towards the congruent types seems to me to be inapplicable to the present analysis. In fact, there appear to be some advantages to certain societies that might recommend the non-congruent cases.

Let me briefly and roughly give some historical examples to illustrate and, I hope, to clarify these remarks. The most obvious field in this connection is technology and science, and for convenience I shall ignore the great differences that do exist between one branch of technology and science and the others, not to mention the differences between technology and science themselves. Further, I shall no doubt loosely give the impression that high inventiveness and high innovativeness and low inventiveness and low innovativeness are discrete variables, whereas I have all along intended them to be understood as points on continua. What I lose in accuracy I strive to gain in boldness!

The following table (see Table 1) is a representation of my suggested typology of societies on the twin dimensions of innovativeness and inventiveness (hereinafter to include potential for discovery).

Cases (1) and (4) are unproblematic and need only a few words of comment. In both nineteenth-century England and twentieth-century North America, as the most obvious examples, inventions and discoveries ran at a very high level in the scientific and technological fields, and the total impact of these inventions and discoveries on the society in general was very great. This is of course another way of saying that science and technology became fully institutionalized in these places at these times, and that a high priority was given to the scientific and technological solutions to the problems that the societies confronted. Progress, as I have argued, was defined in terms of high levels of scientific invention and discovery and the maximum possible impact of science and technology on society. These, then, are the clearly innovational societies in respect of science and technology: they are the societies characterized by innovational progress.

Case (4) requires even less comment. Nomadic societies, for obvious reasons, have a very low level of inventiveness and a low level of innovativeness. Likewise, simple peasant societies tend

Table 1 Typology of societies on inventiveness and innovativeness with respect to technology and science

		Inventiveness	
		High	*Low*
Innovativeness	*High*	1 19th-century England; 20th-century North America	2 Late 19th-century Japan; many contemporary developing societies
	Low	3 *Imperial China; Eskimo society	4 Nomadic tribes; simple peasant societies

to have a very low level of scientific and technological inventiveness, and innovation in the form of the impact that any scientific or technological invention or discovery might have is at a minimal level. In terms of science and technology, therefore, these are the societies that do not attempt to solve their problems by innovational means, and clearly they are the societies that aspire to non-innovational progress.†

Cases (2) and (3) present greater difficulties, but are all the more interesting for that. The clearest example of a society that was undistinguished for its inventiveness and its potential for scientific

---

* It has been suggested that Hellenistic Egypt might fit in this category, and Athens in category (2). This is a good place to re-emphasize the extremely tentative nature of the historical examples given, and to remind the reader that I am here rather less concerned with accuracy of fit than with the utility of the criteria suggested. Further, I am well aware that there are good arguments to suggest that science and technology might develop independently at some periods. All of these points could be dealt with in a more sophisticated table; here I am merely suggesting some possibilities.

† It is at this point that the simplicity of my typology must be checked. The criticism that most easily and most correctly arises here is that which asks: Who, or which group in the society, are you speaking of? R. P. Dore has suggested that a theory of modernization as such is unhelpful and that a piece-meal empiricism that investigates, among other things, the goals of the modernizing leaders must replace it. This approach would suggest that a 'further dimension might be added to my typology, namely the degree of commitment that leaders in society gave to innovational progress in this instance. This is partly covered, however, by the notion that proposed innovational solutions to particular social problems might be unsuccessful for one reason or another. I am at pains to make the suggestion that it is vital to distinguish between failed innovational progress and successful non-innovational progress, and that this is a distinction often obscured by statistical comparisons between levels of economic development.

and technological discovery, while achieving a very high level of innovativeness of other peoples' invention and discovery, was Japan in the last quarter of the nineteenth century. The enthusiasm and the speed with which the Japanese maximized the impact of Western technological and scientific invention and discovery is a unique case of swift, though not painless, industrialization.[23] So impressive was this achievement that one is tempted to wonder if this innovation did not have the essential elements of invention and discovery at its origin. Is it not correct to speak of the 'inventive genius for innovation' of the Japanese at this period? I consider that this is somewhat colloquial, and although one uses words as one pleases my purpose here is to demonstrate that the distinction between inventiveness and innovation is a useful one, and that it can be sociologically fruitful to regard innovation as the impact that inventions and discoveries have on society. This is partly a restatement of the methodological position that I very briefly set out above, in which inventions and discoveries are things that people or groups make, whereas innovation or non-innovation is what happens in societies. People or groups themselves do not innovate, in my sense, rather it is their inventions and discoveries that have or do not have an impact on society (theirs or others') and that are innovated or not as the case may be.

Many developing societies, especially those approaching 'the hump of industrialization', are largely in this category of societies with low inventiveness and high innovativeness in science and technology. Indeed, the well-known idea that the West and the Soviet Union export their so-called 'know-how' to vast sections of remaining humanity supports the existence of this third category.

Case (3), the combination of high inventiveness with low innovativeness, is the most challenging case of all and the pressures and strains that might be brought to bear on such a society in the modern world are too obvious to need pointing out. Certain historical examples do suggest themselves nevertheless, and without going into any detail let me mention Imperial China as a society in which technological and scientific inventiveness and discovery achieved a fairly high level, although innovativeness, the impact of these inventions and discoveries on the society at large, was not at all great. Chinese technology, as Weber comments, 'remained sublimated empiricism', and there was no proper 'transition from empirical to rational technology'.[24] Weber of course explains this situation, the absence of scientific, technological and economic innovation, with reference to certain elements that were lacking in the Chinese value system, but I am more interested here in the curious state of affairs that permits or encourages invention and discovery in these areas and yet precludes its large-scale innovation throughout the society.

K

Marcel Granet sums up this seeming paradox in the following manner:

> With the imperial era, which closes the history of ancient
> China, Chinese civilization certainly arrives at maturity, but
> although, by defining with increasing·strictness its traditional
> ideals, the believers in orthodoxy wished to adorn it with a
> static dignity, it remains rich in youthful forces.[25]

Eskimo society is a variation on the same case. Tales of the inventiveness and the potential for discovery exhibited by the Eskimo are legion.[26] The level of technological and scientific innovativeness, however, remains low doubtless due to overwhelming practical difficulties. This may seem an unduly harsh judgment on a people who were disadvantaged by their environment, and it is indeed not immediately clear what further impact certain technological inventions and discoveries could have had beyond those particular contexts of problems that the inventions and discoveries were originally intended to solve. But this itself is to beg the question of the growth of science and technology and, more generally, the development of civilizations. It is in this respect that we may consider, for example, W. F. Ogburn's study of *The Social Effects of Aviation* to point out the high level of innovativeness of twentieth-century North America in terms of the very great impact that this extremely important invention-discovery complex had on the total American society. No invention or discovery in Eskimo society, even allowing for the vast differences in scale and complexity, had anything like this sort of impact. Eskimo society simply is not innovative to the degree of American society.

All four categories in my primitive typology of societies have tentative historical members, and now I must explain how this foray into nineteenth-century-style societal classification is linked to my eighteenth-century-style foray into the idea of progress!

In my view, the idea of progress is endemic to human societies and, though I would not go so far as to say that it is instinctive to man as a social animal, I do not consider that it is totally misleading to regard it in some respects as we might regard the wish for self-preservation. The social arrangements that make this latter desire of men possible, and indeed justify risks to this self-preservation, have analogues with reference to the idea of progress. Just as in wartime society calls on its members to be prepared to sacrifice their lives for the sake of the preservation of the society as a whole, so too a society may invoke one idea of progress or another in order to meet the needs of its members, in order to solve the problems that the society confronts. In situations of emergency, as above, the society that operates on a predominantly innovational concept of progress may call upon non-innovational solutions to dire problems, and societies characterized by non-innovational progress may be forced to call upon innovational solutions to their problems. The justification of action in each case is progress, as it was, in the previous case, self-preservation.

It is the task of the sociologist to show that certain variables strongly influence though do not absolutely determine the path of short-term and perhaps long-term social change for each society. The short-term continuity of these variables is very correctly taken for granted, unless there is good reason for not assuming this. If these statements are unacceptable, then on the one side a situation of the trendless flux of history is forced upon us, and on the other side there is the rigid determinism that appears to negate any idea of morality in society.

It is therefore essential that progress, whether innovational or non-innovational, be theoretically tempered with some criterion of success. In my account of progress, the satisfactory solution of problems facing men in society, the criterion of success, is defined with respect to whether the solution to a problem or set of problems is sought in an innovational or a non-innovational fashion.[27] As has been seen, the presence or absence of inventions and discoveries is by no means the final arbiter of whether a solution will be attempted on one or other of these modes of progress in the modern world. That is, inventiveness and innovativeness are quite separate though related dimensions. The notions of world communities and world markets for goods, services and techniques, perhaps the most important concepts for a sociology of international systems to emerge in the twentieth century, ensures that most societies have, in theory at least, the option of choosing one type of progress rather than the other. I say 'in theory at least' because the dice are loaded against those who choose innovational solutions to problems that were hitherto solved or approached and not solved by non-innovational means. This much is obvious, for it is usually more difficult to find new things, ideas or processes, and to apply them so that they may have the maximum impact on society, than to continue with the old things, ideas or processes.

An interesting and often critical case is where the old thing, idea or process runs out, through natural or unnatural causes, thus necessitating new and initially innovative solutions to the social problems confronted. What we might discover, for example, is that a society, working on a non-innovational concept of progress in general, was rather successful in solving its traditional problems. With the destruction of very basic resources, both the specific problems and the specific possible solutions would change, with the result that innovational attempts to progress might be quite unsuc-

131

cessful; or that the familiar non-innovational means of problem-solving (where conceivable) were totally inadequate to the new problems to be solved. Doubtless, we would note that conflicting groups in the society would organize around the banners of innovational and non-innovational progress—those who saw the survival of the people in terms of modernization and those who considered that faith in the tried and familiar ways of life, however difficult in particulars, was the only way to progress, to solve the problems of the society. The latter group will wish to minimize the influence of any new things, ideas or processes to which the society is exposed, whereas the former, the modernizing group, will wish to innovate to the greatest possible extent—they will wish to ensure the greatest possible impact of inventions and discoveries, whether internal or from abroad, on the structure of their society.

This may be very easily generalized to a large and increasingly significant part of the contemporary world. One of my reasons for pointing this out in these differing ways is, as I hinted above, a polemical one. Contrary to the belief and the opinion of most writers on the sociology of development, I do not consider that modernization, development of industrial society, and scientific and technological progress, are the *only* options open to twentieth-century man. It is true that they are the most comfortable goals all round, but it is not callousness that leads me to argue that certain non-innovational progress is worth some examination, all the more so because though innovational progress has had some astounding successes it has also had some crashing failures. I am not simply saying that certain problems typically call for innovational solutions and others for non-innovational solutions, though I have little doubt that this statement would be abundantly supported by the evidence from the socio-historical record but I am reiterating the suggestion I made above that different societies define their problems in often very different ways, and so it is not uncommon that the very appreciation of a problem may prescribe the nature of its solution. In particular, the society that operates on an innovational concept of progress will naturally tend to define all problems, or most of them, in terms that are amenable to innovational treatment, and likewise non-innovational societies will define their problems non-innovationally. The two possibilities, innovational and non-innovational paths to progress, are open at some periods and to some men more than to others.

It is very striking that Herbert Marcuse, in reflecting on ideas of René Dumont, expresses a view on these issues in the following terms:

If industrialization and the introduction of technology in the backward countries encounter strong resistance from the traditional and indigenous modes of life and labour—a resistance which is not abandoned even at the very tangible prospect of a better and easier life—could this pre-technological tradition itself become the source of progress and industrialization?

Such indigenous progress would demand a planned policy which, instead of superimposing technology on the traditional modes of life and labour, *would extend and improve them on their own grounds*[28] (my emphasis).

Marcuse, however, is not optimistic about the possibility of the success of such a project.

If a decision is to be made on whether or not a particular society has experienced progress in some or all aspects of its life, and I firmly believe that sociologists and others frequently make these decisions and that it is right and proper for them so to do, then it is clearly of paramount importance that innovational and non-innovational concepts of progress be distinguished for what they are. Before one can even begin to discuss the standards on which a sociological theory of progress might judge one state of affairs to be 'better' than another—the essentially normative realm—it is imperative to make this distinction between the innovational and the non-innovational.

In the long run, unsuccessful societies of any type, that is those societies that systematically fail to solve their problems, will cease to exist as independent entities, whereas successful societies that solve their problems to some extent will continue to exist as more or less independent entities. One would expect that previously successful societies, in one respect or another, on meeting failure might try to overcome it by non-innovational means in the case of mainly innovational societies, and vice versa. It is therefore crucial that each situation is studied carefully, and that we do not assume either that because a society has always tackled x by innovational means that it always will, or that because x, y, z, a and b are tackled by innovational means that c will be so too.

To the innovational man, successful non-innovational progress may be quite incomprehensible as progress, as might innovational progress to the non-innovational man, and so the difficulty of accepting such a thing as someone else's progress that cuts across one's own way of life may be very great indeed. The fire-power, at present, is with the men who espouse innovational progress, and, to put not too fine an edge on it, all that the non-innovational concept of progress appears to promise is the flower-power.

This distinction between innovational and non-innovational progress does not in itself explain anything, though I would claim that it helps to clarify the issue of progress, and to place it in a universal perspective where it truly belongs in opposition to those who would have us believe that the very idea is a recent invention of Western man and linked uniquely to the type of society in which he lives. This latter view is somewhat true of innovational progress, and it is not surprising that the modern development of the idea of progress, traced out in the first part of this study, grew both practically and theoretically alongside the institutionalization of science at the turn of the eighteenth century in Western Europe, and a little later elsewhere.

In the next chapters I shall attempt to construct a sociological ethic which, in conjunction with the distinction between innovational and non-innovational modes of progress, will lay the foundation work necessary for a sociological theory of progress.

Appendix

One of the problems of the sociology of science is to ascertain the degree of independence and isolation, or the interdependence and community of scientists and technologists with respect to their research and development work. The sources of data for this type of study are of uneven quality. On the one hand there are the objective but often misleading statistics on patents, and on the other hand there is the subjective but often very important anecdotal information.

The unreliability of patent statistics has been amply demonstrated by John Jewkes and his colleagues. They appeal to such facts as the unknown number of unpatented inventions, the changing standards of patentability, the difficulty of determining whether or not a patent taken out by a corporation was due to individual inventiveness, and the practice of corporations buying rights from individual inventors, to conclude that 'all kinds of inconclusive speculations can be based upon patents statistics'.[29] Patent systems have often come under attack themselves, whether from those who argue that the individual patentee must be more rigorously protected if technical progress is to be assured,[30] or from those who see the notion of monopolies in ideas as intrinsically inimical to that very progress.[31] The latter view is strongly supported, in theory at least, by the possibility that individuals or collectivities may use the patent system to protect vested interest by patenting an idea in order to suppress it rather than exploit it.

The anecdotal information on inventors is legion, and it appears in a great variety of forms, from autobiographies and biographies to folklore and films. The most systematic work in this field is probably the early studies of Joseph Rossman, written in the 1930s when he was employed in the U.S. Patent Office and was also carrying out the duties of the editor of the *Journal of the Patent Office Society*. In articles published in the aforementioned journal, in the *American Journal of Sociology*, and in his book, *The Psychology of the Inventor*, Rossman examines a series of topics concerned with the life and influences of a sample running into many hundreds of American inventors.

Jewkes and his colleagues present case studies of over sixty inventions in their book to which I have already referred, and there is no shortage of material on the history of science and technology to suggest further that generalizations are most difficult to maintain in this region. The weight of the anecdotal evidence, if only on a cursory reading of it, suggests the picture of the independent and isolated inventor who, by dint of individual genius and/or perseverence, manages to overcome great scientific and technological problems and to contribute to material progress. Even Jewkes, however, indicates that this pattern is changing due to such factors as the ever-increasing scale, complexity and expense of research, and the modern tendency for research teams rather than individuals, necessitated by the factors just mentioned as well as the very great specialization in science, means that any one individual has only a quite incomplete knowledge of fields that vitally affect his own.

The sociology of science further refines these impressions, both with regard to the picture of the lone-wolf nineteenth-century inventor and to the position in science and technology today. The history of independent multiple inventions, of which Ogburn in 1922 catalogues nearly one hundred and fifty examples,[32] suggests most strongly that, in the words of Bernard Barber, 'Scientific discovery [or invention] is not the mysterious outcome of unexplainable individual genius. It is rather the result of a partly specifiable social process in which the individual and society each has an important part to play.'[33] As Barber goes on to suggest, one can overplay the hand of social determination of science just as easily as one can overplay the hand of individual genius, but as this line of argument must slip back into the type of methodological discussion to which I called a halt above, I shall move on to another aspect of the same problem for which empirical evidence can in fact be called directly.

I refer to the actual studies of the working conditions and influences of scientists and technologists who were involved in the industrially important inventions of the nineteenth century. The following is a description, by Burns and Stalker, of those conditions and influences:

In the Scotland of the eighteenth century, for such men [as Black, Watt and Roebuck] to be acquainted with each other was virtually inevitable.

Such circles of personal acquaintanceship served as a social medium for a further decade or so. By the beginning of the nineteenth century, fellow-students and friends sought to institutionalize their informal acquaintanceships. Clubs rather than learned societies, as the Lunar Society and the Royal Society of Edinburgh were, they and their offspring and kindred in Manchester and Newcastle, and the archetype in London, included the persons responsible for scientific advance, technical invention and, to a large extent, industrial innovation.*[34]

None of this is surprising or unexpected, for it is simply that which has made it possible to speak about science as a social system and to deliberate on its norms as Merton has done,[35] and to treat it as a specialized belief system, institutionalized in certain societies, as Parsons has done.[36] The present issue is largely one of the level of communication and interdependence between scientists, and especially inventors, and it is important to find out the details of the practical arrangements that existed for communication and influence to take place.[37] Most of the sources that I have mentioned above give the apparently contradictory impressions that no inventions, or very few, appear out of the blue, yet particular inventors very often seem to come up with inventions that have no discernible links with anything that preceded them. Communication, of course, never proves influence, as indeed 'seeing' something never entails 'noticing aspects' of it.

Nevertheless, the sort of evidence that Ogburn marshalled on independent multiple inventions, the numerous reports of scientific and technical societies and clubs, the patterns in which inventions very often appear, and not least the order that logic imposes on the progress of invention, all suggest that invention or innovation has been rather less haphazard than a purely 'individual inventive geniuses' account would have it. On the practical as well as the internal logical level, the processes of invention and innovation, though not necessarily directed by some hidden hand of complete social determination, exemplify the strong influences of changing societies and changing social requirements. And these changing social requirements are the specific needs of societies with relation to their respective positions on the continuum of innovational or non-innovational solutions to the problems that face these societies. That is to say, a study of the conditions for invention and innovation as preferred methods for the solutions to problems facing societies, the option of innovational progress, presents us with an approach to the sociology of science, for science is the form that these innovational solutions typically take in modern industrial society.

* This statement, and many others made by Burns and Stalker, may incidentally be used to support the arguments in Part One of this book which pertain to the institutionalization of science and technology around this time when the idea of progress was undergoing a radical transformation.

VIII   The sociological ethic (1)

In the previous chapter I have tried to show that on the levels of events, theories and aspirations, a sociological theory of progress was best served by the analytical distinction between innovational and non-innovational progress. That is to say, on my definition of progress which focuses on the 'most satisfactory solutions of any or all of the problems facing mankind', the emphasis is firmly placed on the problem-solving arrangements and capacities and successes of societies. In this chapter I shall suggest how we can make judgments within the spheres of innovational and non-innovational progress. Then, I shall examine briefly some traditional systems of ethics and show that the only way we can find the necessary value-standard for a theory of progress, a sociological ethic, is to redefine the problems of ethics.

Innovational and non-innovational progress
Innovation and non-innovation are two approaches to problem-solving, and the fact that all men always aspire to progress means that there is no final way to judge between the proposed innovational and non-innovational solutions to social problems. I say 'final way to judge' because whether on some inner logic or long-standing habit or the dictates of the ongoing human condition, there appear to be certain self-evidently obvious types of solutions to the more widely-met problems that men face. How much these are due to the substance of social life and how much to the variable attributes is not for me to decide at present—though it will become a crucial issue before I am done. What can be said is that typically there are problems in most societies that call for innovational solutions and those that call for non-innovational solutions. One may persuasively argue, therefore, that the innovational rather than the non-innovational is the more satisfactory solution (or vice versa) to a particular

problem complex, and perhaps one might have the right to be astonished if and when someone disagreed. But otherwise, the choice between innovation and non-innovation as the approach of a society to the solution of its problems, in other words the orientation of the society to progress, is not a matter on which the sociologist or indeed the philosopher can properly make a judgment. In this respect I consider values, in the current terminology, to be normatively relativistic.[1]

We are faced, however, with a totally different problem *within* the spheres of innovational and non-innovational progress. For whereas at the highest level of abstraction there are only two possible paths to problem-solving, namely the innovational and the non-innovational, at the next level of abstraction there are many alternatives within the innovational and the non-innovational. There are apparently no limits in the innovational sphere, as the history of the social impact of inventions and discoveries amply shows. It hardly needs to be pointed out that in modern societies the institutionalization of science has meant that in many areas of social life the structure of society has been significantly planned and controlled in order to facilitate and encourage the maximum level of innovation in the solutions of a great variety of problems.[2]

In the non-innovational sphere there are definite limits to the range of alternatives available, though this range is often rather less limited than one might imagine. It is, however, logically closed in the way that innovational progress is logically open, and so it is rather more easy to predict the course that non-innovational progress might take because the careful researcher has access to all of the options, simply because none of them can be new and their impact is by definition restricted. This is not to say that non-innovational progress is merely the traditional, in the sense in which this term is used by Weber. As this point is essential to an understanding of what I mean by actual non-innovational *progress* and to the moral problem of progress as I now confront it, I shall elaborate upon it in some detail.

Weber's 'traditional' behaviour was the most 'behaviouristic' type of action in his scheme of social action. 'For', Weber says, 'it is very often a matter of almost automatic reaction to habitual stimuli which guide behaviour in a course which has been repeatedly followed. The great bulk of all everyday action to which people have become habitually accustomed approaches this type.'[3] But of course Weber was grinding the axe of rationality and he fully appreciated that traditional action was not always simply blind response to irrelevant stimuli. Men could know perfectly well what they were about when they participated in traditional forms of action. This realism is clearly demonstrated in his analysis of the traditional mode of the legitimization of authority, for here we see the self-conscious use of tradition, like bureaucracy and charisma, as the organizing characteristic of 'a system of imperative co-ordination'. Weber's analysis is however rather individualistic for he concentrates on the person of the chief or the leader, as much as on the system of rules and the structural arrangements which are the distinguishing features of his treatment of the rational-legal bureaucracy.

The point does emerge, nevertheless, that traditional action or traditional authority may be the hallmarks of a distinct societal type, though it is clear that Weber was latterly somewhat more interested in the struggle between bureaucracy and charisma—perhaps tradition represented an insufficiently severe reaction to the trend of rationalization that runs through his work like a binding thread. I should consider this emphasis misplaced. It would seem that both bureaucratic and so-called traditional societies, *very roughly* contract and community-based social structures, are equally susceptible to the surge of charismatic claims on authority relations. The difficulty here is that on Weber's account, although the bureaucratic form of social structure, rational-legal society, is well specified, the picture of traditional society apart from the details of the traditional form of the legitimization of authority is not at all full. It is to Tönnies and Durkheim that we turn, rather than to Weber, for this information. This is not to say that his work does not contain an enormous amount of information on traditional societies, indeed his comparative sociology of religion is replete with such matter, but he did not devote the same sort of theoretical attention to it as he did to industrial-bureaucratic societies. Be this as it may, although it is useful and illuminating to speak of the charismatic legitimization of authority in contrast to the rational-legal and the traditional as Weber very properly did, it is something approaching a categorical error to see these three phenomena in terms of total social structure, for 'charismatic society' does not belong in the same category as bureaucratic and traditional societies. Weber, of course, saw that this was so, and thus developed the notion, crucial to his sociology, of the routinization of charisma.

Traditional behaviour as a type of social action, however, is just as characteristic in many ways of bureaucratic societies as of traditional societies, as the quotation from *The Theory of Social and Economic Organization* above indicates. All societies have elements of habitual everyday activity, and sociology recognizes this by its insistence on some concept of social structure. Traditional society, presumably, is that in which most action is everyday action and where new things, ideas and processes are conceived in a fashion quite remote to that in rational-legal bureaucratic societies. Parsons, in his introduction to Weber's aforementioned work, sums this up admirably in his discussion of traditional authority:

Even actual innovations* are justified by the fiction that they were once in force but had fallen into disuse and only now are brought back to their rightful position of authority. One of the important consequences, and symptoms, of the existence of traditional authority is that there can be no such thing as new 'legislation'.[4]

This represents part of what I mean by non-innovational society, although, as I claimed, it is not all. Traditional society gives the impression of constant repetitiveness and almost complete lack of imagination. This is probably due to the fact that we tend to consider as traditional those societies in which nothing ever 'happens'—in a typically modern usage of the term 'happens'. And this is evidently a fair approximation to a description of traditional societies. With non-innovational societies it is quite otherwise for these societies, like all viable and ongoing societies, try to solve their problems. Non-innovational societies try to solve their problems, and they try to achieve progress by calling upon known and familiar things, ideas and processes.

The truly traditional society is perhaps like the perfectly adapted organism, a closed system with its environment. When anything changes, the organism dies out, unable to cope with new problems even on the basis of old solutions. The traditional society on this stylized view has stopped aspiring to progress because it does not or cannot define any state of affairs as problematic. Life drifts on.[5] In non-innovational society this is most certainly not the case; this is to be expected, for the account that I have sketched of traditional society would perhaps refer only to very special circumstances, for example the complete isolation of a self-supporting community. Non-innovational society, then, differs from traditional society in the atmosphere of aspiration as well as in its susceptibility to social change and to social problems, each of which stimulates the other.

There is another very important sense in which traditional and non-innovational societies differ, and that is in terms of the relevant stock of ideas, things and processes. In the former there is usually one right way to do everything, a general lack of what Merton has termed 'functional alternatives'.[6] In non-innovational society, on the other hand, there is no logical or sociological reason why there cannot be a large variety of things, ideas and processes—a range of functional alternatives. The only restriction imposed by my analytical scheme is that non-innovational societies do not typically look to innovations, to new things, ideas and processes, in order to

---

* Parsons here uses 'innovations' more in the sense of inventions and discoveries than in the sense of impact of inventions and discoveries on society But this does not alter the significance of the statement for my present point.

solve their problems. Progress in these societies is achieved or not achieved on the existing stock of solutions. Further, the impact on society of solutions that do contain new elements, and even of those that do not, is strictly limited.

Here then there is just as much possibility that non-innovational solutions to problems might dictate a choice between alternatives, like the obvious choices possible in innovational solutions. It is within the areas of non-innovational and innovational progress that moral problems can arise, and whereas I hold that we cannot legitimately force a judgment on whether a problem ought to be solved on a non-innovational rather than an innovational basis or vice versa, we can and must force a judgment on the best solution within a non-innovational or innovational context. To force such a judgment it is necessary to find a standard of value that will be universally acceptable and that will be wide enough to cover the whole field of social relations, for it is here in the end that all problems that affect man in society reside. In one important sense, this quest is the history of ethics.

The redefinition of ethical problems

The history of ethics, it is fair to say, consists of attempts to answer the questions around moral progress—what counts as a good course of action and what as a bad one, etc.—but few and far between are the moral philosophers who actually hold that these questions have been satisfactorily answered. I have no intention of reviewing the history of ethics, and I shall simply draw attention to a few examples that demonstrate the impasse which always seems to be reached when ethics confronts the important questions of human conduct.

The great utilitarian systems of ethics, propounded as a hedonist behaviourism by Bentham and as an inductive science of action and morals by J. S. Mill, was the most pragmatically successful general theory of ethics in the last few centuries, not least because of its appeal to common sense before its articulation as a technical theory of ethics. Like Marxism to the sociologist, utilitarianism is to the logically-sophisticated modern philosopher, 'the theory we love to hate', but as many good and true men continue to find out, mere logical dismemberment does not touch the spirit. When a belief system travels the path from science to ideology, cognitive considerations of internal consistency become less important than matters of commitment.[7] However much scorn can be poured on the logical structure of any of the utilitarianisms, it is implicit in my understanding of progress that one of the major groups of problems that any society will confront is that dealing with the happiness (or in its Protestant version, the relief of pain) of its members. That actions leading to happiness or those done with that intention are not *irrelevant* to moral progress is hardly a controversial proposition. Therefore the theory of Mill at least can be seen as an overstatement of the case for *one* aspect of moral progress, and cannot simply be dismissed entirely, on account of the committal of several albeit important mistakes in the total analysis.

Yet another badly battered system of ethics widely ignored, if not forgotten in contemporary moral thought, is that based on some version of evolution. As I dealt with the social applications of evolution at length in Chapter IV, I need only pause to comment that, in the terms of reference of this book, when progress or evolution in a morally distinguished direction is the condition to which social humanity aspires, then evolution as an ideal and therefore as a factor in reality becomes meaningful. Whether evolution or progress take place or not, they are relevant to moral conduct. This is almost a tautology to any but the most abstract and ivory-entowered moral philosopher, for it claims that what happens in the world, the ways in which societies change (progress or regress with respect to some standard), is *relevant* to the morality of conduct in the society.

This is the position of C. H. Waddington with regard to the ethical question, though of course his belief that evolution actually takes place as contrasted to my view that evolution and progress are certainly operative only at the level of aspiration, forces him to conclude more strongly in favour of an evolutionary ethic, whereas I merely note the relevance of evolution for ethics. [8]

The Kantian 'moral law' brings out yet another relevant aspect of moral conduct: namely, that the goodness of an act stems from the motive behind it rather than the hoped-for consequences. It would be impudent of me to attempt to deal with the ethics of Kant here—I only introduce him in order to balance the impressions given by both utilitarian and evolutionist ethics, that the result is all-important and that the motive is nothing. The brief corrective is that both motive and consequences are morally relevant to human conduct, and any theory that emphasizes the one and forgets the other will accordingly fail to reflect the reality of essential features involved in the moral evolution of social action.

Modern moral philosophy has largely forfeited the responsibility for the solution of problems relevant to moral progress. Where what used to be known as 'moral propositions' are held to be merely sounds, expressions making no significant assertions as in the theory of A. J. Ayer, [9] it is not always easy to see how anyone, logicians and psychopaths apart, could take this account seriously as an effort to speak of morals. In the work of C. L. Stevenson the notion of moral philosophy as an examination of moral language becomes a little more convincing, for although neither man appears to be speaking about that part of *life* (as opposed to language) in which conduct is judged, at least Stevenson's theory goes some way to relating moral statements to things that happen in the world, apart from the behaviour implicit in uttering words. But it only goes part of the way, for Stevenson's distinction between the descriptive and the dynamic or emotive use of language and his view that ethical language has a persuasive function can tell us little about moral progress—as Stevenson points out, disagreements in ethics are disagreements about *interests* on his theory, and so 'moral' progress (if it could be given any meaning at all) must consist in the successful redirection of other people's interests.[10] This interpretation is from my point of view too generous, for Stevenson is prohibited on the general line of his argument from allowing such an 'objective' or even 'inter-subjective' notion as moral progress. For him as for all of those philosophers who see in ethics only the analysis of moral language, the implications of moral progress are quite untenable.

Wittgenstein's dictum, the seventh main proposition in his *Tractatus*, 'What we cannot speak of, we must be silent about',[11] is taken all too seriously by the philosophers of language who concern themselves in their idiosyncratic version of ethics. They simply do not speak about the actual problems of conduct that men in society have to solve or leave unsolved in the context of social relations. It is not clear whether with Wittgenstein our average linguistic philosopher feels that there is *something* transcendentally somewhere that is the *real* subject matter of ethics, only it is not sayable in language, or whether he takes his cue from the extreme positivism that dictates that there is nothing meaningful anywhere except that which is accessible to our common senses. Whatever interpretation holds, there is strictly speaking neither point nor possibility of discussing the matter. And incidentally, if thought and language are inseparable, then it is a theoretical miracle that we have come this far . . . where, one might ask, need we stop stretching the limits of our world?

The challenge of the linguistic philosopher's analysis of moral 'problems' can only be met in the last resort by doing other sorts of moral philosophy, for although this whole mode of philosophizing can be and has been vigorously taken to task,[12] this necessary demolition is only half the task and the less important half at that. The real revolutionary project is to construct some new system of ethics.* This is not an easy matter, but it is the only level on which

---

* At least one respected modern moral philosopher has concluded thus. G. F. Warnock has written recently that 'the analysis of linguistic performances has nothing in particular to contribute to moral philosophy'. This is in his paper 'Ethics and Language', in Royal [Institute of Philosophy Lectures, *The Human Agent*, London, 1968, p. 209. Warnock suggests that it is the foundation of morals that constitutes the problem, and this is precisely the way in which I go on to redefine ethics in the following chapters.

the challenge of previous inadequate systems of ethics can be taken up with any chance of success. There are splendid precedents for remaining silent. Bertrand Russell, in a note appended in 1952 to the reprint of his essay 'The Elements of Ethics', of 1910, remarks poignantly, 'I am not, however, quite satisfied with any view of ethics that I have been able to arrive at, and that is why I have abstained from writing again on the subject.'[13] Russell at least does not develop his silence into a theory of ethics!

This then is a problem, and it is interesting to note that the problem is not conceived as such by certain sections of certain societies. That is, certain strategically placed groups have defined this particular problem away, and by virtue of the positions they hold in their respective societies, they attempt to replace this (by definition) insoluble problem with one that is soluble (again by definition). This is of course a very old gambit and it has important applications in all spheres of social life. There is no need to impute crude ideological motives to every attempt at re-orientating some activity in society, to see the impact of the redefinition-of-problems strategy. A few examples will suffice to illuminate this phenomenon.

It is often argued that the two basic assumptions a social theorist can make about how societies are best contemplated are the order axiom and the conflict axiom, and it is further often argued that the choice of one of these axioms in preference to the other will largely dictate the theories, research interests, specific hypotheses, and even the results, of our social theorist. He who operates on the axiom of order will take social equilibrium as the normal state of society, and will conceive of the great problems in terms of explaining, and usually explaining away the pathological state of social conflict. In the same way as one does not need to ask why a man takes his umbrella with him on a rainy day, one does not need to ask why (as opposed to how) social order prevails.

The conflict theorist (let us assume that he comes on the scene to find the widespread acceptance of the axiom of order) *redefines* the problem as a strategy to find the solutions of what he considers to be the great problems. Conflict, as the natural state of social relations, needs no more explanation than the fact that umbrellas are used on rainy days, but social order when it occurs (if ever) is needful of very close attention by the theorist. The revolutionary possibilities of redefining these types of problems are obvious.

The redefinition of the cosmic problem implicit in the version of positivism that Comte advanced is another case. Previous to himself, Comte claimed, the so-called sciences of society had dealt mainly with the metaphysical problem of finding initial causes for phenomena and so, he argued, they could not possibly succeed. The only path to success lay in the search for the more or less orderly association of events in the real world, and until those concerned with social science realized this, there would be no advance. Comte thus redefines the relevant problems of social theory, and his answers of course stem from this redefinition.

Sometimes this redefinition-of-problems strategy works in so far as it persuades strategic members of society, the groups that they belong to and those that are influenced or commanded by them, to stop trying to solve the 'old' problem and to devote all their energies to finding a solution to the 'new' problem, that is, the redefinition of the old problem.* And sometimes, like most strategies, it does not work, and we are left not only with the old problems unsolved but also with a need, practical or theoretical or both, to solve them. This, I suspect, is the case with ethics. The attempted redefinition or reformulation of the problem, carried out for a mixture of purely cognitive and deviously ideological reasons, has not entirely succeeded. To select in accordance with my own biases, I should say that the sociologist, when confronted with the normative problems in his discipline, is like the social theorist who can reject neither order nor conflict as the axiom of social reality, and like the scientist who cannot make the choice between metaphysics and nothingness.

In short, the sociologist and the social philosopher when confronted with contemporary philosophy must redefine the problems of ethics if they are to have any chance of success. This redefinition-of-the-problem strategy does not take place in an arbitrary fashion. The linguistic philosopher redefines in terms of his general theory, and in like manner the sociologist and the social philosopher will normally redefine the problems of ethics in terms of a general theory or (as is fashionable to say) meta-theory. Therefore, from the sociological perspective the solution of the problems of moral progress in society lies in the articulation of a sociological ethic.

John Plamenatz, discussing the idea of progress, gives a simple illustration of this procedure. He writes: 'it may be that knowledge, freedom, virtue and happiness are, as Condorcet believed, so connected with one another, that, if we take society as a whole and not individuals separately, the first brings the other three with it.'[14] As I argued at length in Chapter III, this is what Comte attempted and largely failed to do.

* It is necessary to point out here that problems are conceived to lie on a continuum stretching from 'old and familiar' to 'new and unfamiliar'. Redefining a problem usually involves shifting it from left to right along the continuum, but this is to be taken only in a rough sense. It is clear that many seemingly new problems are, in reality, old problems reformulated rather than redefined. For example, Wittgenstein's supposed redefinition of the problems of philosophy is largely to be found, as Miss Anscombe points out, in Plato's *Theaetetus*. Similar suggestions hold with regard to the atomic theory of the late nineteenth and early twentieth centuries.

L

In the next chapter I shall attempt to set up such an analysis and solution of the problems of ethics. I shall argue that the quest for a rational ethic is misplaced if it operates solely in the category of logical analysis. However, where *social life* rather than logical analysis is the testing ground a sociological ethic becomes not only theoretically feasible but actually attractive. The second part of the chapter presents some reasons why such a project should be the task of the sociologist, and how he can rebut the traditional charges of relativism, moral authoritarianism and arbitrary ethical prejudice.

IX The sociological ethic (2)

In the last chapter, by way of an introduction to the sociological ethic, I discussed moral judgments within the spheres of innovational and non-innovational progress, and the strategy of redefining ethical problems in order that such judgments could be made at all was introduced. Now I wish to go on and redefine the problems of ethics in terms of the sociological ethic and to show that sociology as an activity necessitates these judgments, and that sociology as a body of empirical and theoretical knowledge gives some guidance in this task.

Logical analysis and sociological analysis
One convenient way of summing up the difference between moral progress and, for example, economic progress or material progress is that, whereas the latter are measurable on a variety of indicators, moral progress possesses no such indicators. This is not to say that the distinction is always cut and dried, for it is not uncommon for arguments to take place over the validity of using one indicator, say level of consumption, rather than another indicator, say level of production of heavy industrial units, in order to measure material progress. These different views point to different economic theories and though these theories are often neither conclusively proved nor disproved, we do not on this account consider that material progress is impossible or that the phrase 'material progress' is devoid of any meaning.

Nevertheless, the conclusion is almost always otherwise with moral progress. When people and societies disagree on how moral progress is to be measured, as they very often do, most social theorists consider that the phrase 'moral progress' is thereby rendered meaningless.

There is another side to this coin. Whether consumption or

production is considered to be the main indicator of material progress, and they very often go together, we can all agree that material progress means something—even if it only means that if in two societies starting from the same point, one has a large part of its population dying from starvation and the other has a well-fed population, then the latter has made more material progress than the former. And we should all agree.

On the other hand, the true philosopher argues, moral progress is a matter of preferences, social or individual. Who are we in this particular day and age to condemn slavery in Ancient Greece, or wage slavery in Detroit? Morality is a function of places and times or even of individual decisions, with no higher judgment possible. All the supposed answers to the view that morality is relative, and thus not really susceptible to dispute, are dismissed. Why should good acts be judged on the basis of how much pleasure they produce? Or on what their relation is to some Pietistic good-will? Or even according to how they fit in with some cosmic scheme? Why should good acts be so judged? And no reason is to the point for the variety of redefinitions is inadequate. And this judgment of inadequacy is itself a redefinition of the problems of moral conduct, and must in its turn be judged inadequate.

This is so because it makes not only the difficult questions of moral progress impossible to answer but also the easy questions of material and scientific progress. And if the burden of my argument has shown anything up till now, it has surely shown that I shall cling tenaciously, for theoretical as well as ideological reasons, to the belief that progress as aspiration is *meaningful* and that progress as reality, to a greater or lesser extent, is sensible.

Therefore, I must ask alongside the sceptical relativist, why does feeding a population count towards material progress, why does the principle of asymmetry count as scientific progress, and why does housing more people count as social progress? We may dispute details of these cases as we may dispute details of slavery. But what is the essential difference? One suggestion is that the essential difference lies in the process of measurement and that this process misses the spirit of morals. Indicators of material or scientific progress, once we agree on some particular set of indicators, can usually be measured. For example, the crude percentages of populations receiving above and below the commonly accepted calorific norm of nutrition can be measured with varying degrees of accuracy, but no one will claim that because they cannot be measured with absolute accuracy that the attempt to measure them is a waste of time.

If we take a notion like 'personal freedom', which in one form or another most societies accept and claim to strive towards for all members, then we have an instructive parallel. In the first place (it almost goes without saying) different indicators of personal freedom will be submitted for consideration at the United Nations General Assembly, for example. Some of these interpretations will appear to pervert completely the meaning and intention of this ideal. There appears to be no equivalent among the varieties of 'personal freedom' that corresponds to the calorific norm of nutrition. This latter is, as it were, a distillation of opinions which is arrived at through some process of collecting, sifting and evaluating information on the basis of commonly agreed criteria—the procedures, namely, that scientists follow. The problems around 'personal freedom' therefore stem mainly from the fact that there appear to be no commonly agreed criteria, at least on an international scale and often on an intra-national scale, against which moral concepts can be measured.

It is my contention that the problem of values is not so much that people and societies fail to agree on what is right and what is wrong, but more often that they fail to agree on how to measure how much better one course of action is than another. These questions are of course quite interdependent, and they interact with one another to such an extent that it may be difficult to keep them apart. This distinction between meaning and measurement which leads to the problem of the value-standard or the criteria for moral judgment is useful in pointing out the possibilities of moral progress.

These are threefold. Moral progress is either meaningless, or meaningful and measurable, or meaningful and not measurable. I shall ignore the first possibility for reasons which must by now be clear.*

The view that moral progress is meaningful but not measurable could be taken to suggest either that it is in principle immeasurable, or that it could be measured but not with our present conceptual or other tools. The former of these possibilities would leave us with the difficult situation that there is such a thing as moral progress, but we would never be able to recognize it, for we would never be able to tell whether one pattern of action was 'better' than another, that is whether moral progress had taken place. This would be, theoretically, a most unsatisfactory state of affairs, though it might conceivably enhance some mystical system. The suggestion that we have not yet developed (or discovered) the tools with which to measure moral progress is a fascinating proposal, but is unlikely to be true. (An interesting version of this view is that *others* do not *recognize* the way in which we measure ethical progress, that is the ideological enemy fails to recognize *our* moral truth.)

An understanding of moral progress that considers it to be both meaningful and measurable is the only one on which a satisfactory

* A modified version of the rest of this section is published as 'Moral Progress and Social Theory' (op. cit.).

theory of progress could be constructed. If moral progress is measurable, even in the minimal sense of a crude hierarchy of states rather than a precise calibration of scale, then it will be legitimate to speak of one action, institution, social system or society being morally better than another, or of these units progressing in a moral sense over time. To do this it is necessary to start with what moral philosophers and writers on ethics have generally termed 'a rational ethic'.

It is difficult to discover exactly what is meant by a rational ethic, but simply, if not simplistically, it may be characterized as a set of values which can be rationally defended to hold good for all men at all times. This must be seen in opposition to the view that has been called ethical relativity and in relation to the thesis of the diversity of morals. Ethical relativists argue that each culture or society must be judged on its own merits and on these only, and that the observer who evaluates in terms of his own standards or in terms of some abstract ideal is reasoning in an illicit fashion. Therefore, on this theory a rational ethic is neither desirable nor possible. The diversity of morals argument is less extreme and certainly more helpful in the solution of these problems. This points out that there is no denying the very great differences that are to be found in moral and social practices carried out by people living under widely divergent social arrangements, but (in the words of the foremost modern proponent of the view) 'there is no necessary connection between the diversity of morals and the relativity of ethics'.[1] Ginsberg goes on to suggest that behind the apparent diversity of moral content there exists an essential and universal similarity of form of the moral life, which he summarizes in six main categories.

The logical objections to any rational ethic are formidable, and it is as well to examine briefly the notion of rationality in this connection. It would be pedantic to attempt a precise definition of the term, nevertheless most usages of it approximate to something like 'a rational act is one which makes use of the most efficient or suitable means to a given end'. Max Weber distinguished two types of rational action, namely *zweckrational* and *wertrational*, and the key to this distinction is to be found in Weber's analysis of ethical attitudes, as Parsons points out.[2] Briefly, *zweckrational* action is the normative type logically implied by what Weber terms the 'ethics of responsibility', roughly the recognition of several different, legitimate values; while *wertrational* action is implied by 'ethics of absolute value', total commitment to a single specific value. It is significant that a deeply pessimistic strain runs through a great deal of Weber's work in so far as he considered the difficulty of reconciling these absolute values to be immense. The ends of action, on this view, are not susceptible to scientific or rational study, as are the means of these ultimately arbitrary ends. The principles for the construction of a hierarchy of ends or values will not be rational principles, though those for the attainment of the ends or values may be *zweckrational* or *wertrational* depending on whether the end or value is an ultimate one or not.

It seems clear that if a request for a rational ethic is pushed back to logical analysis, and to analysis alone, then the request must be refused. If facts and values are logically separated, then no amount of manipulating premises will justify a moral conclusion from a set of non-moral premises. Let me cite, as an example, the argument used by many which proposes that a rational foundation for ethics might be found as a result of researches into human nature and human needs. The logical objection to this line of argument is based on the impossibility of demonstrating that the satisfaction of human nature and the fulfilment of human needs are to be valued any more (or indeed any less) than any other item or items. Would it be irrational of man to deny these seemingly basic proposals? If we care to make the distinction between the logic of the situation and the definition of the situation, then this denial may make sense. If we are to find a rational ethic, then, paradoxically, we must retreat from logical analysis *per se*. As Ginsberg comments, 'the attack on humanitarian values made by the Nazis has made the doctrines of ethical relativity . . . emotionally untenable'.[3] Logic and social life clash head-on.

Does it make sense to suggest that though a rational ethic is logically impossible in a strict sense, it is nevertheless sociologically possible? This statement requires some explanation. Not all things that are logically possible are physically possible, and similarly not all things that are logically possible are sociologically possible. This is partially explained by the observation that the scope of social relations is more limited than what we might term the scope of 'cognitive' relations having to do with social life. Numerous as the combinations of structural units in societies appear to be, there are some combinations which simply would not work. For example, although there is nothing logically impossible in the co-existence of a thriving industrial society and a population increasingly distributed in rural communities, the fact of the matter is that urbanization is found in combination with industrialization. Similarly, social groups are rarely, if ever, found to combine the dominant value of social mobility with a predominantly feudal economy. There are, of course, very good reasons why this should be so, and no one worries unduly that what is logically possible can be said to be, in an important sense, sociologically impossible.

In order to link the foregoing with any statement of a sociological ethic, it is necessary to expose certain sociological assumptions and to emphasize that only where the assumptions are sociological and *not* ethical or moral will this line of argument have any chance of success. These assumptions are concerned with the minimal conditions under which it is possible for a society to exist, survive and thrive, although for the present this need be in no more than a crudely biological sense. (Note, however, that man's biology, as the biology of other species, has its peculiar requirements.) This approach derives from the search for the functional requisites of society.

The functional requisites of a society are best described in terms of structural units whose absence would lead fairly directly to the disintegration of a society. M. J. Levy, in his exploratory work, *The Structure of Society*, analytically distinguishes ten such functional requisites (he reserves the term 'prerequisite' for the condition that assures the functional requisite). These range from the provision for the satisfaction of physiological needs to role differentiation, and from communication to adequate socialization and institutionalization of the normative system.[4]

Parsons, acknowledging his debt to previous work of Levy and others, while departing from their analysis, is somewhat more sophisticated in his treatment. For Parsons it is rather less a question of functional requisites, though he does use the term, than of functional imperatives and, even more significantly in his work of the late 1950s and early 1960s, the notion of functional problems on whose solution depends the survival of the social system or society. Such features as the motivational problem or order, the 'plasticity' and 'sensitivity' of human nature, and the integration of the cultural system, appear to be most important.[5] In a section of *The Social System* entitled 'The Constitution of Empirical Societies', Parsons narrows down the essential units to four: namely kinship, community, ethnic group and class. He asserts, 'What might be called a "minimum society" might as a structure be describable exclusively in terms of these four categories if the requisite discriminations, of differentiated roles within each of them, were made.'[6]

The functional problems approach—Parsons' ambitious attempt to analyse social systems in terms of the necessity of solving the problems of adaptation, goal attainment, integration and pattern maintenance or tension management—is very relevant here. In the next two chapters, I shall go on to make specific suggestions for a viable set of functional requisites of society. Here I am only concerned with showing that this type of approach may contain the seeds of the sociological ethic.

My definition of progress, it will be recalled, is also in terms of problems to be solved, either by innovational or non-innovational means, and any suggestion as to the problems that all societies must inevitably face and solve cannot but be helpful. It is not the specific aspects of Parsons' or Levy's analyses that are important here, but rather that they select basic and universal elements of human society. I am by no means ready to elaborate the details of a sociological ethic, but this argument is intended to point to the possibility of an ethic based on sociological grounds.

Many writers on ethics claim that if any moral principle is self-evident and would qualify as an essential basis of human society, then it is the principle of justice. A recent series of papers by the philosopher John Rawls attempts to place the concept of justice firmly on sociological grounds, and thereby throws some light on the sociological ethic. Rawls, in an onslaught on the utilitarian position, sees justice as 'a virtue of social institutions'.[7] His argument is developed from a contractualist basis, regarding the reciprocal arrangements of a set of social practices as some sort of irreducible foundation for the proper conduct of social relations. Two principles support Rawls' theory of justice as fairness. Firstly, each person should have as much liberty as makes similar liberty for all possible; and secondly, genuine inequalities, the principle of equity, should be considered.

Let me once again point out my distinction between logical and sociological possibility. Logically, there appears to be no reason to prefer liberty to bondage, sociability to rampant selfishness, or social rules to arbitrary power, but sociologically the latter of these alternatives works less well than the former. Indeed, both Levy and Parsons, and many others, point out that the war of all against all is one of the conditions for the disintegration of a society. Conditions which lead to the disintegration of society are in this sense sociologically impossible.*

Rawls' work is radically criticized in an issue of *Nomos* devoted entirely to 'Justice'.[8] John Chapman shows that Rawls' concept of justice as fairness is deficient in the historical, the linguistic and the meta-ethical senses. In logic the critique appears to be most damaging—Rawls' concept of justice does lose the significance of needs; it does obscure the linguistic significance of fairness as applied to processes contrasted with the 'weighing of considerations' relevant to justice; and it does neglect the concept of man as a moral person in its emphasis on reciprocity. But Chapman, no matter how many questionable implications he may derive from Rawls' theory, has yet to show why we should prefer the recognition of needs or the notion of man as a moral person over any other moral concept. The

---

* This statement needs qualification. Many tendencies are found to exist which, if they were permitted to become more widespread, would unquestionably lead to the breakdown of society. However, as Durkheim argued with respect to crime, these may be necessary to a limited or tolerated degree for the satisfactory functioning of a given state of society.

strength of Rawls' position lies in the fact that he is not simply presenting 'justice as fairness' as a morally better state of affairs, but is presenting principles which presumably will be to the advantage of all in all possible situations. As Rawls puts it, 'the principles of justice define the constraints which institutions and joint activities must satisfy if persons engaging in them are to have no complaint against them'.[9] Therefore we may safely hold that all social men will prefer justice, and that as an ideal, whose actual content may nevertheless vary considerably from society to society, it provides an indisputable basis for the construction of a system of social relations.

To say that this is itself a value-judgment one would have to argue that men would rather or could conceivably rather prefer to live in institutions against which they could have complaints. Notwithstanding the very real perverseness of much of social life, this is an important marginal objection, though not a fundamental one.

To reiterate the point that informs much of Ginsberg's work: it is the form and not the content that provides us with the possibility of finding some universal and basic moral principles, principles on which, I should add, societies as systems of social relations must be based in order to be sociologically viable.

These, then, are the types of sociological assumptions on which it is proposed that a sociological ethic for societies, rather than for the individual treated as a moral being, will be constructed. And through this I hope to specify the concept of moral progress. The work of Professor Macbeath, delivered as the Gifford lectures for 1948-9, provides an interesting framework for this task.

Macbeath sets out to 'study the nature and foundation of ethics or morals in the light of recent work in Social Anthropology'.[10] His fundamental distinction is that between the inner and subjective and the outer and objective contexts of morals. The former only is the uniquely moral sense, while the latter, which is embodied in the form of life of a people, is the one that anthropologists and Macbeath tend to discuss. Clearing away the debris of ethical controversy in the past, he sees rules and ends, the deontological and the teleological, as having relations of 'mutual implications. Each is a different but necessary condition of living a good life or doing a morally good deed'.[11] In their interrelations they constitute forms of life, and 'it is men's ideas about these which vary from age to age and from people to people, while moral goodness is the same in all ages and among all peoples. . . . Progress in moral goodness, therefore, consists in increasing loyalty to one's own ideal'.[12]

To this progress in moral goodness or increasing loyalty to a set of ideals, Macbeath adds progress in moral enlightenment which concerns the nature of these ideals. This progress in enlightenment 'seems to take the form of an increasing recognition of the fundamental importance of personality and of the distinction between persons and things'.[13] This is a most important distinction and serves to clarify the whole problem to a large extent, though there is little but disappointment to be found in the use to which Macbeath puts it.

Why, we are bound to ask, do the recognition of personality and the person/thing distinction constitute progress in moral enlightenment? Macbeath asserts these factors as ethical arguments based on a generally Western liberal-democratic bias. There is no hint that progress in moral enlightenment is the basis of sociological continuity in any sense. It is not much less than astonishing that Macbeath concludes his book with the principle: 'Be a person and recognize and treat others as persons', after having previously shattered ethical intuitionism in the light of anthropological evidence. His claim to have derived this from his analysis of the literature on primitive societies rests on an intuition that the notions of individual responsibility show progress in moral enlightenment over notions of collective responsibility and so forth, and by Macbeath's own arguments, this is illicit. Again, the attempt to set up some logically rational ethic appears to fail, as I have argued that it always will.

The form of Macbeath's argument, and especially the distinction between progress in moral goodness and progress in moral enlightenment, is worthy of consideration. Macbeath's criterion of moral goodness and progress within this, as it is seen to refer internally as it were to the ideals of a society, is an interesting though potentially dangerous idea. The principle that it is good to demonstrate loyalty to one's ideals must be linked to the content of these ideals as they rate on the scale of moral enlightenment. The problem of progress in moral enlightenment is also difficult and, as I have suggested, Macbeath's solution is unacceptable. Progress in moral enlightenment (the improvement of ideals), in terms of my general approach, would have to take into account the development of society and the necessity for different types of value systems in those societies which solved problems on totally different bases. Progress in moral enlightenment would have taken place where more people in a society were having more of their problems solved over a greater area of social life. This, obviously, is a very complex matter.

An example of what is meant by progress in moral enlightenment is provided by H. L. A. Hart in his discussion of the nature of the law. In a statement which is most germane to this whole debate, he asserts that 'the introduction into society of rules enabling legislators to change and add to the rules of duty, and judges to determine when the rules of duty have been broken, is a step forward as important to society as the invention of the wheel'.[14] This statement is valuable because it steers carefully clear of ethics as such and it can be looked upon as an objective truth, if indeed it is true, about the development of society. It is with this intention that Ginsberg elaborates his five criteria of moral levels as an integral part of his diversity of morals argument, for these are firmly tied to man in society. Calling for attention to be paid to middle principles referring to specific ends and values rather than those of the highest generality, Ginsberg, in his essay 'Reason and Experience in Ethics', states that: 'It is in this field of middle principles that knowledge of the ways in which institutions affect the individuals concerned, directly or indirectly, is of vital importance, and in which ethics most needs the co-operation of the social sciences.'[15]

The future of ethics, therefore, lies not with moral philosophy, but with the study of man in society. Social research is discovering and will continue to discover the conditions that make life possible for men in society, and will show how these conditions will vary from one social system to another. For the problem of moral progress, progress in moral enlightenment, it will hardly be surprising to find that much that has had to be rejected on purely logical grounds in the fruitless search for a rational ethic will re-enter the scheme under the auspices of social rather than logical need.

Why a sociological *ethic?*
The gist of my argument in this chapter so far has been that logical analysis itself is unable to provide us with a satisfactory basis for a rational ethic, and that we must look elsewhere in order to establish some viable standard or set of standards on which to base our moral judgments. That is to say that logical analysis is not a sufficient basis for judging moral progress. I tried to show that the sorts of assumptions we should have to rely upon, that we might speak meaningfully of moral progress, were not so different from the assumptions inherent in speaking of other types of progress. The basic value difference, and one that seems to me often to be beyond any moral standard, sociological or otherwise, is between innovational and non-innovational progress, in morals or politics or any other sphere of human relations in which progress is possible. What we can do, I have argued, is to judge whether one course of innovational problem-solving is ethically better than another, or whether one course of non-innovational problem-solving is better than another in the moral sense.

To this degree I agree with the intent of Weber's ultimate despair. In the last resort—in the choice between innovational and non-innovational modes of progress—there can be no final arbitration, for at this level ends are in chaos. But this is because in my view we are not simply counterpoising two styles of life or two varieties of social action; we are in effect contrasting two different *conceptions* of living that reach down into the very foundations of social organization. This, however, does not and cannot prevent us from making moral decisions and applying moral judgments about situations and events that take place within these two dimensions of living. And this of course is a position that Weber could never accept, for he could never allow the sociologist to commit a value-judgment and to remain a 'scientist', in the peculiarly German usage of the term 'science'. The view I shall go on to elaborate is that there is something about sociology, as a field of human *activity* as well as a field of human study, scientific or not as the latter may be, that positively dictates certain forms of value-judgment on the grounds of its own advance. There is a sense in which this view is irreconcilable with 'science', and another sense in which these value-judgments can become increasingly 'scientific'. I shall not argue with the purists who say that sociology cannot be both scientific and concerned with making value-judgments, *unless* their label of unscientific in this respect condemns the approach to nonsense or mystery, or even metaphysics. This approach is, on the contrary, fully intended to cover the levels of reality that provided the framework for my analysis of the two modes of progress: namely those of historical fact, theories about these facts *and* the aspirations of men in societies. It is this last level of reality with which sociology is uniquely concerned in any theory of progress.

The question: 'Why sociology?' is indeed a curious one. There is no *a priori* reason why sociology rather than, say, political economy, anthropology, psychology, history or law should supply this sort of theoretical synthesis.* This view of sociology as a framework for a theory of progress—almost a systematic philosophy of history—is in one important aspect the truly Comtean plan of establishing sociology as the 'Queen of the sciences', but with a genuinely ethical ideal as its driving force and its end-point.[16]

It is largely a matter of historical accident that the social sciences have developed the divisions that now act as barriers between them, and though we may agree with Comte on the ideal role of the study of man in society, we need not subscribe to his restricted views on the logic of the order of the progression of all the sciences to the positive stage. As I have now and then tried to show in the first part of this work, the history of ideas or theories cannot be properly

---

* A word is perhaps needed here to explain why 'philosophy' is not in this list. The main reason is that philosophy as such does not exist in the same way as these other disciplines, though professional organization and the rigidity of the university system has helped to prolong the myth that it does. Philosophy, or more properly the philosophical approach, is a way of looking at and/or a way of structuring questions about practically anything. I cannot go into the intricacies of this account of philosophy, but it is not as idiosyncratic as it first appears.

157

studied apart from the history of actual events and aspirations of men in society, and a satisfactory understanding of social change, a viable philosophy of history, can be grasped only with respect to these levels of reality.

Sociology is eminently suited to sire a theory of progress in terms of social change. There is no argument necessary to support this statement for, on the basis of my definition of progress as a problem-solving activity carried out in society, he would indeed be a strange sociologist who did not find this concern at the centre of his activity. It is when we confront the moral element in progress, that which makes one solution to a problem *more satisfactory* than another, that the case for sociology has to be made. I have above indicated some of the ways in which sociological* findings and concepts are relevant to moral progress. Rawls' argument on just institutions, Macbeath's suggested distinction between loyalty to one's ideals and moral enlightenment and Ginsberg's concern with the spread of certain social arrangements which he takes to be morally commendable are all items in the dossier of evidence I wish to present for the redefinition of the problems of ethics of which I spoke above.[17]

There are negative and positive aspects of this evidence. On the negative side there is profound discontent with the state of modern moral philosophy, whether in its emotivist or revamped utilitarian forms. Neither retains what distinguishes (in both senses of the term) moral as opposed to immoral or amoral conduct—namely the dignity of the moral act. This much at least is the strength of the Kantian system of ethics. What Kant neglected, however, was the social dignity of the moral act, in terms of its consequences.

The positive aspect of the evidence for redefining the problems of ethics lies precisely in the partial recognition by the authors cited that both the sociality *and* the dignity of acts is what makes them moral. The paradoxes which may and perhaps must occur in social life when we are forced to choose between sociality and dignity are a necessary part of the sociological ethic. The desperate urge to solve such paradoxes, which has provided most of the grist for the mill of philosophical controversy in ethics, seems to me entirely misplaced. Briefly, the reason for this is that society itself and the possibilities of man in society are such that paradoxes and even contradictions may be irreducible features of social organization. And so if this is the case, any theory that 'resolved' these paradoxes or confusions would be quite literally unrealistic. There is a great difference between denying rational principles of investigation, condoning logical error, contradicting oneself and acknowledging this sort of

---

* I do not of course preclude other related disciplines from this possibility of contributing to our understanding and solution of moral problems.

fact, if it be a fact, about social life.[18] This is not to suggest that reality is in continual, chaotic flux, and not amenable to systematic study. Neither does this imply that progress in the moral sense must break down, for although there may be certain solutions to a problem that are equally as commendable according to the sociological ethic, this does not mean that there are no other solutions that are morally unacceptable on the basis of the sociological ethic. That one action is as right as another does not imply that there are not many other sociologically possible actions that are less right.

That it is conceptually, not to say empirically, fruitful to look at what happens in societies, theories of societies and the aspirations of men in these societies, in order to learn something about the nature of morality, is therefore the weak form of my hypothesis. The strong form is that we shall find the standards on which to make moral judgments only in social life and the ways in which it is organized. I do not feel it necessary to specify meticulously to which hypothesis any particular set of remarks is addressed, for my arguments where they are strong will make my strong hypothesis more persuasive, and where they are less strong will serve only to bolster up my weak hypothesis. My intention is to establish an ethical system on the grounds of what I have suggested to be the important levels of social research.

It is obvious that to carry out this proposal and to erect a sociological ethic is a long step away from simply arguing for the relevance of material about man in society to ethics, which I have been doing. The substantive argument about a sociological ethic will be presented in the next two chapters, where I shall critically examine the work that has been done on the functional requisites of a society. In this way the sociological ethic will be given content. Here I am more concerned with some of the formal characteristics of the sociological ethic, and these will be illustrated with reference to the type of criticisms that any ethical system has to undergo, both from the friends and the enemies of morality, as a meaningful category of discourse and social action.

These criticisms are threefold—interlinked but amenable to separate discussion. They are the ethical relativist objection, the imputation of moral authoritarianism and the charge that any standard of conduct will merely express the arbitrary choice of individuals or groups. Let me deal with each of these in turn, starting with the third which I consider to be the least serious. It is convenient to assume here that a sociological ethic, a moral standard against which we can measure the differential moral progress attributable to different solutions to problems faced by men in society, is a going concern. The reason for this is quite simple: it would be most unfortunate if one were to spend all the effort

159

involved in setting up a sociological ethic in detail only to find that it was unable to deal with the common objections raised against other ethical systems. Therefore, I am saying: let us get the form established, and we may fill in the details later. And further, we may gain some very valuable hints on the substantive details of the sociological ethic from exposing it in a purely formal sense to the objections.

The claim that all standards of conduct are really arbitrary choices of individuals and groups, and therefore moral progress is chimerical, suggests that we have no reasons for coming to particular moral decisions that would tie up with the reasons of others, for making sense of one moral decision, or for enabling a group of moral decisions to be studied systematically. This view is as incorrect for the sociologist as it may be correct for the philosopher of mind or the psychologist. It is clear that, whatever sociological school to which one adheres or if one adheres to no school (as is the more likely), a necessary assumption that has to be made about social life involves the rejection of the view that moral decisions are made and organized in an arbitrary fashion. Generally, there are reasons behind moral decisions and perhaps moral decisions behind these reasons, and so on. It is not anticipated that the sociological ethic will run up against any great difficulties here, for these reasons, far from being absent or even irrelevant to the matter in hand, are sure to be located in the activity of man in society. The demands of social life make it extremely unlikely that this objection in fact applies. Moral decisions, as understood by the sociologist, are for the most part organized in groups or systems, and moral consistency, especially when not observed, is the important expectation. Social life would be impossible without it. And this leads me on to the next objection.

If, it is argued, moral decisions are not arbitrary and there are societally-wide groups or systems of moral decisions, does this not imply some authoritarian standard which deprives 'morality' of all moral worth? This is a powerful objection which derives much support from actual historical events. As an empirical objection against the worth of modern moral standards against which we judge moral decisions, it might well prove conclusive. But as a formal objection to a formal sociological ethic it leaves many things unsaid. If one of the defining characteristics of a societally-wide moral standard is that it must be authoritarian in the pejorative sense in which this label is used, then discussion stops here; the dispute is over words alone and not over words and things. If on the other hand the authoritarian character of these standards of moral judgments is hypothesized, then we are at perfect liberty to suggest that it is quite conceivable, though very difficult in practice, to organize our standard so that it is not in fact authoritarian.

This, then, is precisely what I meant when I commented that the formal consideration of objections to a formal sociological ethic might furnish us with some useful hints in the actual construction of such an entity. Accordingly, it is carefully recorded that if the sociological ethic is to be successful, then it must not be open to the charge of authoritarianism. Moral authoritarianism in its many forms is thus suspended as an objection to the sociological ethic in principle, and we must await further testimony, which I hope to provide in the next chapters, to decide the matter.

The third formal objection, that of the relativity of morals, follows naturally from the first two. Granted that moral judgments are not arbitrary, and the sociological ethic gives a satisfactory account of the reasons involved in making them; granted that the sociological ethic might produce a value-standard that is not authoritarian; granted even that all of the relevant communities to which this work is directed accept the sociological ethic and are happy to organize their social activity around it; granted all these things—why *should* anyone not sharing our particular socio-historic position accept it? What permits the sociological ethic to transcend the time and place of its conception?

The answer to these objections, implicit in the whole of this study, may be framed in two general propositions which lie somewhere between a very high degree of corroboration on the basis of social experience and sociological self-evidence. These are, very roughly:

1 If you want to live in society, then you must behave in certain ways.

2 Moral progress depends on sociological possibility.

The proof of these two propositions lies in the set of requisites that I am to develop in the next chapters, and I shall here show only how they are related to the sociological ethic and thereby show how ethical relativism may be discarded as an objection to this enterprise. The requisites of society are the conditions that make social life possible. The assumptions that have to be made are numerous in this context, and I shall mention only the most important. In the first place, we must assume that although societies change, forms of social organization change, and indeed whole civilizations change, there is a basic minimum set of conditions without which *no* human society is possible. This is axiomatic for if any alternative were to be entertained then it would no longer apply to human society in the particular sense in which this phrase is intended. This does not preclude certain other forms of society, for example non-human society or inhuman society. These latter states are not meant as any kind of a joke, for it is precisely states like inhuman society with

M   161 which the sociological ethic is incompatible. The point of controversy is that point at which human society appears to be entering the non-human or the inhuman state. There are other possibilities, perhaps too dreadful to consider. The important point to remember in an axiomatic exercise of this sort is that the category of morality, of social actions being right or wrong, and more or less good, is a necessary though not a sufficient condition of what I mean by human society.

Next, it is axiomatic that the existential problems of birth, life and death remain in a state of conditional insolubility. As long as they remain open questions and men are capable of finding them problematic, of disagreeing in their interpretations of them, then we may speak of human society. It is entirely mistaken to expect the sociological ethic to solve these problems for then it would face the charge of unrealism. Rather, the unique contribution of the sociological ethic to the solution of these existential problems is its ability to frame the questions in a satisfactory fashion. Lastly, it is axiomatic that under tolerable circumstances the continuation of society and the maintenance of social life are *morally* commendable. This is neither a 'better red than dead' argument nor a crude parody of functionalist harmony-consensus analysis. There are obviously certain conditions under which the continuity of society is not morally commendable, and here we simply confront again the axiom of human versus inhuman society. But more properly, it is a particular state of a particular society that is not worth conserving. In this case the sociological ethic will guide our judgments as to the propriety of change, this of course being the paradigm case of progress in the solution of the vital set of society's problems.[19]

Given these axioms on which, it seems to me, a serious sociology of whatever shade must rest, the objection of ethical relativism levelled against the sociological ethic must fail. When the sociological ethic is developed it will be an error to suggest that it may be invalid for some society at some time. Any such criticism will miss the point. Simply, the sociological ethic is the standard that all societies need from a sociological point of view and have an obligation to strive for from a moral point of view. To deny this will be a denial of the activity of social life, and this is not a possible position.

It must be emphasized that the sociological ethic is an ethic for societies and social groups rather than for particular individuals in them. In the extreme case the life of each individual is the responsibility of himself or herself whereas the life of society is a collective responsibility. The extent of man's responsibility to his society must be a matter of choice, and with rights go particular obligations. No one is forced to accept either, beyond those necessary to the assumption of basic age-sex roles.

There are five formal requirements at least of the sociological ethic. Each must be fulfilled in order that the proposed standard of conduct, the measure of moral progress, will be universally relevant. These requirements are not equivalent to the value axioms that were called upon to rebut ethical relativism, though they are similarly necessary assumptions.

1 The sociological ethic is not a final and immutable standard but is amenable to change on the basis of social experience.

2 The sociological ethic operates on the conception of constraints on social actions, and the possibility of moral responsibility.

3 The sociological ethic must accommodate all sociologically viable value systems.

4 The sociological ethic will only apply where the biological changes in man are of degree and not of kind.

5 The sociological ethic is based on intersubjective rather than objective criteria.

These form the bare bones of the sociological ethic which I have tried to picture in this chapter. In the next two chapters I shall fill in the details of the sociological ethic through an analysis of the functional requisites of society, and thereby complete the second part of my theory of progress. When the concepts of innovational and non-innovational progress are brought together with the detailed sociological ethic, then I shall be ready to articulate the sociological theory of progress.

X The search for functional requisites

I have argued in the previous chapter that the activities of the sociologist as manifest in his understanding and explanation of social life are morally relevant. Indeed, practically *anything* we may learn about human societies may have some moral relevance. I have gone further, by implication, and suggested that not only does this moral relevance exist but it is a part of the sociologist's job (perhaps, in the long run, the most important part of his job) to take account of it, and that if he ignores it, then he is not doing his job properly. It is not difficult to see why sociologists have been reluctant to involve themselves in the moral implications of their work, for there are powerful practical as well as ideological reasons for this, and they are shared by workers in all the sciences and even in the humanities. The present chapter is an attempt to prove by persuasion, rather than by demonstration, what most of these men have known all along, namely that certain solutions to social problems are morally better than others, and that even if perfection or utopia seem presently unattainable, at least improvement (moral progress) is a sensible goal.

As I have indicated, I propose to do this through an examination of the requisites of social life, thereby filling up the presently empty, though in principle formally attractive, sociological ethic.* My procedure will be to analyse critically some attempts to set up requisites for social life and to select, reject and modify for my own purposes. This done, in the next chapter I shall construct my set of requisites with a view to showing how the moral end of my theory of progress operates.

---

* In the following the terms 'requisites', 'needs', 'requirements', 'necessities' and 'imperatives' will be used interchangeably. The qualifier 'functional' simply reminds one that the fulfilment of the need has consequences for some social unit.

Malinowski and the functional theory of basic needs

According to Malinowski, the starting-point for any heory of human behaviour is to be found in the biological impulses that have to be satisfied in order that men will survive. In his long essay, *The Scientific Theory of Culture*, published in 1944, he presented a scheme whereby for each biological need an accompanying cultural arrangement or variety of them could be located. The link between the attempt to find basic requirements for social life and the problem-solving approach, to which I have often alluded, is clearly expressed by Malinowski as a 'General Axiom of [his] Functionalism'.

Culture [he says] is essentially an instrumental apparatus by which man is put in a position the better to cope with *the concrete specific problems* that face him in his environment in the course of *the satisfaction of his needs*[1] [my emphasis].

In the course of an analysis not notable for its simplicity, the theoretical task is attacked in several ways and from several directions. The three main elements of scientific anthropology according to Malinowski may be fruitfully distinguished in this connection: they are a theory of institutions, a functional theory of basic needs and, thirdly, a derivation of what he terms 'instrumental and integrative imperatives'.[2] Added to these, a list of 'universal problems' with their correlative 'real solutions' appears briefly, standing in some unclear relation to 'cultural universals' and 'cultural imperatives' or 'derived needs', which latter appear to be on the highest level of generality. These cultural imperatives act as stimuli and the responses forthcoming are the major institutions of society. Therefore, the imperative of consumption and production elicits the response of economics; regulation of behaviour elicits social control; renewal of institutions, education; and authority relations, political organization.[3]

The basic biological needs from which these cultural imperatives are derived are somewhat scattered around in the body of the theory, though the nearest thing to a definitive list appears to be that which is contrasted to yet another set of cultural responses which is less general than the previous list but still general enough to cause some concern over the relations between the two schemes. The basic needs with the corresponding cultural responses are as follows: metabolism, commissariat [sic!]; reproduction, kinship; bodily comforts, shelter; safety, protection; movement, activities; growth, training; and health, hygiene.[4]

Notwithstanding Malinowski's very great contributions to anthropology and the way we think about social life, his scientific theory of culture, at least in respect of that part of it dealing with basic needs, is quite inadequate.[5] It is neither logically consistent nor theoretically persuasive. In the first and most fundamental instance, he gives no satisfactory list of basic biological needs and his choice of 'cultural responses' is in some cases, to say the least, idiosyncratic. Protection, activities, training, and perhaps hygiene, are more vague than general. There would seem to be a case for arguing that activity, understood as goal-oriented movement, is as much a 'biological' need as safety. The link between growth and training seems to be dubious. It is just as reasonable to assert that safety arrangements are the cultural response to the basic need for protection as vice versa—not that either formulation tells us much.

The root cause of Malinowski's difficulty seems to me to be tied up with his uncertain social and cultural behaviourism, which is at times so strong as to constitute a veritable philosophy of history.* The reliance on physiologically-based explanations that usually support behaviourist sociologies obscures at least two vital points. In the first place, very great care has to be taken to distinguish biological or primary needs of the individual from the biological needs of society, in the sense of those needs of significant aggregates of people. This is not to say that society must be treated as an organism, though (as with many analogies) it is useful up to a point, but that precisely where the analogy tends to break down, societies and individuals have quite different 'tolerance levels' with respect to biological needs. It is here, for example, that Spencer said some interesting things.[6]

Secondly, the relations between the biological-primary and the social-secondary drives[7] must be clearly specified in any attempt to analyse the requisites of social life. Clearly, both have a part to play, and there are significant differences which I shall develop below. Further, the first point on the individual and society distinction holds equally for the secondary as for the primary needs.

Malinowski, it must be admitted, pays little attention to these considerations, and his so-called 'vital-sequence' of impulse→act→ satisfaction superficially describes in a truistic fashion what has always been known to be half true. Of the complexity of actual social life it says almost nothing. The verdict, however, is not entirely negative for, as is so often the case, the mistakes of great men are instructive. Malinowski, in diverting our attention and the attention of a good part of twentieth-century anthropology and sociology from the 'process' thinking of evolutionism to the 'entity' thinking of functionalism,[8] succeeded in showing the importance of minute

---

* In *The Scientific Theory of Culture* Malinowski often uses the language of stimulus-response (S-R), and also speaks of the way in which the mechanisms of reinforcement ensure the continuity of culture.

dissection in social investigation. Gellner has argued that as a method the value of functionalism is very great indeed, but as a doctrine or a general theory it leaves much to be desired,[9] and this is certainly the judgment that I should wish to pass on the work of Malinowski that I have briefly examined here. It might be added that the contrast between the undisputed merit of his field-work on the Trobriand Islands and his exclusively theoretical endeavours is the case in point. *The Scientific Theory of Culture* will not directly influence the analysis of the requisites for social life in the following pages.

The functional prerequisites of a society

In 1950 there appeared a paper jointly written by five American social scientists in *Ethics*, a journal of social and legal philosophy.[10] I mention these details not simply because of their intrinsic interest (why *five* men? why publish a sociological article in *Ethics*? what is the significance of 1950?), but also because I feel that it is important to note the intellectual climate in which this and subsequent work was done. One of the authors, M. J. Levy, tells us in a later publication that the five men had come together in a seminar at Harvard in 1947 to work out 'the definition of the concept of society and the list of functional requisites'[11] that he, Levy, was to develop. Briefly, and this will come as no surprise to those familiar with the recent history of American sociology, the whole enterprise must be considered in the context of the development of structural-functional analysis in the sociology of America in the 1950s. Before I turn to a more detailed account of the relevant literature, two general points must be noted.

It is necessary, in this time of ideological sensitivity and the quite proper suspicion of eclecticism in social thought, to stress that an interest in the requirements of social life, and indeed the consideration of a set of 'functional requisites' for any society in order that it does not collapse, will not inevitably lead to an acceptance of the total and highly complex apparatus of sociological functionalism. It is really an essential though largely implicit part of my argument that *any* social theory that is to be near adequate must pay due heed to the question of these social requirements. It is, of course, no accident that at this time the Functionalists paid much attention to social needs, for both the methodology and the doctrine in their language, as much as in any other factor, lead naturally to such concerns.

The other general point is that whereas in the early 1950s the attention of the Functionalist was very much on 'functional requisites', by the later years of the decade and the early 1960s, it had switched to 'functional problems', to the 'four functional sub-system problems approach'.[12] As I remarked earlier, this shows quite clearly the link between the social requisites approach to sociological theory and the social problems approach.*

Therefore, the article by Aberle and his colleagues of 1950 was one of the first shots in one of the most important battles in recent sociology—a battle that is still raging.[13]

The paper begins by justifying itself in terms of the claim that finding out *what* must be done in any society is an essential preliminary to finding out *how* in fact these things are done. The three tasks that the authors set themselves are to define society, to articulate the conditions for its breakdown, and to list the functional prerequisites of society (the prefix seems somewhat arbitrary here, though Levy in his later work does go on to justify it). It is notable that the whole enterprise is explicitly placed within the framework of the structural-functional theory of action, first presented by Talcott Parsons in his seminal study of 1937.

The definition of society offered is very interesting and deserves to be quoted in full:

A society is a group of human beings sharing a self-sufficient system of action which is capable of existing longer than the life-span of an individual, the group being recruited at least in part by the sexual reproduction of the members[14] [italics in original].

This goes some way, but not far enough, towards incorporating the demand on which I have criticized Malinowski, namely the recognition that societies have different biological characteristics to individuals. The crux of the definition, however, is the notion of a 'self-sufficient system of action', and the writers explain this by speaking of the 'integrity' rather than the 'fixity' of the system. This self-sufficiency or integrity of the system of action or organization of social relationships in society depends on the lack of what are termed 'the conditions for the termination of society'.

These conditions are biological extinction or dispersal of a sufficient proportion of members; apathy; war of all against all; and the absorption by another society. We are offered the hypothesis that the greater the rate of social change then the closer a society draws to these conditions of self-termination. Revolution leads to the breakdown of society. There is at least one serious contradiction in this view. Complete absorption by another society must be resisted by those wishing to maintain the integrity of their own society. This often means revolution, especially in colonial situations. But revolution leads to breakdown, on the hypothesis, and thus to the loss of the

---

* It almost goes without saying that the 'social problems' of the Functionalists are theoretical rather than practical problems, and at the very highest level of generality at that.

integrity of the society. The scheme, thus, is shown to be inconsistent to this extent.

The functional prerequisites, nevertheless, give the semblance of independent utility apart from the functionalist doctrine that here suggests the sociological primacy of the *status quo*. In a list that is proclaimed to be provisional, nine social requirements are put forward, and I shall examine each one in turn.

1 Provision for adequate relationship to the environment and for sexual recruitment. This single requirement encompasses many elements and appears to cover, in a diffuse rather than a specific manner, all of the biological needs on which Malinowski based his analysis. Again, it fails to make explicit the distinction between primary and secondary needs, and one is left wondering about the precise referent of such items as 'adequate relationship', 'environment' itself, and the ambiguous 'sexual recruitment'. It suggests nothing more than the success axiom, which has been presented by the latter-day *bête-noire* of functionalism, Professor Homans.[15] 'Adequate relationship to the environment', seemingly any environment, is what successful societies achieve, and if a society wishes success then it must achieve 'adequate relationship to the environment'. You cannot lose as long as you keep winning, and vice versa! The value of the whole enterprise of finding the basic requirements of social life depends entirely in avoiding such viciously circular arguments. 'Adequate' is a term fastidiously to be laid aside.*

2 Role differentiation and role assignment. As it stands, this requisite is sociologically vital, and in one form or another it must find a place in any significant list of requirements for social life. The way in which it is developed, however, by Aberle and his colleagues and by a generation of Functionalists, into the so-called functionalist theory of stratification is at least controversial. As Tumin and others (including in his own distinctive manner Marx) have shown, differentiation does not necessarily entail stratification.[16] I shall devote more detailed attention to this important and contentious matter when I come to build my own list of social needs in the next chapter.

3 Communication. Aberle *et al.* point out, in my view correctly, that this requisite demonstrates that the items on the list are *analytically* rather than *empirically* distinct. Communication, accordingly, is relevant to all the functional prerequisites and cannot be empirically distinguished from the others, though analytically it is useful to do so.

---

* I am more than aware that the definition of progress with which this study began, incorporating as it does 'satisfactory solutions', is precisely open to this charge. The purpose of this book is to correct this by setting out a sociological theory of progress.

4 Shared cognitive orientations. With this requisite we reach the hinterland of functionalist doctrine, and the outlines of the consensus approach in sociological theory appear. Again, at this stage I am only prepared to concede that there is something in this requisite that repays investigation, and I shall return to it and attempt to show how it might be used in specific ways.

5 A shared, articulated set of goals. Where requisite (4) above issues a subtle warning, this requisite provides the blinding, flashing red lights. I do not wish to overstate the case in opposition to the social need for a shared, articulated set of goals, but in the way in which it is presented in the work under review, the conclusion is inescapable that either this is not a functional prerequisite of society, or that many if not most past and present *actual* societies have lost their integrity. This requisite must be rejected in its present form, though it will reappear later to be discussed anew in the guise of the ubiquity of a shared value-system.

6 The normative regulation of means. This is obviously an element of the first importance for my stated object of deriving a sociological ethic from a list of requirements for social life. Aberle and his colleagues rightly stress that alternative as well as imperative norms must be considered in this context, but as to the contents of these normative regulations, in the best tradition of *wertfreiheit*, they have nothing to say. As I have already suggested, this particular tradition is one that sociology must outgrow. I shall argue below that not only is there a sociological necessity for *a* normative code, but also that there is a *sociological* necessity for a limited variety of normative codes. To put this negatively and perhaps more acceptably, there are certain normative codes that are sociologically impossible, that is unacceptable.

7 The regulation of affective expression. This is a rather fascinating requirement and, it must be admitted, the use of the term 'regulation' it less than happy. As with requisite (4), there is something in the suggestion, and it is as well to bear it in mind and to reserve judgment at this stage.

8 Socialization. There is no doubt whatsoever that socialization is indeed a functional requisite of social life, especially 'functional' in that it directs attention to the ongoingness and the perpetuation of particular forms of social life. It is only when this attention leads to the neglect of social change and denial of its normalcy, that it must be checked. Further, in some versions of the functionalist doctrine, change or rather attempts to bring about certain types of social change, usually in the political sphere, is attributed to some deficiency in the mechanisms of socialization. Where the argument takes this

turn, I shall be forced to oppose it. These considerations lead on to the final prerequisite in the list.

9   The effective control of disruptive forms of behaviour. Control mechanisms are held to be necessary because of the impossibility of perfect integration due to the scarcity of means, the frustration of expectations and imperfect socialization. The host of problems that are raised here makes it unlikely that this requisite can be accepted without severe modification. There is undoubtedly a difference between the necessity of, say, socialization without which society could not survive, and social controls whose 'necessity' seems to be contingent upon certain forms of social organization. Indeed, here Aberle and his colleagues may justly be charged with confusing the formal with the substantive level of analysis. Socialization as a formal requirement of social life, given the comparatively long period of reliance of the human child on others, is not in question. However, the effective control of disruptive behaviour (the examples of force and fraud are given) will only qualify as a social necessity if it is clearly agreed that 'disruptive forms of behaviour', like the long period of infant dependency, are essential and enduring elements of human life.

Where 'disruptive forms of behaviour' are equated to *any* form of social change and the opposition or support of it, as implied by some versions of the functionalist doctrine,[17] then clear agreement to the ubiquity of 'disruptive forms of behaviour' must be given. But the use of the inflammatory term 'disruptive' surely rules this argument out of court, for one man's disruption is another man's development. Thus, in a future in which justice is fairness, and where well-known and trusted mechanisms exist for resolving disputes over the whole vista of societal problems, the necessity for these social controls is obviated. This is, it goes without saying, an important element in moral progress, and the myth that there must always be 'disruptive forms of behaviour' and hence that 'effective control' of them is a functional requisite of society serves to perpetuate the very condition the ubiquity of which the analysis purports to establish.

The article concludes with the conviction that it gives the lead in constructing a system of structural prerequisites, by showing how the functional needs might be met. The general impression conveyed is that though the great task is in its first, exploratory stages, and the provisional nature of the theory is constantly implied, nevertheless, tampering with the total edifice in any of its details is less encouraged than total commitment or total rejection. This is an invitation that (perhaps most) sociologists have not been able to resist, though I have tried to evaluate the statements of these Functionalists, as I shall go on to treat others, on their merits. It is thus heartening and, in the light of recent sociological polemics, somewhat surprising that some of these statements have been found to be useful and have been retained, while others have seemed questionable, have in fact either contradicted or led to deductions that contradicted the more acceptable statements, and have thus been rejected. Functionalism as a doctrine has no place in sociological discourse (other than as yet one more social ideology), while functionalism as a method sometimes works and sometimes does not.

Levy—research and development

One of the authors of the *Ethics* paper of 1950, Marion J. Levy, Jr., published a book in 1952 that may properly be seen as the expected research and development, to use a phrase from modern technology which is not entirely misplaced, from the earlier pilot study in functionalist ideas. Once again, the link with the growing school of American structural-functional theory must be kept in mind, and the influence of Talcott Parsons, the undisputed leader of the school, is always strong and widely acknowledged.*

The most striking superficial fact about *The Structure of Society* is that it is published in typescript, so that (in the author's words from the first page of the preface) 'the tentative nature of this volume cannot be emphasized too strongly . . . the reader, it is hoped, will be constantly aware of the extremely elementary stage of development of the task that is barely begun here'.[18] Notwithstanding these protestations, there follows more than five hundred pages of close prose and no lack of definitions, classifications, deductions, analytical analyses, and even empirical evidence presented in a most positive, confident and in some places seemingly definitive manner. I shall, accordingly, treat Levy's book in the normal critical fashion and pay little attention to the supposed delicacy of its stage of conception.

It would be mistaken to equate the 1950 paper with the book of 1952, but it would be even more mistaken to consider them entirely apart. The position of Levy is that the later book, with respect to the definition of society and the list and treatment of functional requisites, is a 'somewhat modified' form of the earlier work. There is a fifty-page chapter on functional prerequisites in *The Structure of Society*, and the whole book is a prolonged and systematic exposition of these concerns, with the notable and very detailed expansion into the realms of structure in addition to the more implicit treatment of

---

* Chronologically, Parsons should be dealt with before Levy, for major relevant works of the former, *The Social System* and *Toward a General Theory of Action*, were both published in 1951. However, as Parsons has more recently amended and developed his approach to a considerable degree, I have chosen to deal with Levy's book first.

function. But here I am concerned mainly with the revised list of functional requisites and with the extended discussion, clarification and theoretical boldness that distinguishes Levy's solo effort from the previous co-operative venture. The numbers of Levy's list correspond to the previous list, with the addition of a tenth requisite, and I shall go through the list as before.

1 Provision for an adequate physiological relationship to the setting and for sexual recruitment. The most important modification here is that 'setting' replaces 'environment', and for human society the setting 'consists of the factors of human hereditary and non-human environment', the limits of which may be empirically found.[19] These two factors of the setting, the non-social factors, plus the existence of other societies, referred to in terms of the need for *defence*, are thus lumped together. But that 'such apparently disparate features ... [are] under one heading is by no means arbitrary ... [for they] are all part of the setting of action'.[20] The reasoning is clearly circular, and there is still no satisfactory case to justify not simply the collapsing of the biological needs that are specific to men and human societies, but also the inclusion of *defence* against other societies in this bulging package. It must be concluded that the requisites for the continuity of social life with reference to the biological problems faced by men in society are as poorly covered by the over-parsimony of Levy's scheme as by the excesses of Malinowski.

2 Role differentiation and role assignment. Apart from a rather laborious, almost anal redefinition of 'role', the main interest in this section is with 'one particular type of role differentiation that is a requirement for any society, i.e. *stratification*. ... that differentiates higher and lower standings in terms of one or more criteria'.[21] The argument is based on the universality of scarcity and the assumption of greater responsibility of élites. These arguments, as was indicated above, will be dealt with later.

3 Communication and

4 Shared cognitive orientations may profitably be discussed together, for Levy shows clearly that the shared cognitions make up a large part of that which is to be communicated, and his analysis, analytical distinctiveness notwithstanding, suggests two requisites for the price of one, or rather one for the price of two. The interdependence of the functional requisites in Levy's scheme is, if anything, even more blatant or marked than in the *Ethics* paper. This forces a confrontation with the issue of whether certain elements, and especially the four conditions for the breakdown of society which

173

Levy reiterates almost literally from the previous article, and the whole set of functional requisites are *a priori* constructions or empirical generalizations. Levy claims that:

> No society, however simple, can exist without shared, learned, symbolic modes of communication because without them it cannot maintain the common value structure or the protective sanctions that hold back the war of all against all.[22]

This statement is the supreme suggestion that the whole exercise consists of one great, complex, ingenious tautology. It is here that the mode of criticism of Dahrendorf, for example, against functionalism is very difficult to understand. The argument runs that the Functionalists train all their attention on consensus, 'the common value structure', and neglect conflict and its potential in society.[23] Precisely the opposite is true. The Functionalists are so neurotic about the permanent possibility of conflict of one sort or another, manifest in the four omnipresent conditions for the breakdown of society, that they devote by far the greater part of their theoretical concern to the construction of systems of sociological categories that explain how conflict has been and will be contained. It is in this sense that functionalism like 'conflict-theory' regards conflict as only too natural—with the difference which is of course very significant, that the latter school 'encourages' some forms of conflict for political reasons, while the former 'discourages' most forms of conflict for the opposite political reasons. Coser's well-known development of Simmel's work, in *The Functions of Social Conflict*, is therefore an example of a hybrid that is becoming less uncommon, namely the combination of the functionalist method and the rejection of the Functionalists' doctrine. The Functionalists view conflict as the Dutch view the sea, and where the Dutch construct dykes the Functionalists construct their requisites. Both must be built strongly, must be well maintained and must be regularly tested, and the public must be constantly reminded of their importance for the survival and the integrity of society. The issue for sociology is to decide whether conflict is a natural phenomenon that will always be with us, part of the human condition as the sea is part of the human environment; or whether conflict is like, for example, atmospheric pollution, a necessary condition of the type of society in which we choose to live.

Therefore, communication may be a requisite of social life, but not for all the reasons that Levy gives. Shared cognitive orientations, that by and/or about which members of a society communicate, presents a similar but more specific set of problems. Levy makes some interesting distinctions in this context. He points out, correctly in my opinion, that there are different levels of these cognitions and that in fact some need not be shared generally at all. In the first place, however, there are the 'basic cognitive orientations which must be institutionalized for full social actors'—the common pool of knowledge that those from other societies might be expected to pick up after a fairly short time, years rather than decades perhaps. The cognitive orientations of this sort are institutionalized in the sense that they are expected to be known, and if they are not known then others will be indignant and make some moral protest. (There is further comment on this issue when I come to deal with institutionalization as a functional requisite below.) All other cognitive orientations are termed *intermediate*, and they may be either institutionalized or not. The former obviously refer to special though not extraordinary skills, and people who call themselves diamond cutters *should* know how to cut diamonds. Non-institutionalized intermediate cognitive orientations is the name given to the residue, and includes, curiously, such things as the theoretical discoveries of science. Possibly Levy intends to make the point that members of the general public would not know a 'theoretical discovery of science' if it were shown to them, whereas most of us have at least some idea of diamond cutting.

Further, Levy classifies cognitive orientations as he does the social institutions, into crucial and strategic, the latter being subdivided into substantive and critical. These classes seem somewhat arbitrary, linked as they are by definition to the requisites of society with no clear empirical referent.

The hypothesis immediately presents itself, though to my knowledge no Functionalist or any other social theorist has yet taken it up, that with the increasing specialization and role differentiation of modern society basic cognitive orientations *necessary* to social life are bound to decrease, while intermediate cognitions are bound to increase. This is of course extremely germane to the whole question of communication, both in its formal and its more popular connotation, and one need only mention the great Snow debate on the two cultures, which still rages at a leisurely pace, to highlight the point.[24]

5   A shared articulated set of goals. Levy devotes nine pages to this requisite, a degree of attention equalled only in his discussion of role differentiation and stratification. Goals, or 'a state of affairs deemed desirable by the actors concerned', are distinguished as the middle ground between 'immutable and ultimate ends of action' and 'motivations'.[25] And it is goals in the plural rather than the totalitarian goal that is predicated, for alternatives in this matter will reduce conflict. Nevertheless, goals like cognitions are either basic or intermediate, and presumably the liberal tolerance of alternatives does not apply to basic goals. Indeed, when speaking of 'basic goals' or values,

Levy tends to define away the problem of competing goals, for example when he argues that:

> Some goals may be mutually incompatible without being destructive to the society, though this cannot be the case if both are functional requisites for the society and affect the same members at the same time.[26]

A fine piece of question-begging, one might say! One cannot accuse him of ignoring the common-sense objections to the notion of the ubiquity of common value systems, for he is well aware of them. He concludes his analysis with the words:

> despite the mixture of empirical and nonempirical goals, the indeterminacy of goal systems, the presence of mutually incompatible goals, and the lack on the part of each member of the society of complete knowledge about the total goal system of the society, without a relatively well-articulated and clearly defined set of goals a society would invite extinction, apathy, or the war of all against all.[27]

If it is suggested that a society cannot continue to survive when one basic goal or value is rejected by a significant section of the members of that society, and as a corollary, the proponents of the basic goal or value reject the basic goal or value of the other section, class, group or what have you, then the suggestion does violence to both experience and reason and gives no commensurate stimulus to the imagination or the theory. As I have argued above, the fundamental goal or value of progress, innovational or non-innovational, is the only such value, and other goals, when considered as goals, may co-exist with one another or not, contingent on the other sociological characteristics of the society in question. This naturally leads on to a consideration of means, the next requisite; but let me briefly draw attention to a theoretical step which is concealed by a smooth semantic transition. I refer to the way in which the term 'goal or value system' is quietly inserted in the argument in place of 'set of goals or values'. *System* seemingly gives the impression of interdependence, of mutual support, even of control over contradictions and incompatibilities. A *set* of values does not entail a *system* of values, and it is at this point of transition that the consensus theory strains on its weakest link.

6   The regulation of the choice of means. Goals, it is pointed out, may be seen as means from some positions, and means as goals from others, and so just as goals are necessary for social survival, means are too. And not simply means, but 'legitimized means' are necessary, for failing this, goals must either 'be devalued' or their 'attainment must be left open to considerations based solely on instrumental

efficiency'.[28] This is curiously Maoist in tone, for it seems to exemplify the ideologizing approach to *all* matters of social action, drawing pointed attention to the legitimate sources of means and values. Not the little red book, but the large blue book, Parsons' *The Social System*, contains the ritual incantations. I shall suggest below that there are indeed requisite forms of means for satisfying the conditions of survival of societies.

7   The regulation of affective expression. It is no accident that Levy is very interested in Chinese and Japanese social life, for it would take an orientalist to conjure up a functional requisite of this type. As before, I shall merely note it.

8   Adequate socialization and

9   effective control of disruptive behaviour are not developed in any manner that leads me to revise my previous comments on them. A word again on the term 'adequate' is, however, in place. Levy writes that 'an individual is *adequately socialized* if he has been inculcated with a sufficient portion of the structures of action of his society to permit the effective performance of his role in society'.[29] 'Adequate', 'sufficient' and 'effective' could all of course be interchanged and the meaning would not be altered. This is a very poor statement indeed, for it gives no indication of how effective is effective role-performance, etc.; whether this mysterious level is the same for all roles; whether some relatively independent test of this is possible or whether the only test is post-factum when society has already broken down (the 'I told you so' proof); and how 'inadequate' socialization can become 'adequate' in the course of one or more generations.

10   Adequate institutionalization. The same strictures on the use of 'adequate' naturally obtain here as before. This functional requisite is explicitly located in the tradition of the normative orientation of action that has informed the work of Talcott Parsons from the 1930s, though, as Levy stresses, all the functional requisites involve normative orientations. Institutionalization as a process is in fact only analytically distinct from the other nine items on the list, and it is instructive to prefix each functional requisite with the phrase 'the institutionalization of . . .'. This exercise demonstrates the real significance of the basic theory on which the enterprise is founded—to elaborate the normative springs of action, to discover why people make societies work and the roots of their commitment in the social order. The eternal insight of functionalism is 'let us not rock the boat', and this does not prevent the movement of the boat in any case; it is a theory of adjustment to each disturbing wave. Institutionalization of some social unit or process means, roughly, getting people to agree to it and to disapprove of those who do not agree.

The methods used to encourage people to agree have elicited little critical attention from the Functionalists, and we may be rightly suspicious that the theory tends to place maintenance of the social order, even in the assured short term, in a more sociologically desirable position than any disruption of the social order, for whatever reasons. Given this dogmatic assertion of doctrinal functionalism, that it is always best to avoid those conditions that might lead to the breakdown of society, contradictions follow, as I pointed out with respect to revolution against colonialism. In addition, an ethic of expediency, as the functionalist ethic undoubtedly is, is no ethic at all and can have no place in a theory of moral progress.

The dogma of functionalist doctrine, as dogma, must be rejected, but as a working hypothesis in both sociology and ethics it is quite obviously of the greatest interest and value. Violence, an extreme form of conflict, for example, is very often socially wasteful; rapid change may create more difficulties than gradual change; and a high level of personal and moral involvement in the activities of a society by its members will certainly contribute to solving problems of some types more than apathy or opposition. What I am trying to make clear is that sometimes all these social phenomena have consequences which turn out to be different from those that the functionalist doctrine would lead one to expect. This is an empirical question, although political and ethical considerations can never be entirely excluded. Lewis Coser's *The Functions of Social Conflict* is a case in point. Coser showed, on the basis of the insights of Georg Simmel, that social conflict could in fact contribute to the integrity and the cohesiveness of a society in many and sometimes devious ways. This of course is quite contrary to the expectations of someone reading Levy's *The Structure of Society*. (I infer this, for there is no mention of 'conflict' as such in the book.)

With these remarks I shall move on to the work of one of the most influential sociologists in the modern world, Talcott Parsons.

*Parsons and the functional problems**

The work of Talcott Parsons, now spanning forty years of remarkably prolific publication, is best seen as an elaborate, sometimes ingenious and sometimes vacuous, attempt to solve the Hobbesean problem of order. This problem, expressed in everyday terms, is bound up with the reasons why society does not fall apart, why people do what has to be done and, a more recent aspect of Parsons' work, how social evolution guarantees more efficient solutions of these problems. The persistant emphasis on the means-end schema as the main focus of

* A modified version of this section is published in *The British Journal of Sociology*, XXI (1970), pp. 30–42, under the title of 'The Fate of the "Functional Requisites" in Parsonian Sociology'.

the analysis of social relations, in terms of goal-seeking and problem-solving activity, has run through Parsons' sociological enterprise as a unifying thread, linking *The Structure of Social Action* (SSA) of 1937; *Toward a General Theory of Action* (TGTA) of 1951; *The Social System* (SS) of 1951; *Working Papers in the Theory of Action* (WP) of 1953; the revised edition of his *Essays in Sociological Theory* (EST) of 1954; *Economy and Society* (ES) of 1956; his long contributions to *Theories of Society* (TS) of 1961; and the small volume *Societies: Evolutionary and Comparative Perspectives* (SEC) of 1966.[30] In addition to these, Parsons has written and contributed to scores of books, journals, symposia, etc., and has rarely missed an opportunity to explain, develop and broadcast his theoretical aims—no less than 'the establishment of a general theory in the social sciences' (TGTA, p. 3).

It is impossible to restrict oneself to any one aspect of the Parsonian edifice to the total exclusion of the construction as a whole, for there is no doubt that the theory of action or structural-functional analysis is intended to be a unified approach to the social sciences and that its internal consistency is at a premium. The vast changes of particular emphasis over the years, at best theoretical development, at worst the brushing under the carpet of notions found to be useless or even complete liabilities, has caused much confusion in the sociological ranks, and so this investigation of the fate of 'functional requisites' in Parsonian theory may serve the dual purpose of tracing the development or otherwise of the concept and of reflecting the changes in the general theory. Again, my intention is to approach functionalism more as a method, attempting to evaluate the worth of positions as they are stated, than as a doctrine to be wholly accepted or wholly rejected.

It is very important that Parsons' original theoretical position be considered, for if it is ignored or merely acknowledged in a ritualist fashion, as many modern commentators are apt to do, then there is grave danger that the whole point of his considerable exercise may be missed. As he himself has said as recently as 1964, '*The Structure of Social Action* (first published, 1937) . . . is the basic reference point of all my subsequent theoretical work . . . not only in terms of content, but also for what I may call the strategy of theory-building.'[31] It is just this strategy that has been consistently misunderstood by critics and disciples alike. It is summed up in SSA (p. 733) as follows:

> the action frame of reference . . . involves no concrete data that can be 'thought away', that are subject to change. It is not a phenomenon in the empirical sense. It is the indispensable logical framework in which we describe and think about the phenomena of action.

TGTA further reinforces the impression just given of the logical status of Parsons' theory of action. The monograph, 'Values, Motives, and Systems of Action', begins with the claim that it is an extension and revision of the position previously outlined by Parsons in SSA, and refers the readers to the very page from which the above quotation is taken. After some introductory material, Parsons, Shils and Olds make the following expository statement (TGTA, p. 76):

> Those who have followed our exposition thus far have acquired a familiarity with the definitions of the basic elements of the theory of action. There are further important conceptual entities and classificatory systems to be defined, but these, in a sense, derive from the basic terms that have already been defined. The point is that the further entities can be defined largely in terms of the entities and relationships already defined, with the introduction of a minimum of additional material.

Thus, there can be no doubt whatsoever that the theory of action or the action frame of reference is not intended to be a *theory* in the accepted sense of the term,[32] but more of a system of logical categories arrived at, presumably, on some basis other than the actual empirical study of on-going societies.

Compared to the attention paid by Malinowski, Aberle and his colleagues, and Levy, to the functional requisites of society, on the surface it seems that Parsons has not been very concerned with this approach. However, on a more careful examination of the books cited above, one is forced to the conclusion that the name of the concern, functional requisites, might have dropped out of common Parsonian usage, but the concern itself, to elucidate the conditions necessary for social life, has always been and remains at the very centre of Parsons' work. The best way of demonstrating the truth of this contention is to trace the path of the requisite analysis through the changes in the theory.

Let it first be noted that nowhere in all his many published writings does Parsons ever give a systematic list of functional requisites which could be remotely compared with those of the authors treated above. In lieu of this, one finds widely scattered throughout most of his volumes numerous references to functional requisites, functional exigencies, functional imperatives and, most importantly, functional problems, from which one may tentatively construct some list of relevance to social requirements.

Parsons certainly acknowledges the fundamental importance of these items for, at the beginning of SS, he discusses 'The Functional Prerequisites of Social Systems', referring to the Aberle paper, but noting that 'the present treatment . . . departs from it rather radically'

(SS, p. 26, note 1). The orientation is almost identical; Parsons argues that if 'a system is to constitute a persistent order or to undergo an orderly process of developmental change, certain functional pre-requisites must be met' (SS, pp. 26-7). He then goes on to distinguish between the personality, social and cultural systems, and one is left wondering whether the functional prerequisites are simply the harmonious relations among these systems or whether they refer to relations within these systems, or both.

At least three functional prerequisites may be extracted, with the greatest difficulty, from Parsons' discussion at this point, and it is notable that he speaks of 'classes' of functional prerequisites rather than unitary needs. The first class is 'the biological prerequisites of individual life ... to the subtler problems of the conditions of minimum stability of personality' (SS, p. 28). This class also contains socialization, at least to a minimum level. The second class, the obverse of the first, again with specific reference to the individual actors, 'is to motivate them adequately to the performances which may be necessary if the social system in question is to persist or develop' (SS, p. 29). Here we begin to understand that the prerequis-ites are indeed *pre*-requisites and that, at this level, it is the 'per-formances which may be necessary' or rather 'the performances which *are* necessary' for social life (when and if Parsons comes to discuss them) that will be more directly comparable with the previous studies. However, included in this prerequisite of 'adequate motiva-tion' we find a negative aspect (control over potentially disruptive behaviour) and a positive aspect (the motivational problem of order). This prerequisite is obviously of the first importance. 'The pre-requisite of adequate motivation gives us one of the primary starting points for building up to the concepts of role and institutionalization.' (SS, p. 31.)

The third class of prerequisites concerns 'the integration of cultural patterns ... [which] imposes "imperatives" on the other elements ... [and is a] major functional problem area of the social system' (SS, p. 33). This class includes such items of cultural significance as language, general communication, 'empirical knowledge necessary to cope with situational exigencies, and sufficiently integrated patterns of expressive symbolism and of value orientation' (SS, p. 34).

Perhaps the most noteworthy shift in this account as compared to the previous functional prerequisites examined is in the case of 'role'. The difference between the functional and the structural requirements according to Aberle, etc., it will be recalled, was that the latter answered the questions of 'How?', whereas the former answered questions of 'What must be done?'. Parsons, however, wittingly or not, quite categorically sees role as answering the question 'How?' rather than 'What?'. 'Roles are,' he states, 'from the point of view of the functioning of the social system, the primary mechanisms through which the essential functional prerequisites of the system are met' (SS, p. 115).

It therefore becomes fairly clear that these three classes of functional prerequisites are organized around the three major systems, personality, social and cultural, and that role in some way acts as a mechanism of 'translation' among the systems. This is certainly a conceptual advance on Malinowski, Aberle and his colleagues, and Levy, in so far as it distinguishes individual, biological-personality based needs, from social, societally-based needs. This satisfies my earlier criticism, but the addition of the cultural system, with the hypothesis of a set of specifically culturally-based needs, might prove to be unnecessary in terms of social requirements, however much it means to Parsons' general theory.[33]

A further and most interesting development in Parsons' analysis comes with his discussion of 'The Constitution of Empirical Societies' (SS, pp. 166 ff.). Following a speculative investigation of what he calls 'empirical clusterings of structural components', that is the facts that certain characteristics such as the high level of instrumental competence and high rewards, for example, tend to 'cluster' together rather than to spread randomly throughout a society, Parsons reflects on the 'functional exigencies' that seem to account for these structural patterns. It is worth quoting him here, for what he has to say is of much significance for the relations of social needs and moral conduct. He argues (SS, p. 167):

> These exigencies are of two classes: first, the universal imperatives, the conditions which must be met by any social system of a stable and durable character, and second, the imperatives of compatibility, those which limit the range of coexistence of structural elements in the same society, in such a way that, given one structural element, such as a given class of occupational role system, the type of kinship system which goes with it must fall within certain specifiable limits.

The first class of universal exigencies or imperatives therefore corresponds to the functional requisites of social life, and are obviously related to Parsons' earlier functional prerequisites of the personality, social and cultural systems. The second class of exigencies or imperatives of compatibility closely resembles the content of 'sociological possibility and impossibility' that I introduced in the last chapter during the discussion of the sociological ethic.

Without going at all into the considerable complexity of Parsons' reasons, it is advisable at this point to report that he describes the mechanisms by which these imperatives are met as 'adaptive structures' and that the universal exigencies, like so many items in the scheme, disappear all of a sudden and pop up again in the most unexpected places. There is, however, one excellent and clear reason for this concentration on the imperatives of compatibility, for they *are* the structural imperatives of the social system. This means, and incidentally is the most radical departure from Levy, that whereas functional prerequisites or universal exigencies must be met for social life to be possible at all, the structural imperatives or exigencies of compatibility apply to particular social systems. To put it more simply, but not I think to distort seriously Parsons' meaning, *what* societies must do to survive is common to all societies, but *how* they should go about it is not similarly common, with the proviso that once a particular society begins in a certain way many options appear to close.

TGTA bears a curious relation to SS. Whereas the latter is a solo attempt by Parsons to apply the theory of action to the social system as exclusively as possible, the former is a collaborative work written by sociologists, anthropologists and psychologists on all three systems—social, cultural and personality. There are, of course, many points of coincidence (not to say repetition) between the two volumes but, just as naturally, there are differences in emphasis. Perhaps the main difference is in the treatment of 'value-orientations' in TGTA, and it will serve us well to examine this with respect to the fate of the functional imperatives.

The place of the cultural system, as I have already suggested, throws up special problems, and indeed it has often been treated as different in important respects to both of the other perhaps more intuitively acceptable systems. 'Apart from embodiment in the orientation systems of concrete actors, culture ... is not itself organized as a system of action,' the authors of TGTA explain in the General Statement that introduces the volume; and they continue (TGTA, p. 7): 'Therefore, culture as a system is on a different plane from personalities and social systems.' However, we later learn that the part of culture that is exceptional and that is organized in action systems, namely *actor orientation*, is in its most important form extraordinarily important. Thus, 'Patterns of value-orientation have been singled out as the most crucial cultural elements in the organization of systems of action' (TGTA, p. 159). To complete this particular picture we are told that there are different *types* of imperatives for each system. Those for action systems, personality and social systems which are functional, have imperatives of compatibility; while cultural systems have imperatives of coherence, logical imperatives.*

---

* This is all explained in a footnote (TGTA, p. 173, note 12). It is worth mentioning that whereas the imperatives of compatibility were the structural imperatives in SS, in TGTA they seem at this point to suggest functional imperatives. It is rather confusing!

It is almost impossible to list the requirements for social life in any systematic manner from TGTA because the treatment is so uneven. The problems that Levy, for example, classified in his list of functional requisites hold TGTA together whenever there seems to be a need for some fundamental statement. They certainly do not act as organizing principles. The insight of the distinction between universal and structural imperatives is quite obscured. For example, we find in the General Statement cross-cutting and blunt claim that 'the functional problem of social systems may be summarized as the problems of allocation and integration' (TGTA, p. 25). Much later on we are blatantly informed that 'Order—peaceful coexistence under conditions of scarcity—is one of the very first of the functional imperatives of *social systems*' (TGTA, p. 180). These are clearly imperatives on different levels of generality, and they are symptomatic of the whole treatment of the topic in this volume. The former, allocation and integration, link up with perhaps the major organizing features of SS, the pattern variables of action-orientation, and these variables are—if not derived from the consideration of social requisites—at least one analytical consequence of this direction of thought.

These pattern-variables, or patterns of value-orientations, are a set of five choices on dimensions rather than polarities that each actor must make (*a priori*) in any social situation. This mode of analysis clearly reflects universal imperatives, conditions for social life in any case, and not the structural imperatives or the exigencies of compatibility. In the conclusion to 'Values, Motives, and Systems of Action' Parsons and Shils seem to hold on to the distinction between universal and compatibility imperatives, but in a weak fashion. They say that 'some conception of *functional imperatives*— that is, constituent conditions and empirically necessary precon- ditions of on-going systems, set by the facts of scarcity in the object situation, the nature of the organism, and the realities of coexistence —are necessary' (TGTA, p. 241). This statement is best understood as an inexact reiteration of the approach outlined in SS, where the functional prerequisites were dealt with in terms of the needs of the personality, social and cultural systems. In TGTA, however, as has been suggested, the emphasis on value-orientations and thus on the cultural system leads into the exercise by a somewhat different path— and a less satisfactory one at that.

This is not the place to discuss the limitations of a social science that speaks in words compared with a natural science that is not by necessity always so bound. TGTA loses its grip on its vast subject- matter at so many crucial points that on balance the whole enterprise is of doubtful value, and it is not surprising that much of it is simply forgotten. The vacillation and inconclusive array of comments, some couched in such categorically certain terms, on the requirements of social life is, I believe, only one of many examples of the confusion that runs deeply through this unfortunate volume.

Temporary salvation in the person of Robert Bales and his small-group experiments was soon forthcoming, and this juncture marks the most interesting aspect of Parsons' thinking on imperatives and the problems of social systems. Briefly, in a series of experiments Bales and others had conceived of small groups as functioning social systems, and had made the analytical 'discovery' on the basis of their experimental findings that each group as a system had four main functional problems. These were, roughly, adaptation to the environment, instrumental control over the environment, expression of sentiments and social integration.[34] This subject is broached in WP and some interesting analogies between these four functional problems and the original pattern variables of action orientation are drawn. Unfortunately the possible large steps that could have been taken in this volume were obscured by a bad attack of scientism, perhaps encouraged by contact with the experimentally minded Bales! After an attempt to establish four sociological principles, those of Inertia, Action and Reaction, Effort and System-Integration (WP, p. 102 ff.), on the basis of four-dimensional 'social space' suggested by the four system problems, the very term is dropped. 'These terms [the dimensions] now take the place of what we formerly meant to designate by the "four-system problems" as named by Bales.' (WP, p. 189.)* Thankfully, this type of analysis has not exclusively prevailed.[35]

The link between the pattern variables and the functional problems, now taken firmly out of Bales' hands and implanted with the unmistakable characteristics of Parsonian functionalism, is worked out most fully with respect to the economy in ES. Parsons and Smelser indeed place the reconstituted functional problems at the very centre of their theory of society and its major institutions. The four functional problems are as follows: goal attainment, the problem of ensuring that society is trying to achieve its goals; adaptation, the way in which means to the goals are mobilized; integration, the problem of social co-operation; and pattern maintenance/tension management (originally called latency), the problem of the satisfaction of the units within the system. This scheme is commonly known as AGIL, and as societies develop the agencies or institutions for satisfying these system needs and for solving these functional problems become more and more specialized. This process is termed structural differentiation, and 'the primary basis of this differentiation

---

* It is ironic that another devotee of the application of principles from the natural and biological sciences to sociology was the very Herbert Spencer at whose intellectual post-mortem Parsons presided in the introduction to SSA.

is the process of meeting the functional exigencies of a system in relation to its situation' (ES, p. 37). Thus the economy of an advanced society is the differentiated sub-system specialized to meet the adaptive exigencies of the system as a whole, and the political structure of a society is the specialized institution that deals with the exigencies of goal-attainment. Less definitely, the legal system deals with integration problems, and the kinship system with pattern-maintenance and tension-management.

Before examining these functional imperatives further, it is important to point out that each social institution (the economy, polity, education, military, etc.) may itself be regarded as a functioning social system with the full complement of four functional imperatives. Thus, and this is mandatory for any *functional* analysis, the relevant system under consideration must be stated and kept firmly in mind. Only if this proviso is strictly adhered to does it become useful to speak of some unit or process as function, that is functional for a particular system in that it makes some contribution to the survival of that system, and perhaps dysfunctional for another system, in that it contributes to its breakdown. One unsolved problem of functionalism is that some units or processes appear both functional *and* dysfunctional *at the same time* for the same system. However, as long as the functional imperatives do not throw up problems whose solutions are mutually contradictory, in the sense that the solution to one inevitably makes another worse, then the system-problems approach may be fruitful.* This is certainly a matter that has to be dealt with in view of the opposition between the 'task-performance' problems and the 'system-maintenance' problems.[36]

The other important focus of attention in ES is the beginning of what might be termed 'cybernetic functionalism', the analysis of social systems and sub-systems and so on in terms of inputs and outputs and hierarchies of controls. I do not wish to become too deeply involved in this aspect or stage of functional analysis, but it is essential that I mention it in light of the development of Parsons' thinking about the functional problems in TS. Here Parsons speaks of the three 'cross-cutting—but also interdependent, bases or axes of variability, or as they may be called, bases of selective abstraction' (TS, p. 36) for the analysis of social systems. The first axis involves the distinction between structure and function; the second involves the distinction between dynamic problems which lead to structural change and those that do not; and the third concerns the hierarchy of relations of control. We are told that the behavioural organism is 'controlled by' the personality system, the personality by the social

---

* To say this much is to grant, for the moment, the doctrinal assumption that *all* on-going societies tend towards 'equilibrium'—an assumption which is, to say the least, controversial.

system, and the social by the cultural system, or, to use Parsons' own words, the cultural system is 'a system of control relative to social systems' (TS, p. 38). This is of course theoretically necessary from the analysis of action in all the volumes from SSA onwards which makes the basis of all action a normative problem and which locates value-orientations within the cultural system. The vital twist for the purposes of this discussion comes when Parsons states that 'it is possible to reduce the functional imperatives of . . . any social system, to four, . . . pattern-maintenance, integration, goal-attainment, and adaptation. These are listed in order of significance from the point of view of cybernetic control of action processes in the system type under consideration' (TS, p. 38).

This is not entirely new, however, for in both WP and ES the notion of 'phrase movements' was introduced to deal with the ways in which the particular systems dealt with their problems in cycles, some problems having to wait their turn, as it were, till others were seen to. The cybernetic hierarchy of control elaborates this idea in the direction of clarifying the relative importance of problems to systems. This mode of analysis suggests a set of interesting empirical problems, with respect to the satisfaction of individual and social needs in on-going societies. It remains to be seen whether or not this theoretical reflection can be successfully applied to the solution of social problems if and when it has illuminated sociological issues.

The most controversial of these issues concerns the explanation of social change, and it is here that the views of one of Parsons' most astute critics, Alvin Gouldner, may be usefully recalled. Gouldner raises the problems of allocating differential importance to 'functionally autonomous parts within a social system . . . because these aid in identifying possible loci of strain within the system', that is elements for change.[37] Although there is no point in suggesting that any of Parsons' system problems or requisites is any more 'requisite' than the others, there would seem to be a case for considering the possibility of temporalizing requisite analysis to accommodate and benefit from Gouldner's contribution. By this I mean that an historical analysis of a revised set of individual and social requisites for society might reveal that different sorts of arrangements and emphases were given to certain requisites at one point in the development of a society, and other arrangements and emphases were given at later points.

However, Parsonian sociology has chosen other paths. Mention of 'functional requisites', 'imperatives', and even 'functional problems', has gradually faded from the works of Parsons. The emphasis has swung from the problems to be solved in order that social life might be possible, with the constant exception of the ubiquitous 'problem of order' in its many and various forms, to the primary functional categories, as the four system problems may have been relabelled (for example in SEC, pp. 28-9).

A rather novel and stimulating aspect of Parsons' recent work is his foray into what can only be called 'evolutionary functionalism'. This is particularly interesting from the point of view of this study in general, as a modern sociological theory of progress, and in particular for the light it throws on Parsons' views on the requisites of social development. Generally, he argues along the lines suggested in ES that social development or evolution is a matter of increased structural differentiation, the specialization of certain crucial institutions. It is interesting that Parsons uses the category of 'innovation' extensively in his argument, but in a way that differs in important respects to its use in previous chapters of this work.

Any attempt to evaluate or sum up Parsons' contributions to our problem must perforce be inadequate, and I have tried to restrict my remarks to those aspects that seemed to be directly relevant to the matter in question. Some general comments are, nevertheless, in order. Firstly, the caveat quoted from SSA on theory-building has held over the years, at least with respect to 'universal imperatives'. They are not subject to change and they are not empirical realities; they are, however, real, in their consequences for social systems. Secondly, Parsons has made the important distinction between personality and social systems, and has paved the way for an analysis of individual and social needs. Thirdly, the important though badly obscured distinction of universal and structural requisites presaged by Levy may be usefully retained and developed. Fourthly, the link between functional problems and pattern-variables, the dilemmas of action, though it has not been discussed in detail, is close to the very heart of this investigation. It is yet another confirmation that the choices that human beings must make in the activity of social relations, some of which have moral significance, are related indissolubly to the conditions for the survival of society. The long-standing and consistent emphasis of Parsons on the normative basis of social action is ample testimony for this contention.

Having examined in some detail attempts of social scientists to build up a satisfactory account of the conditions necessary to the survival of society, and having rejected some items and accepted others, it remains for me to give my account of the matter. In the next chapter I shall present my list of individual and social requisites and show how these are related to the sociological ethic.

XI Needs, morals and society

In constructing yet another list of essential requirements for social life I am striving to show how, at the very least, these needs are relevant to morality. This is of course a long-standing assertion of many writers, both ancient and modern, though no one has yet satisfactorily shown precisely in what this relevance lies.[1] The Greek conception of good as a functional judgment is profoundly disturbing, emphasizing as it does the role-fulfilment aspect of social acts at the expense of the intrinsic nature of the conduct and the results it brings. The curious sociology of Kantian moral theory implies that we must find out what others do and think, but suggests that we may carry out this task purely by reflection and through the fortunate intuitions of our moral sense.

The Utilitarians tried to link happiness with morality, and by a strange mixture of philosophical intuition and empiricist common sense they welded a powerful bond between psychological and sociological findings and ethical judgments. In the words of a recent and sympathetic commentator, the Utilitarians considered that 'the whole of morals can be summed up as the taking of everyone's point of view, and not just our own, when we act'.[2] Obviously, a well-established set of requirements such as I have been discussing would save the Utilitarian a great deal of time and trouble. If 'everyone's point of view' was based on a set of universally necessary principles, without which social life would not be possible, then many of the practical objections to the theory would disappear. (The logical objections, however, would remain.) The Utilitarians, by banking their all on happiness, pleasure and the absence of pain, have a list that is much too restricted.

More recently Ginsberg, from the standpoint of the social rather than the moral philosopher, has dealt with these problems. While he gives a place to sociology and psychology in clarifying moral issues, he remains sceptical about the possibility of what I have termed the 'sociological ethic.' In criticizing Durkheim for just such an enterprise, Ginsberg states: 'All that sociology can do is to reveal the discrepancy between the existing conditions and the ideal and possibly to suggest methods for removing the discrepancy. But it cannot of itself define the ideal.'[3]

The philosopher, Stephen Toulmin, in his widely discussed book, *The Place of Reason in Ethics*, has pointed out the link between sociality and morality, though his argument never proceeds beyond hints and suggestions in this connection.[4] As I have already mentioned, other philosophers such as Macbeath, Edel, Ladd and Dorothy Emmett have devoted attention to sociological and anthropological data in an attempt to clarify the problems of ethics. Solutions still elude us, and as I have suggested most modern moral philosophers have either ignored or redefined the traditional problems with which this study has been concerned.

Therefore, although there is little cause for celebration in the ranks of sociologists and others concerned with values, there is more than a faint glimmer of encouragement in the contemporary tendency to discuss together the 'facts' of social science and the 'values' of moral philosophy. It is in this spirit that my classification of needs is to be taken.

The requirements of social life refer to the conditions that must be satisfied if (1) human life and (2) human society are to be possible. This gives us the basis of a first and vital classification of human needs, namely individual and social. The basis for this distinction is the fact that certain needs must be satisfied for each individual to survive (for example nutrition), whereas others (like reproduction) are not needs of individuals as such but of social survival. A second and equally important principle of classification is between the biological or physiologically-based needs and the derived needs. Thus, both individuals and societies will have biological and derived needs. For convenience I shall call these latter primary and secondary needs respectively. The rationale for this second distinction is that there are some individual and some social needs whose basis is to be found in man's biological nature, and others whose basis is to be found in the nature of social relations. Before I illustrate this classification of requirements for human life, it is proper that I make clear a number of assumptions on which I am operating.

In the first place, I assume that there is *some* sense in which we may speak of social needs, but this is not to extend the organic analogy of society beyond reasonable limits. It does *not* imply the sort of circular teleology for which I have chastised the Functionalists, for it says nothing yet about the success of societies in fulfilling these needs. Furthermore, the notion that only a certain number of the

members of a society require to have their primary and secondary
individual needs fulfilled for the society to survive as a unit is
sufficient evidence for the existence of a category of social needs. The
actual number of individuals involved is of course an empirical
matter, and one may surmise that this number or proportion will
vary with social and political circumstances in any particular society
over time.

As a corollary, the assumption is made that psychological and/or
biological explanations of an individual nature are insufficient to deal
fully with sociological phenomena. The arguments above apply
equally well to this assumption as to that of social needs.

Lastly, I am assuming that the human species will continue to
manifest the same or similar characteristics in the foreseeable future.
This is largely a matter of definition. This problem would solve
itself in any case, for if and when we carry out biological tricks like
'genetic-programming', moral considerations may turn out to be
irrelevant. We would cease, in the moral sense at least, to be human.

My classification of basic requirements for social life is laid out in
Table 2 below.

Table 2   Individual and social needs

	Primary	*Secondary*
INDIVIDUAL	Nutrition; shelter; sleep	Stability of personality; cognition
SOCIAL	Reproduction; communication; socialization; motivation	Role differentiation; preferences; institutionalization

Let us now examine each of these items briefly in turn, beginning
with individual primary needs. These are largely self-explanatory.
With nutrition, shelter and sleep and nothing else, the individual
could survive as an animal, as a member of the human species, on the
basis of the satisfaction of his biological needs. This level of existence,
truly, would constitute a bare minimum and there are doubtless many
who would hesitate to dignify these conditions alone as human.
Perhaps it is only with the satisfaction of the secondary, non-
biologically based individual requirements that we begin to enter
properly the realm of human persons. Two such requisites appear to
be basic, namely stability of personality and cognition. Stability of
personality, which derives from Parsons' discussion of the personality
system in *The Social System*, refers to the need for the individual

to have sufficient control over his reactions in the physical world. There is an element of what can only be termed 'character' in my meaning, in the sense that each individual has a typical stock of reactions and modes of responding to the world, and displays a remarkable emotional consistency in the vast majority of cases. Some sense of identity, therefore, is a secondary need of the individual. The final individual need is that of cognition. Again this stems from Parsons' discussion, though I have adapted what he has said to my own purpose.

I am *not* referring to a set or system of *shared* cognitions, as is abundantly clear from the fact that I place it in the individual and not the social category. The need is not so much for people to *share* cognitive orientations, or ways of looking at the world, but for people to *have* cognitive orientations. There are practical as well as theoretical reasons for this. The natural environment will always pose a physical threat, if not from wild animals in certain times and places then from even more lethal machines; if not from swamps and chasms then from chairs and stairs. The hazards have to be recognized and avoided, and this is the minimum level of cognitive orientation. Further, the environment must be manipulated for all sorts of reasons, not least of which is the satisfaction of the biological requirements of nutrition and shelter, and so the necessity for cognition from the most primitive arrangements to advanced science and technology must be established.

These then are the individual requirements for human life. To put it at its simplest, the isolate on a lonely desert island, conveniently supplied with food and means of shelter, would need to satisfy these five needs—three biological and two secondary—to survive as a recognizable human being. Man in society, however, has additional needs.

The primary social needs based on his biological nature are reproduction, communication, socialization and motivation. The case for reproduction is clear. Although no individual requires to reproduce to survive individually, society if it is to survive must ensure a certain level of reproduction. Therefore reproduction is a social need and not an individual need, though it is biologically based. In a similar fashion, there is no necessity for any individual to be socialized, as long as he is fed and sheltered until he can take care of himself. He will, under these conditions, probably survive.

However, for a society to survive, develop, change or simply stay as it always was, socialization of a certain proportion of its children is necessary. By socialization is intended the process whereby an agent introduces another into the ways, the customs and the rules of the society to which he belongs. Consideration here must be given to the relatively unstructured nature of much of this instruction.

Here, I believe, the Functionalists once again over-emphasize the consensual basis of society and neglect the very real differences that can and do exist within and between societies, and that simply cannot be dismissed as variants which may be subsumed under some general value system.[5] Socialization is classed as a social need for the reasons stated above, and it is biologically based for a negative reason. Although as an individual the child might survive without socialization, as a social actor he would not, for he does not have the given material, the physiology to know what to do and what not to do. In other animals these capacities, sometimes termed 'instincts', are much in evidence, and the human child is by comparison very poorly endowed. It is thus the physiological lack that lies behind this social need for socialization.

Much the same holds for communication. It is a social requisite for the trivial reason that individuals on their own, far from having a need for communication, have no real use for it. In society, however, it is utterly necessary, so much so that languages, extremely specialized tools that they are, have emerged with most known societies. Again, communication must be taught in some way to compensate for the lack of instinctive skills in this respect, as with some animals and birds.[6] Some interesting and widely important work on language and the grammatical universals underlying all natural languages is being carried out by the American professor of linguistics, Noam Chomsky, and the possible repercussions of his findings may have a profound effect on philosophy and the social sciences.[7]

The requisite of motivation, suggested by Levy, Aberle and his colleagues, and Parsons and his colleagues, raises some very fundamental issues. Again, the Functionalists go too far in attempting to coagulate the problems of motivation, control and order. They are no doubt related, but in the functionalist scheme everything is interdependent with everything else and this theoretical massification only confuses the issue.

Motivation refers to the need to ensure that things are done at the correct times, in the correct manner, by the correct people. In all societies there can be distinguished activities that are totally unorganized in the sense that there are no correct times, places and ways in which to do them, and no correct people to do them. On the other hand there are the more or less organized activities that must be carried out for a variety of practical, ritual or therapeutic reasons, and around which the strictest rules and regulations obtain. For the individual there is no problem—when he becomes hungry he tries to find food; when tired he sleeps. Motivation as an explanatory factor in these cases is superfluous, and for the individual there is no necessity to organize it for he can exist well enough on the basis of his needs.

o

For society, however, it is otherwise. Even if a man is not hungry he may be required to find food, or sleep when he is not tired. The organization of motivation in a certain proportion of members of a society is socially necessary to cope with the other social needs. It is thus analytically independent of the other requisites, though empirically interdependent. It is biologically based in so far as society must make arrangements to fill in a gap in man's physiological properties.

The secondary social needs of role differentiation and institutionalization may be understood together as the bases of social structure. Even in the smallest and most communal society different tasks have to be performed, a division of labour operates, and skills emerge or are passed on to certain individuals or groups. Institutionalization refers to the organization of these social phenomena into fairly predictable patterns. So far, Parsons and his functionalist colleagues have made important contributions to the analysis of societies, or social systems. However, as I have indicated above, when these valuable insights are extended to set up the so-called 'functionalist theory of stratification'[8] in which the present system of inequalities in all known societies is transformed into a functional requisite of social life, then the position must be closely re-examined. In so doing, I shall indicate the way in which the final secondary social need, *preferences*, enters the picture.

The functional theory of stratification has, over the last quarter of a century, occasioned a veritable flood of writings and emotions for the good reason that it serves as a front to what is probably the most important political, not to say moral and sociological, debate of all time. I speak, of course, of equality and justice. Roughly, the functionalist theory attempted to explain why it was sociologically necessary that different rewards must accrue to those carrying out different tasks in any society. This argument has correctly been construed as a justification of social inequality, and it is a morally relevant argument precisely because its proponents wish to disabuse us of the notion that inequalities of income, prestige, power, etc., are inevitably unjust in themselves or lead to injustices. Stratification would merit a place on my list only if it were clear that societies could not operate without it, for even if it were shown that it was the most efficient or most just system of social organization, and these demonstrations have not transpired to my knowledge, then it would still remain to be demonstrated that without a stratification system a society would fail to survive.

I must point out that both motivation and role differentiation do find a place on my list and that I am not so naïve as to expect that by dint of mysterious and all-pervading mechanisms socially-necessary tasks are carried out. All I am claiming is that the sorts of stratification systems discussed by sociologists and others do not exclude alternative schemes of social organization which do not make the questionable and too often *post hoc* association between 'functional importance' and rewards. The functionalist theory of stratification tends to condone inequalities rather than to justify them.

The issue of stratification and that of common orientations, especially value orientations, so crucial to the functionalist doctrine, meet at the point that I should like to label 'the preference structure of society'. The basic idea behind the Parsonian emphasis on common value systems and similar consensual and integrative concerns is very sound, as everyone, from the wildest revolutionary through the most piecemeal reformer to the rare conservative who actually knows what he wishes to conserve, is well aware. However, as with so many good ideas, it contains the seeds of its own destruction. What I label the preference structure of a society is, I maintain, a more realistic version of the common value system imperative of the Functionalists, though I fear that it will be quite unacceptable to them as it has the disadvantage of rendering the functionalist doctrine unnecessary.

My view is, simply, that there is a sociological necessity for the preferences of people, most usually in groups of one kind or another, to be taken into account by other people or groups. These of course can be and have been developed into value systems, and sometimes we even find that one set of preferences, one value system, obtains in a particular society at a particular time, to the exclusion of any others. To suggest that this must happen if a society is to survive is both ridiculous and untrue. The notion of preference structure seems to me more useful in this context than that of value-system, for the latter implies a consistency and a coherence that is not always and certainly not necessarily present when judgments are made in and about social life. The preference structure of societal members may of course be organized into a coherent system, consistent over time,* but, and this is just as important, it may not be and it need not be. These scrappy or unstable or ill-conceived or schismatic preference structures (where each 'or' signifies 'and/or') might for all we know constitute a majority of such phenomena in the world. Neat common value-systems, one suspects, are in a distinct if not a potentially extinct minority.

There are some societies, it goes without saying, where the preference structures of significant groups are systematically ignored. This is a death-blow, it seems to me, for the functionalist use of value-sharing, though it is not quite so serious for the notion of preference structures. In a society that kept slaves and survived, it is only possible to maintain a belief in a common value-system shared by all members

* Indeed, we typically characterize certain strategically placed social groups in this way.

by excluding the slaves, or by arguing that in their own way the slaves shared some utterly fundamental value-orientation with their masters. This defence is not only artificial but repulsive, and perhaps a little less repulsive but equally as artificial when used with reference to economically or otherwise exploited groups in the modern world.

The defence of preference structures as socially necessary items in a slave or otherwise exploitative society stems from the premise that no relationship is so coercive that there are no elements of co-operation, even on the most unequal terms, involved in it. The slave and the master must take each other's preferences into account for a relationship to be possible and for social life to persist. There is a continuum stretching from maximum injustice, where almost all of the preferences of one party and almost none of the other party are taken into account, to maximum justice, where each party equally takes the other's preferences into account. There is no need to point out the parallels between this line of reasoning and, for example, collective bargaining in industry, the art of diplomacy in international relations, 'swapping behaviour' in children, and other arenas of social interaction. The difference, even more instructive than the parallel, is that I am not discussing bargaining or games theory or exchange in social life, but the fact as I conceive it that society is impossible without the preferences of people in groups being taken into account by those in other and the same groups. Further, I hold that justice prevails insofar as this process is carried out, and injustice occurs when we neglect other people's preference structures.

It should now be clear that the functionalist theory of stratification explains to some extent why stratification and its attendant, nay necessary, inequalities persist and how this aspect of societies works; it should also be clear that stratification could not occupy a place in any list of the requisites of social life. Simply, this type of social arrangement, stratification where rewards correspond to 'functional importance' (assuming for the moment that this latter term is unambiguous), might satisfy the preference structures of certain groups at certain times, and again it might not. It is the fact that preferences are taken into account to a greater or lesser extent that in this context makes social life possible, and not any particular consequences of some set of preferences. The Functionalists would have us believe that certain preferences, and the value-systems that harbour them, are necessary for society to survive. My contention, to reiterate, is that in order to keep chaos from the door and prevent the dreaded war of all against all, men need not have the same preferences, far less share them in the form of common value-systems, but that preference structures must be taken into account, whether common or widely disparate, and for whatever reasons ideologically feasible at the time in question. I mean by this that coercion and continual brute force is neither convenient nor efficient, especially if spatially and/or temporally extended, and so one often finds reasons of one sort or another for taking others' preferences into account rather than not.

An interesting illustration of this is the development of the informal structures of bureaucracies and of most organizations.[9] Formal structures are almost always unable to plan for the variety of people's preferences, especially where they are apt to change suddenly, and so the informal structures that grow up, whether encouraged or not, may be seen as arrangements to meet this requisite of preferences. It would be instructive to examine the relations between the central command and the local activities in the great empires and in modern states in this light.

Having introduced the list of individual and social needs that must be satisfied if social life is to be possible, it remains for me to draw the ethical implications, that construct what I have termed the *sociological ethic*, from it. Let me repeat that I do not consider ethics, the study and prescription/proscription of moral conduct, to require utter certainty or complete verification. As I have commented, the criteria of scientific plausibility have been traditionally so much less stringent than those of moral plausibility that moral and social philosophers are continually castigated by themselves as well as by others for not producing impossible goods. If a sociological ethic seems plausible in form and in its suggested substance, if it can clarify the moral choices open to men in society and if it can make sensible and workable statements about the conduct that should ensure more justice, or whatever, rather than the lesser justice of alternative conduct, then it will be worthwhile. Its flexibility will guarantee that additions to our knowledge and sophistications of our future reasoning will not go unnoticed. A sociological ethic will be, in short, a potentially progressive activity.

The sociological ethic is intended to provide a framework for decision-making, specifically the making of moral judgments in the context of an on-going society. In the first instance, and as a guiding principle, the survival of human society is taken to be morally worthy in itself, with the proviso that men will decide what will count as 'human society' as opposed to 'inhuman society'. Thus, although my argument has similarities to what has been crudely termed a survival ethic, it differs in the critical respect that not all societies or forms of social organization are considered to be worth saving. A second assumption (unproved but not without strong support from several sources) is that social justice, mainly a matter of taking other people's preferences into account when social arrangements are being made, is on balance the most satisfactory basis of social organization. This is not simply a weak suggestion that most people would wish this in the long run, or simply a claim that in most respects this would lead to more efficient or more convenient social life for the majority, though all of these factors seem to me to support my argument. The moral position that I am taking depends upon the view that these factors *are* relevant to what is right and what is wrong, and even more so in that they *do* help us to choose one moral judgment and the action that flows from it over another, as a morally better solution to a problem.[10] The problems are of course those that I have outlined in my classification of individual and social needs.

These needs, therefore, are conceived as goals or ends with positive moral value for which men strive in society. Perhaps it is more in the spirit of our times if the position is stated in negative terms: namely, that where these needs are not fulfilled then there is something morally wrong in the world, and societies so afflicted are morally regressive compared to societies not so afflicted. At a certain point, as I have argued, in the extreme case such morally and otherwise regressive or stagnant societies will fail to survive because individual and social needs have not been met. At the other extreme, progress persists as long as these needs continue to be met in increasingly more satisfactory ways.

The sociological ethic is based on the necessity of ensuring that the individual and social needs of human life are fulfilled, and that when a morally relevant decision has to be taken, when one is faced with a problem pertaining to social life, the morally preferable solution will be the one that contributes to the general end of the fulfilment of these needs, The interesting cases, where conflicting interests and contradictory preferences arise, would present insurmountable difficulties for an instrument whose maker claimed infallibility. I make no such claim for the sociological ethic. It is quite possible that for various reasons such a decision as to the lesser of two evils or the better of two goods might never be made with any degree of certainty. *What the sociological ethic does make possible is the choice between evils and goods, between what we have always known to be wrong and what we have always known to be right, but have never been able to claim for fear of offending the sacred canons of a logic that could never deal with the human complexities of social life.*

The guidelines for the sociological ethic thus correspond to the satisfactory solution of the prototypical problems of man in society, the individual and social needs of life. Generally speaking, anything that prevents people from having nutrition, sleep and shelter, and from developing stability of personality and cognition, is morally wrong. Likewise, anything inhibiting sufficient reproduction, communication, socialization, motivation and role differentiation, preferences and institutionalization, is morally wrong. It follows that those

198

things that encourage the satisfaction of these needs will be morally right.

This crude statement must be immediately qualified in a variety of ways. First, it is apparent that there is an optimum level of satisfaction for each of these needs—where does eating become gluttony; sleep become sloth; reproduction, over-population; motivation, unthinking obedience to authority; role differentiation, soul destroying specialization; and so on? The answers to these questions are not at present known and might indeed never be conclusively known, but there seems to be no reason why intensive and imaginative studies cannot help us to make up our minds about them. To dismiss this attitude as Utopian is to dismiss an important part of the work of the contemporary biological and social sciences.

Secondly, and more seriously, it must be admitted that some of these needs will and indeed do conflict. How are we to decide between them, especially in a situation where certain social and other commodities are in short supply? The short answer is that we simply cannot set out hard and fast rules for such choices. In each age there will be groups that will take these sorts of decisions upon themselves, whether they be small and closely-knit élites who ignore the preferences of the large part of their society, or groups coterminous with the society, each taking the preferences of the others along with its own in making such decisions. Once again let me state that final definitive answers, as in the explanatory nexus of the natural sciences, are never forthcoming. As our knowledge grows, and especially in sociology as we become more adept at seeing the unintended consequences of social action, we shall be increasingly better placed to resolve the difficulties presented by the conflict of needs. This brings me to a third point, an extension of the second, around which a great deal of controversy has occurred.

It will be recalled that my classification of needs distinguished the individual from the social, and the organically based from the derived (primary and secondary needs). The former, the case of individual and social needs, in one form or another has been the focus of social and political thought for many centuries. It is therefore only proper for me to comment on the ways in which the sociological ethic deals with this age-old dilemma. How do we decide between individual needs (or in a more recognizable version, individual rights) and social needs? This is sometimes posed in the form of an opposition between man and the state, society and its members or, in our own times, the struggle against bureaucracy.

As a special case of the possible conflicts between needs in general, this issue deserves special mention. The most convincing answer to this question, in theory, is that of Marx. He argued that moral progress would consist in the state of affairs where the interests of each coincided with the interests of all—where individual and social interests coincided.[11] This is not as opposed to my distinction between individual and social needs as might at first sight appear. Marx's point is not so much that individual and society will in this state have the *same* interests (or needs), but that it will be *in the interests* of each individual and of society at large that his interests and those of any and all other individuals should have their interests served (or needs satisfied). Thus, as far as the sociological ethic is concerned, we need not choose dogmatically between the individual need and the social need, but we must always be sensitive to each, until the day that their coincidence resolves the issue into a satisfactory synthesis. But even then there will still be individual and social needs, though men might in fact fail to perceive the distinction. A hint of this possible future development in social relationships is to be found in some recent works of the late Pitirim Sorokin, emanating from his studies on 'Creative Altruism'.[12]

These, it seems to me, are the most important qualifications that have to be made to the sociological ethic at this stage. I have not here reviewed any anthropological, sociological, historical or other data on moral codes or systems of ethics that actually now exist or have existed. This is not because I consider this information to be unimportant, indeed in the long run it is the *most* important item in any scientific study of ethics, but because I have here been concerned mainly with other aspects of the sociological ethic and individual and social needs. This whole approach to the problems of ethics, with its intended sociological bias, permanently stresses the relevance of what actually occurs in societies to the facts of moral progress and its determination. Moral progress, accordingly, is the recognition of these individual and social needs and the performance of social acts that enables them to be satisfied, or combats those things that are obstacles to their satisfaction.

To speak of moral progress in a particular society, therefore, is to find evidence that individual and social needs are being satisfied in ever more satisfactory ways—specifically that each need is taken into account and that none is being neglected.

The sociological ethic cannot be authoritarian. This is clear for both theoretical and empirical reasons. Theoretically, an authoritarian moral standard is one against which there is no appeal, let alone redress. But based as it is on the individual and social needs of human life, the only 'authority' that is involved is the authority of these needs, which includes the central social need of preference structures that I have discussed above. To consider the fulfilment of these needs as a dictate of an authoritarian moral code, one would have to argue that there were really no good reasons for the moral rule in human society, and further that we might expect men to object to it, if not now, then at another time and in another place.

The reasons I have given in the preceding pages are intended to persuade and not, obviously, to broadcast revealed doctrine. The very admitted flexibility of the sociological ethic and the complete acceptance of the possibility of changes in its formulations, that increases in our knowledge, our understanding and our powers of explanation might bring, are certain guarantees against moral authoritarianism.

The empirical reason, following on from my comment on the worth of the actual data of ethics, is that the sociological ethic must and does deal with a great variety of ethical codes and moral judgments. Some will be shown to be morally progressive and others to be morally regressive, but the diversity of morals *within* each category of judgment is so great that this surely renders any objection of ethical authoritarianism most unconvincing. This is the situation that necessitates the assumption that the sociological ethic must accommodate all viable social systems. Furthermore, the emphasis I have laid, contrary to Parsons, on the *contingency* of common and shared value systems, suggests that by means of the sociological ethic different moral conduct is not evaluated on the apparent differences we may see, but on its relations to the individual and social needs of human life with the qualifications acknowledged above.

Two points remain to be clarified in this context, namely the difference between human and inhuman society, and the fundamental conviction that the persistence of human society is morally commendable. Briefly, human society is morally better than inhuman society because there is more good in the former and because the former is more just. Inhuman society is the case where, as I have argued, injustice prevails and the preferences of some consistently ignore those of others. It is clear that the secondary social need, preferences, is of particular relevance for moral progress.

As with the task of showing that human society as defined is morally commendable, a task to which this whole endeavour is devoted, the task of showing that human society is morally superior to inhuman society rests on a commitment of faith. I have here been arguing that this faith requires strong reasons, and has them. Inhuman society is society in which no attempt is made to achieve progress in terms of the sociological ethic. Where the needs of the people are not being satisfied, society is to this extent inhuman.

The condemnation of some societies, past and present, as inhuman is of course a matter of degree, and indeed our standards of humaneness change in quite dramatic ways. Modern social science, as I claimed above, is not in a position to give definitive answers to questions, though some societies like Nazi Germany, Stalinist Russia and South Africa under *apartheid* are clearly inhuman, in

201

terms of the sociological ethic. This is not to say that certain elements of these condemned societies are not present in many other societies that would be characterized as human on the same criteria. The point is that, contrary to the opinion of some radical Marxists, the three inhuman societies mentioned above *are* qualitatively different from the bourgeois and social democracies of the contemporary world.

In the next chapter I shall go on to show how some of the requisites outlined in this chapter are specifically linked to certain spheres of progress. Some criticisms of progress will then be examined, and the sociological theory of progress outlined in the preceding chapters will be defended against them.

XII The sociological theory of progress and some criticisms

Some progress is innovational and some is not. The sociological ethic helps us to decide instances of progress in the context of morals. These are the twin pillars on which my sociological theory of progress is built. It is important to be clear that progress in different areas of social life may be morally relevant to different degrees and that although their interaction is of interest, so too is their independent operation. Thus, it is instructive to begin this synthesis by focusing on the different areas in society in which it is proper to speak of progress or regress. This is conveniently and usefully accomplished with respect to the classification of individual and social needs outlined above. I do not suggest that each need specified in that classification corresponds exactly to an area of possible progress, but it is not very difficult to link some of the needs with some areas of progress.

The organically based individual needs of human life, the provision of nutrition and shelter (and perhaps, though not usually, sleep) are often characterized by the term 'material progress'. It almost goes without saying that for perhaps the majority of people in the world the needs of nutrition and shelter, that is enough food and satisfactory housing, are simply not being fulfilled. It is with little exaggeration the greatest continuing tragedy of modern times that this should be so, and it is striking that much work in the social sciences can be condemned as utter unrealism for simply ignoring this fact. Here I can do no more than note it and yet again reiterate the intended relevance of this work for the sociology of development and as a contribution towards a framework within which some of these problems might be solved.

The secondary or derived individual need for stability of the personality suggests the progress of mental health. In an address to medical psychologists, the particular relevance of this issue for our times has been outlined: '. . . "mental health" is an emerging goal and a value for humanity of a kind comparable to the notions of "finding God", "salvation", "perfection", or "progress" which have inspired various eras of our history, as master-values which at the same time implied a way of life.'[1] While not sharing this view entirely, Dr Soddy and his colleagues, working through the World Federation on Mental Health,[2] give valuable information on how progress is to be made in satisfying this need.

Cognition as an individual need suggests the area of intellectual progress in a more sophisticated version. As man and society develop, more opportunities present themselves for conceiving the world, and of mastering the natural environment by means of science and technology. I do not wish to be coy about this matter. The whole burden of Part One of this study, tracing the history of the idea of progress and showing that a crucial change in it took place at the start of the nineteenth century in causal interdependence with the process of the institutionalization of science and technology, in a sense leads up to this point. To put it sharply and briefly, our historical experience implies that science and technology become identified with progress. This is the reason, of course, that I have found it necessary to distinguish innovational progress, the paradigm case of which is science and technology, from non-innovational progress. I shall go on to develop this theme below.

Closely linked to this is the primary social need of socialization, and educational progress. It is an instructive example of the interrelationships of these phenomena to point out that in a society characterized by the scientific mode of cognition, for its 'serious business' at any rate, socialization must introduce new members of the society into the rudiments of science or, more widely, rational appraisal; as this is a task outside the competence of large numbers of socializing agents, the educational system continues the process in the rather more specialized sectors.

Role differentiation, in its most important aspect, is usually taken to be related to economic and/or industrial progress, through the agency of specialization and training in specific skills which entails a certain division of labour. However, as I have argued previously, this does not imply social stratification or unequal rewards for the performance of different roles. The primary social need of motivation is relevant to this discussion. One could almost identify satisfaction of the *social* need of motivation with social progress, *per se*. This is so with respect to the integration of society, the goal that Parsons shares with Marx. Society on both accounts will be fully integrated to the extent that all its members feel fully a part of the social whole. I have shifted the emphasis from the Parsonian common value-system to the Marxist stress on the unity of individual and social

interests, or needs. In this latter case, the social problem of motivation would be assured of solution for, by definition, individuals
would want to do what was in the interests of their fellows, for it
would be in their own interests. There would be an autonomous
motivation to pursue the social good.

Communication, in an important sense, may be connected with
both scientific and artistic/aesthetic progress. For scientific progress
the link is obvious, for it is the ability to communicate facts and
theories about the world and men that transforms science into
scientific progress. In the context of progress in the arts and literature, it would be a special theory of aesthetics or criticism to claim
that progress in these fields depends on more satisfactory means of
communication. Professor E. Gombrich, in an essay on the idea of
progress in art, does not come to any firm conclusions, reserving
judgments on the considerable complexity of the field.[3]

Institutionalization occupies roughly the same ambiguous position
in my classification as in the others I have discussed, being something
of an organizing principle for the establishment of patterns of social
action for the satisfaction of any need. In a purely illustrative sense,
it may be regarded as the parallel secondary social need to the
secondary individual need of the stability of the personality. The
degree of institutionalization in a society, then, is metaphorically
analogous to the mental health of the individual, and is similarly
concerned with the organizing principles of levels of predictability,
defence mechanisms against stress. This notion derives from the
remarks of Parsons and his colleagues on the relations of pattern
maintenance and tension management, seen by them as a single
functional problem.[4] It should be added that just as personalities
can become too stable, rigid or inflexible, so too is there an optimum
level of institutionalization of any social institution in any society.
Concepts such as anomie and alienation mediate between the structural and the personality levels, and at least one recent sociologist
has, significantly, seen alienation as the concept diametrically
opposed to progress.[5]

Preferences, as has been made abundantly clear, refers to moral
progress and is thus relevant to each of the other areas.

Each of the individual and social needs that must be fulfilled for
social life to be possible at all, therefore, has one or more roughly
corresponding dimensions of progress linked to it. As I have argued,
these fundamental conditions of life in societies give us good reasons
for establishing a sociological ethic that will enable us in a great many
cases to judge whether one act is morally better than another or
worse than another, and so allow us to speak of progress or regress
in human affairs. The rule of thumb is that where an action contributes to the satisfaction of one or more of the individual or social

needs, then it constitutes progress in the relevant area or areas; where it frustrates any need, it does not do so. There is no reason to believe that the difficult and contentious cases will outnumber the simple and straightforward cases, under present world circumstances at any rate. However, there are bound to be many difficult cases, and indeed it can be plausibly argued that as there is more progress the probability of contentious cases will rise in so far as the more apparent social evils are eradicated.

The cases would fall into a few main types.* First there would be those in which a choice had to be made between two incompatible actions, each of which would tend to satisfy one particular need. Then the problem becomes that of deciding between needs rather than between actions, and a hierarchy of needs will often be set up in societies to deal with such problems. The distinction between non-innovational and innovational progress will be particularly relevant in this context, for it will very frequently be the case that a proposed innovational solution to a problem that has perennially been dealt with in a non-innovational fashion will present this type of quandary. As I mentioned above, I join Weber to the extent that, in the last resort, nothing that the sociologist or the moral philosopher can say will ultimately decide between the choice of innovational or non-innovational progress, though of course if a particular innovational solution to a problem satisfies more needs or the same need in a better fashion than non-innovational attempts, *ceteris paribus*, then the former will be morally preferred and the 'progressive' option. Where this is not clearly the case I have little advice to offer, except to reiterate the wise hope of Ginsberg that the social sciences will increasingly provide factual and theoretical material that will help men to ascertain more precisely what is the case.

The second main difficulty occurs in those cases where the needs of one group are opposed to the needs of another. I do not, of course, intend this in the sense that the *interests* of one are opposed to another, but in the sense that one group selects one or more individual or social needs as paramount, and another group makes a contrary selection. Situations such as this can become extremely complicated, especially where they relate to scarce resources. In general, some notion like 'balanced progress' might be fairly useful in order to ensure that progress is spread evenly throughout a particular society and its different groups. Perhaps this notion begs fewer questions than it raises. Let me remind the reader at this stage that in terms of what I have termed 'preference structures' the goal to which progress is directed is the coincidence of individual and social 'preferences', and in this utopian state such problems could not arise.[6]

---

* I deal here only with the theoretical possibilities of such difficulties.

The third type of contentious case is that where genuine disagreement exists as to the consequences of different solutions to some problems for human needs. This is in fact only a matter of degree for all states of affairs, given the now unassailable sociological role of the unintended and unrecognized consequences of social action. Some actions or solutions to problems, nevertheless, are very much more problematic than others, or at least they seem so after the event. For those that seem so before the event, the issue is much more severe. It is no accident that the place of the expert is vital in societies characterized by innovational progress. It is in such societies that such issues must frequently arise, for the introduction and diffusion of new things, processes and ideas will obviously generate more doubt than non-innovation, and the expert is the man to reduce or even to eradicate doubt.[7] Once again, the possible conflict between the innovational and the non-innovational modes of progress comes to the fore, though the type of difficulty I am discussing might also occur within each mode of progress. The guiding lines around this difficulty, as before, are to be found in careful study of each situation on its merits, primarily to discover whether or not the purported advantages of one solution will involve the eventual greater satisfaction or frustration of one or more human needs than the original or alternative solution. It is clear that proposed innovational solutions to certain problems will create other problems that may turn out to be more serious in terms of needs than those original problems rather less well solved by non-innovational means. A tragic example of this is where the reduction in infant mortality rates condemns children to eventual starvation in very poor countries.

Given the moral premise that I attempted to substantiate in the previous chapters, that progress consists in the satisfactory solution of problems of men in society and that satisfaction of needs, both individual and social, is the criterion of 'satisfactory' as here used, then we can begin to speak meaningfully about the problems of progress with which this study is concerned. Given the distinction between innovational and non-innovational progress, explicitly elaborated in Chapter VII, then we may extend our understanding to the major oppositions, not to say contradictions, of any theory of progress. For this purpose I shall examine the traditional criticisms of any theory of progress, such as might be found in a normal textbook on sociology or the social sciences,* some of which I have used

* That is, if it mentions 'progress' at all. A good number give no indication of the fact that the idea of progress as much as and probably more than any other single idea provided the initial and in many cases the subsequent framework for sociology. This tendency to ignore the socio-historical roots of current ideas is altogether deplorable, though some ideas fare better than others in this respect.

in the first part of my study to chastise the theories of others. The first and most common criticism of the idea or any theory of progress is, in the words of the author of a typically unsophisticated textbook: 'standards of progress are a matter of faith or belief, and . . . values are not the proper subject matter for objective scientific evaluation.'[8] The same sentiment is expressed by Ogburn and Nimkoff in their influential handbook. Distinguishing evolution from progress, they claim that the latter implies values and that 'for values, like taste, there is no measuring stick'.[9] Finally in one of the most sophisticated, learned and well-argued of recent introductions to sociology, Bierstedt comments that 'if progress means development in a desirable direction, then what seems desirable to some may seem undesirable to others . . . the concept had to be abandoned for sociological use'.[10]

My answer to these strictures should by now be abundantly clear. In the first place, in the largest choice between whole civilizations in the sense that the concepts and social life of the population at large are characterized by innovational or non-innovational solutions to problems, one cannot dogmatically prefer one style to the other as a moral choice. However, on the criterion of satisfying human needs, both individual and social, specific solutions to specific types of problems will often clearly impress themselves on the participants. Bell, Ogburn and Nimkoff, and Bierstedt cannot *really* mean that there is never any moral difference between giving people food and allowing them to starve to death, or that comfortable housing is in no way better than slums. They similarly cannot *really* doubt that the organization of social life is in some way morally preferable to chaos and/or a war of all against all. Yet these statements are precisely what they imply. I do not for a moment claim or even secretly expect that such statements will *always* hold good, or that there will not be many occasions on which men will argue over which of two courses of action is the better. But this is no reason whatsoever to surrender to despair, and to deny many things that seem to have a great weight of diverse evidence to support them.

The next common textbook criticism is to a large extent a derivative of the first. Here the critics complain that progress is confused with, and often smuggled in on the coat-tails of, the notion of evolution. Bierstedt puts this case very cogently in the passage following the one I quoted above, which describes the abandonment of the idea of progress.

In the process the concept of evolution, in so far as it is applied to society or to history, was also abandoned. . . . There is reason to believe, however, that this second abandonment was perhaps a little hasty and that certain changes do occur in both groups and societies, as they grow or age, which can reasonably be analysed as evolutionary.[11]

MacIver and Page, in one of the most widely-used introductions to sociology ever written, argue that whereas evolution can be demonstrated with certainty, progress cannot. Evolution they define in terms of continuity and direction of social change, whereas progress is evolution to an ideally determined final destination.[12] They accuse Comte, Spencer, Ward, Giddings and Hobhouse of confusing the two concepts and thereby falling short of the scientific ideal in their respective analyses.[13]

The same sentiment emerges from a guide to social institutions: 'Progress implies a movement toward given goals, ordinarily regarded as advancement or improvement. But institutional development may be and often is in any direction, progressive or regressive, or perhaps in no clear direction at all.'[14] Ginsberg, as mentioned in previous chapters, has distinguished clearly between development, evolution and progress, and there is now no excuse for confusing these terms. There is, however, good reason to re-examine the relations between evolution and progress in the light of my general argument, especially with respect to man's part in all of this.

One of the sometimes implicit and sometimes explicit assumptions of the sociological theory of progress is what might be termed 'the axiom of sociological voluntarism'. Voluntarism has had a bad name recently in some sections of the sociological world, partly because of the often paradoxical development of the thought of Talcott Parsons, from his 'voluntaristic theory of action' of the late 1930s to the social behaviourism/social determinism of the 1950s, and his cybernetic model of action of recent years.[15] A further complication is that provided by the current battle between the methodological individualists and the methodological collectivists,* and as I have taken the side of the spiritualists in this matter, and yet wish to espouse some form of voluntarism, my argument is needful of a dialectical turn. This last remark is not simply flippant, for I firmly hold that Marxist writers, more and more successfully than any others, have faced up to this problem seriously. It is here too that I would reintroduce the idea that oppositional rather than dialectical (especially triad-style) thinking will best deal with this issue, as in my discussion of Hegel in Part One. Put briefly, as I have already indicated, the methodological issue is one where persuasive argument rather than deductive demonstration is the order of the day.

There is naturally an enormous pressure on anyone concerned

---

* Or 'sociological spiritualists' as Peristiany calls them in his introduction to Durkheim's *Sociology and Philosophy* (London: Cohen and West, 1963 [trans. by D. Pocock], p. vii).

with these problems to maintain the autonomy of man and the freedom of human action, so the individualists on the whole have an easier time than their opponents. Few social thinkers, though there have been some, have denied man any freedom of choice in any situations, and most social, cultural, economic, geographical or theological determinists have left at least some loopholes through which man can freely clamber and exercise his will, however limited.[16] Many examples of oppositional thinking occur in this context, in the sense that actual contradictions, in the way in which the world operates or in the ways in which man operates in the world, are expressed and appreciated rather than glibly resolved.

Comte did make a serious attempt to come to grips with sociological voluntarism. As will be recalled, Comte as much as anyone conceived of progress as the natural evolution of man's thought and of his affairs. What is important here and what links his theory of progress to the methodological question is the addition of a higher field of study than those originally proposed, to the hierarchy of the sciences. This is the moral science (ethics), a late addition that transcended sociology.[17] The significance of ethics is that it appears to modify the sociological determinism of the original scheme and to give man once more the possibility of semi-autonomous action. But obviously we cannot forget the prior claim of the 'queen of the sciences' as the prime framework for social explanation, and so Comte displays an element of oppositional thinking on this issue.*

The point to be noted here is that the evolutionary interpretation of progress, in the sense of gradual unfolding of latent potential (progress through order in Comtean terms), gives rather less scope to the free choices of the individual or of groups, and rather more to a deterministic flow of history. Durkheim too comes up against difficulties in this connection, and as Ginsberg has indicated[18] the ethics of Durkheim and his general sociology and methodology are basically incompatible. But Ginsberg intends his analysis as a criticism of Durkheim, whereas I should consider it an example of basic theoretical honesty—the clash and interaction between sociologist and man that necessitates oppositional thinking if we are to

---

* Another writer who has drawn this conclusion from a study of Comte is McQuilkin DeGrange in *The Nature and Elements of Sociology* (New Haven: Yale University Press, 1953, ch. 8). This is an altogether remarkable textbook, written explicitly from Comte and Sumner. It must be the only textbook of its period from America to mention Weber only once, and to make no mention at all of Sorokin, Parsons or Merton, to mention only a few of the ignored leaders of the field. I must add that I am not entirely persuaded by DeGrange's view of Comte's addition of ethics, though I am obviously not wholly opposed to it. There would seem to me to be a strong element of physiological determinism in Comte's account of ethics—in parts it reads almost like a proto-behaviourist moral theory—though, as I have argued, the overall impression is 'oppositional'.

understand the social world. Plekhanov, in his essay 'The Place of the Individual in History',[19] argues in a dialectical (or oppositional) fashion to the same ends as Comte, Durkheim and the Marxist writers in general. That modern sociology is at last beginning to catch up is suggested by the recent study of Berger and Luckmann on an everyday sociology of knowledge. They quote Durkheim's maxim that social facts are things, along with Weber's insistence on the subjective meaning-complex of action in society and history. They continue:

> These two statements are not contradictory. Society does indeed possess objective facticity. And society is indeed built up by activity that expresses subjective meaning. . . . It is precisely the dual character of society in terms of objective facticity *and* subjective meaning that makes its 'reality *sui generis*', to use another key term of Durkheim's.[20]

It is incorrect, thus, to consider this situation as in need of resolution, for if we employ oppositional thinking and, as it were, learn to live with this dual character of society, then we shall be true to ourselves as men and as students of social life and thought.

In studying progress, therefore, it is instructive to look at the reasons that have led writers to confuse and/or identify it with evolution in these terms. Where the identification is made, and especially where social evolution is conceived as somehow a part of or analogous to organic evolution, then progress tends to emerge as an automatic aspect of social change, and not as a state that men can make or spoil for themselves. My emphasis on sociological voluntarism, intending to indicate that within certain limits men can make or spoil progress for themselves, points to the way in which social evolution differs or can differ from organic evolution.

In so far as the aspirations of men are taken to be important to any social change, though not of course the only important factor involved, and in so far as men will act to satisfy not only their individual needs but also social needs, there *must* be room for this sociological voluntarism. Again, the dimension of 'preference structure' plays an important role. Organic evolution takes little notice of preferences, whereas the notion of progress that I am developing is very much bound up with them. Social evolution on the other hand, comparable only in a metaphorical sense with organic evolution[21] if it is understood in terms of sociological voluntarism, suggests one type of progress. Where social evolution implies that men, within limits, may control the ways in which their society evolves, if conscious choice has some part to play in the process of change and if this change is judged to be more or less morally commendable on some value-standard, then we are justified in speaking of progress or regress. If we consider evolution in this sense and contrast it to revolution, then it is clear that these convey two different ideas of progress.

This special though not at all unusual sense of evolution suggests a notion of non-innovational progress, progress based on the unfolding of potentialities and not on the construction and diffusion of new ideas, things and processes. In the context of problem-solving, non-innovational progress in terms of evolutionary change does not look to innovations to solve problems, be they old or new problems.

The use of revolution in this context is not entirely idiosyncratic either, though I am extending a point made by many sociologists. The innovator as a rebel[22] or a deviant[23] is a fairly well-known figure in the literature, and it is a short step from here to the label of revolutionary progress. Indeed, the novelty of original conceptions, the scope and rate of change envisaged, and the sweeping attitude towards problems, have always characterized the revolutionary (at least before if not after the revolution). These characteristics are, of course, the hallmarks of what I have termed innovational progress.

Bierstedt, as quoted above, is quite correct in bemoaning the fact that evolution has tended to be abandoned along with progress,* but I should argue that new thinking on both evolution *and* progress might find a place in a revitalized and socially relevant sociology.

The third criticism of progress typically found in introductory textbooks in the social sciences is in fact more of an explanation and a plea than a proper criticism. This is that progress is an ideology and must be judged as such, and perhaps utilized as such. Even the positivistic writer, with whose curt disclaimer of progress I began this section of the discussion, admits that 'the idea of what constitutes progress is an important force in bringing about and directing change within a particular society'[24] (italics in original). Ogburn and Nimkoff similarly remark that 'conceptions of progress, like general ethical principles, are of great value'.[25]

Summing up a very common attitude to progress, as Part One of this study had abundantly documented, Kimball Young has exclaimed: 'If made less utopian and mystical and more practical, the doctrine of progress might become a fighting faith, a slogan or even a *principle* and a *tool* to be used in tackling problems of a given time and place.'[26] MacIver and Page are even more definite, and in my

---

* This is a rather premature judgment, however. In the writings of Ginsberg and MacRae (amongst others), the notion of social evolution is strongly defended, and as both of these point out, and demonstrate, it still has some vitality. As I have remarked above, even Parsons has returned to it. The *coup de grâce*, however, is that Professor Popper, in his lecture, 'Of Clouds and Clocks' (1966), nobly admits that there might be something to social evolution after all. Nevertheless, for the vast majority of professional social scientists, Bierstedt's comment holds true.

opinion with every good reason. After a notably subtle and careful analysis of the problems that progress holds for the sociologist as a man of science, they conclude powerfully by claiming that 'as human beings we cannot get rid of the *concept* of progress'.[27]

This is, of course, the basic position of my work that, as I argued with respect to philosophies of history, social life involves some notion of progress. Even more clearly, the notion of progress is inevitably linked to the problem-solving nature of man within the context of social morality. MacIver and Page therefore take progress one step beyond ideology, as I would wish to do, and place it in the centre of the human condition. As they very correctly point out, the reality of progress may or may not be true, but that men aspire to progress, whether mistakenly or not, is in general the case.

The analysis of Bottomore straddles the issue of progress as an ideology, and is the final textbook criticism of progress I shall examine. This is the point that progress runs into insurmountable problems in its application to the modern world, especially that part of it that is affluent. Bottomore argues cogently that Marxism, the embodiment of progress as an ideology, is currently receiving more support from the underdeveloped part of the world than from the developed part. This is not very difficult to understand, says Bottomore, in terms of

the uncertainty about what ends are worthwhile in societies which already enjoy high standards of living . . . [for] . . . once the major social evils of ignorance, poverty, and oppression have been largely overcome, the ends and means of progress become more complex and less easy to determine.[28]

The argument around progress as an ideology is best seen as a consequence of the process linking the great nineteenth-century theories of progress to the institutionalization of science and the corollary growth of scientific organization. The twentieth century heralded what has been termed the further 'empiricization' of progress. Therefore, progress as an ideology is a version of science as an ideology, and they are almost interchangeable. This is to equate progress *per se* with innovational progress, in the terms of my argument. MacIver and Page provide the balance-wheel: men generally have no choice but to operate on the possibility of progress, though in reality progress is another matter—in theory, too. Bottomore has himself, in an unpublished thesis, subjected Marxism as a theory of progress to critical scrutiny and has found it inadequate.[29] Theories of progress, like most if not all other social theories, have greater or lesser elements of ideology in them.

What I have tried to do is to provide the opportunity of comparing different styles of progress and, more especially, to show that pro-

gress is most relevant to specific solutions of specific problem complexes. The sociological ethic is precisely an attempt to show this
sociological theory of progress in a non-ideological light, in so far as
it focuses on what is common to all men and all societies. The
individual and social needs of human life, and my list may be
modified at any time, are common to man as social beings and to
societies as human societies. If it is acceptable as an inventory as it is
set out, then it can be ideological only in contrast to beings that are
non-human, in form or intent. Thus, I have suggested a distinction
between human and inhuman or non-human society with this in
mind. This theory of progress will indeed seem ideological to those
who would destroy or remake much that is morally commendable in
social life.

The final point in this connection is the notion that progress
becomes problematic only in the modern world. W. Sprott argues
that this is so because of the great power of destruction controlled
by the few, the blaze of publicity that has replaced the formerly
private and isolated acts of the many and, what he terms, 'the moral
problems of a shrinking world'.[30] Howard Odum, fully conscious of
the dilemmas of technological civilization, though perhaps somewhat
over-dramatic, asks the significant question: What new things should
not survive? What shall it profit to gain a world of civilization and to
lose the folk-soul?[31] There is no need to reiterate the familiar
gemeinschaft-gesselschaft dichotomy, never absent from sociology
since Tönnies wrote his major work on the subject. Its role in this
controversy is plain.

It is here that the category of non-innovational progress appears
to me to be particularly useful. One need not necessarily accept every
aspect of technological society if one is to be 'progressive'. In the
same way, a preference for 'folk-society' in many of its aspects need
not commit one to all of its aspects. Innovational progress and non-
innovational progress can and do co-exist in the same society, and
the 'best' solutions to all the problems men face are no doubt mixed.
The sociological ethic directs us to judge problems or problem-
complexes on their merits; it is an ethic because it does guide moral
decisions and it is sociological because it does take every account of
the problems and the consequences of varying attempts to solve
them for men in society. There can be no justification whatsoever, on
my account, for deciding on innovational or non-innovational
solutions, one to the exclusion of the other, for *all* problems. Some
types of problems have been typically solved on a non-innovational
and others on an innovational basis, and there is little doubt that
excellent *a priori* reasons can be found for each. This is not to suggest
a politics of contingency or that there is no principle that informs
what I have been saying. The principle is that although it is realized

that in some cases the choice between innovational and non-innovational progress will not ultimately be amenable to the type of analysis that I have been pursuing, in general the contribution of solutions to the satisfaction of individual and social human needs will be the deciding factor in whether or not a particular piece of social action is progress.

Bottomore places sociology in the centre of this concern, as I have tried to do. He sees a necessary connection between sociology and progress: 'as a discipline,' he asserts, sociology 'must be justified in part by the contribution which it can make to human progress.'[32] It is difficult for the sociologist not to sound immodest in this context, and immodesty is perhaps a lesser fault than paternalism. As always, it rests with the varieties and persuasiveness of *reasons* for a stated position, and the dispositions of the relevant community to which the arguments are directed, for the result of any serious non-violent dispute. The paternalist will not demean himself to give many, or any, reasons for his dictates—the sociologist must. But there is a limit to which reasons and reasoning can go, and the sociological ethic is precisely an attempt to argue that it is not logical analysis itself but sociology that sets the limit. In his book, *The Place of Reason in Ethics*, Toulmin makes the not dissimilar point in answer to a reported criticism of Bertrand Russell that Toulmin's account of ethics 'would not have convinced Hitler', by replying, 'but whoever supposed that it should? We do not prescribe logic as a treatment for lunacy, or expect philosophers to produce panaceas for psychopaths.'[33] The great danger in the form in which Toulmin expresses this view, which I generally support, is that it places the onus of deciding who are the lunatics and who are the psychopaths on someone, unnamed, or society, unspecified. But this takes us back to the question of the moral desirability of social life, an assumption of this study, rather than in Toulmin's format, to the philosopher-king (or Royal Commissioner).[34]

The basis of this analysis of progress is to discover what are the requisites of social life, individual and social, while assuming that their fulfilment is morally commendable. The list of requisites given in the last chapter is corrigible, and is to a large extent a function of our knowledge at this stage of the development of the socially-relevant studies. That social life, the continuity of *human* society, is morally commendable is an *a priori* judgment; it is a limit of our reason.*

* In a strange sense it is an *a priori* synthetic judgment for I am only too conscious that the *fact* of the potential goodness of life might be largely conditioned by the lucky chance of having been born in the affluent West. One's experiences of life, and especially the sure knowledge that the majority of human beings are underfed and underprivileged in many ways, might even create this moral position and not simply reinforce it.

That human society is morally commendable is the link between innovational and non-innovational progress, for they are both styles of progress. The differences between them are only as important as the fact that they both portray man in society as a problem-solving being. Sprott, Odum, Bottomore and others are basically correct in considering that progress is particularly problematic for modern, advanced industrial societies. The reason is that 'progress' as used by these writers means 'innovational progress', and that this is the style of progress of such societies. But this is incomplete, as I have argued at length, for non-innovational progress must be considered too. If it is, we do not find ourselves in the ludicrous state of affairs of having to condemn certain 'progress'.[35] With the two types of progress at our command, 'condemning' one may 'assert' the other.

In the next chapter I shall turn from the general use of the sociological theory of progress to a specific application of it. As has been argued throughout this book, science and technology occupy a particularly strategic place in any discussion of progress, especially with respect to the development of modern society. Some important problems concerning the role of science and technology in society will therefore be discussed in the context of the sociological theory of progress.

XIII Progress and some problems of the sociology of science

Science has always had a special place at the banquet of progress and many would argue that it provides the main dish. In the past two centuries, as I have previously pointed out, the progress of science and technology has come to be identified for many as a measure of progress *per se*. Indeed, this study may be seen partly as an attempt to expose this position and to correct it where it has erred.

Two of the major problem-complexes of science and technology in modern societies seem to demonstrate this point. These are (1) what has recently and somewhat sensationally been termed 'the biological time-bomb'; and (2) the 'space race'. These problem-complexes throw up a whole host of specific problems and some of these will be discussed with a view to showing how the sociological theory of progress elaborated in the preceding chapters can suggest answers to the problems. These solutions will, of course, represent progress in the context involved. This progress will be classified as either innovational or non-innovational, depending on the circumstances, and it is important to make explicit a point that has lain largely implicit in all that has gone before. This refers to the difference between progress within the institutional spheres of social life, scientific progress, political progress and so one, and the way in which progress within these spheres is related to innovational and non-innovational progress in society. Various solutions to problems can be found within and among these spheres, but it is in the context of innovational and non-innovational progress as judged on the basis of the sociological ethic that *progress*, in my sense of the term, occurs.[1]

The biological time-bomb
There is more than a current suggestion that the present half-century will prove to be as notable for the spectacular advance of human

biology as was the last for physics. And, in at least one very real sense, the impact of the biological revolution on individual and social life may turn out to be the greater and to pose more problems of a *personal* nature than the previous revolution in physics.* Some recent semi-popular books and some recent medical events have sparked off an interest and an apprehension in lay circles that testifies to this view. I am not, of course, competent to discuss the technical aspects of any problem of human biology and no overall theory of progress could hope to do this in each field in which it had to guide judgments. What can be done, however, is to weigh up the problems of the relevant areas as they might affect social and individual life, their proposed scientific solutions, *their* consequences for man in society, and the consequences of solving the original problem some other way, and/or of redefining the original problem. This weighing up is accomplished in terms of the satisfaction or frustration of the individual and social needs of human society. Solutions may be innovational, on the basis of the perceived novelty and the impact on the social structure, or non-innovational.

Let me begin with a fairly general problem of science with special reference to human biology. It has been recently and influentially expressed by Sir Macfarlane Burnet, the man who shared a 1960 Nobel Prize with Sir Peter Medawar for work in immunology. Basically, Burnet sets out to challenge the seemingly insatiable curiosity of the biologist, in particular of the geneticist, and he suggests that there might be things that are better left alone.[2] For example, Burnet indicates the enormous danger of producing micro-organisms in the laboratory whose properties are not known and, worse, whose uncontrollable effects might prove to be catastrophic. As Gordon Rattray Taylor points out in the book that gives this discussion its heading, Burnet is by no means alone in these fears and misgivings. Taylor cites, amongst others, Lederberg, Bentley Glass, Salvador Luria and Thorpe, as leading biologists who have also expressed similar feelings.[3]

It is important to distinguish the scientific from the social consequences of such work. Comments on these consequences will therefore be extremely interesting in determining what notion of progress is used by the scientist. For Burnet, the answer is quite remarkable. He is reported, shortly after the publication of his *Lancet* article and on hearing the comments of some colleagues, to have been 'just as rigorous in his approach to the subject. He certainly did not advocate withholding financial support from molecular biology or anything like that, but "the results from molecular biology immediately

---

* See, for example, the headline in the London *Evening Standard*, 24 November 1969: 'Genetic "Bomb" Fears Grow'.

applicable to human affairs will be bad rather than good," he said firmly.'[4]

That this opinion appears to contradict the spirit of the original article is quite clear. To John Kendrew, another Nobel prize-winner, this implication also seems clear for, as he is quoted as saying: 'Of course there are dangers in acquiring new knowledge . . . but to suggest this as a reason for not trying to acquire it, would be to deny the validity of human endeavour to find out more about man and his environment.'[5] It is only in the case of the particular problem that this issue can be satisfactorily resolved and the road to progress for man in society indicated. This is obvious, for we can neither dogmatically call a moratorium on all work in a particular field, nor dogmatically agree with Kendrew's implication that *any* experiment is justified by 'the validity of human endeavour to find out more about man and his environment'. There are no doubt scientists who would be most interested to find out the effects of a full-scale nuclear holocaust on flora, fauna and man. This burning curiosity does not itself justify the necessary and simple experiment.

One specific problem is that of how to manipulate genetic materials so as to control certain factors in matured organisms or, more popularly, to make babies to order, and to ensure that they grow into adults with predictable and predicted characteristics. It is difficult for the non-specialist and almost impossible for the non-biologist to understand fully the significance of these and related problems, and even more, to assess the importance of widely hailed experimental and/or theoretical breakthroughs. For example, the work of Dr Teh Ping Lin at the University of California was reported at the beginning of 1966 by one science columnist who headlined his account: 'A New Breed of Men?'. Dr Teh had, by means of micro-injection techniques, made possible 'rigorously controlled study of developments and genetic effects. . . . It might, in time, lead to the possibility of deliberately manipulating foetal developments so that a predetermined end product is obtained.'[6] This, and the maturation of human embryos outside a particular female womb, artificial inovulation, is not apparently just around the laboratory corner, but certainly in the foreseeable future. These and similar possibilities are discussed in recent works based on 'scientific speculation and forecasting' by Hermann Kahn and others.[7]

Another move in the same game, that of exposing to the public the possible consequences of what scientists are doing, was played out in the correspondence columns of *The Times* in December of 1967. The conjuncture of two events (a television programme, 'Assault on Life', showing certain biological experiments, and some advances by three American molecular biologists working on 'the activating of D.N.A.' and picked up by President Johnson as a major

219

step in the direction of creating life) stimulated a spate of letters on the responsibility of the scientist. A rather shocked Mrs S. Harrison (in a letter published on 14 December) condemned 'the deeply immoral attitude' of scientists conducting biological experiments 'solely to satisfy their curiosity'. On 20 December Professor Waddington, who had been involved in the television programme in question, and G. Rattray Taylor (his book mentioned above two months from release) rushed to defend biology and by extension scientific experimentation.

Waddington rejects Mrs Harrison's charge of 'irresponsibility' and, rather weakly, claims that few people will disagree with him, because funds for these experiments are administered by 'level-headed officials' who scrutinize all research plans 'to ascertain that they offer real possibilities for improving our understanding of . . . human ills'. Waddington goes on to make the point that it might not be possible to cure cancer, for instance, without at the same time providing knowledge which might lead to 'most unpleasant' things, and that the International Union of Biological Sciences had been set up to 'work out some effective form of world forum, or warning system'. He ends his letter by making the interesting suggestion that in biology, as in atomic energy, there will be benefits as well as dangers, but that in the latter the dangers came first whereas in the former the benefits come first. This theme requires development, but from Professor Waddington, and not from me.*

Taylor similarly castigates those who see science as irresponsible but feels that the television programme misled Mrs Harrison. 'Of course,' he admits reassuringly, 'all knowledge can be misapplied.' The last paragraph of his letter bears quoting in full:

> The moral is not that research should be stopped but that society should consider whether to make use of research results and if so how. Several scientists, notably the late Lord Brain and, in the United States, Professor Joshua Lederberg, have pointed out the dangers of the misuse of biological discoveries. Society has not so far heeded their warning: it is imperative that bodies now be formed to consider these researches and recommend public policies, preferably on an internal basis.

Taylor is very difficult to pin down on any issue in his book. His discussion of the unknown dangers of as yet undiscovered viruses, the problem adduced by Burnet which Taylor labels the 'Promethean Situation',[8] would seem to make nonsense of the apparently sensible

---

* Is it simply mischievous to remind the reader of Waddington's previous appearance in this production? As a leading light in the school of evolutionary ethics a generation ago he argued that science generally progressed and took society with it.

proposal from his letter to *The Times* that the problem is whether and how to make use of research results. If the result of some future research is the spread of some epidemic disease then the principle rather loses its point. (As we are not able even to control, let alone eradicate, some major communicable diseases about which we know a great deal, this seems to be a *serious* issue, even if it is improbable. Helminthic infections [worms] were estimated for 1963 at a rate of 1·1 infections for every man, woman, and child on earth, from about 2·1 in Africa to 0·3 in North America.)[9] Similarly, altering genetic material, according to the caveats of some very influential biologists, holds like perils. In a generally sympathetic review of *The Biological Time-Bomb*, Anthony Storr comments: 'I share Mr. Taylor's alarm that the human race might be overwhelmed by an epidemic disease against which it has no protection.'*[10]

But Taylor merely reports and does not himself show such alarm, though Storr might be forgiven for thinking that he does. For if Taylor meant what he said in his letter to *The Times*, written without doubt after his researches had uncovered the risks of modern biology, then alarm is too mild a term to describe his feelings if he were consistent. But he like Burnet before has found it impossible to be consistent in this context when to be so would threaten the never-ending and apparently unstoppable march of science that will, on most sober assessment, destroy man sooner or later.

In a discursive fashion I have tried to put this problem-complex of biology in perspective, and resisted the temptation to wrench it out of its setting and present it as a clear-cut issue. The problem of altering genetic material and breeding in and out certain human characteristics in order to control the physiological and the psychological properties of human adults is a special case of the general problem of weighing up the expected and unexpected scientific and extra-scientific consequences of particular solutions.

As in all such matters, the first question must be: what is the problem? In this case, the problem is, for example, what is the best way to deal with a sex-linked disease? If the best solution that the medical biologist can furnish is to control it genetically and the only consequences of this solution the condition that certain women will be precluded from having, say, female offspring, then (to be pedantic here) on the basis of the satisfaction of human needs this solution

---

* Compare this review with that of Dennis Potter in *The Times*, 27 April 1968, as an example of how the assured and confident medical-scientist (Storr) and the rather nervous, swingeing layman (Potter) react to this type of material. Potter concludes his review thus: 'And in the meantime, perhaps, those revolutionary biologists might do something about the common cold. Or shall we yet reach the comedy of a two-headed man with both his noses streaming? There is something peculiarly, perversely reassuring about such a thought.'

appears to be the most satisfactory. Controlling the disease in this way is thus an incident of progress—innovational progress in societies where this type of solution represents a new departure and where it has a maximum impact on the relevant population.

Let us now take a difficult problem, one that refers to the controversial alteration of a human faculty, rather than the obvious decrease of an unwanted characteristic. I refer to the situation implied in the above problem, namely the sex-determination of children before birth. The problem is: how can we have boys when we want boys, and girls when we want girls? There are of course a great variety of what could be termed non-innovational solutions to this problem in terms of such proto-magical variables as position during intercourse; types of food and drink consumed before, during or after the act; concentration; and even ritual incantations. The birth rate, as is well known, is about evenly divided between males and females, with the result that most people are mostly contented, and no doubt the rate of correct prediction is one that would make many social scientists rather pleased if attained in *their* work. The innovational solution is one that is well under way, if we are to believe the biologists. The manifest, expected and intended consequences of this innovational solution are, on the first level, that parents will have the means of choosing the sex of their offspring, and societies will have the possibility of so ordering this information as to be able to plan in a more informed manner, for the future provision of educational, welfare and other facilities. Societies could of course make similar arrangements now or at any time past by the simple expedient of selective infant 'mortality', and indeed many societies through choice or necessity have done so for a variety of reasons.[11] But infanticide, apart from being socially wasteful and often individually painful to a high degree, offends the moral feelings of most moderns. If we wish to have control over the sex of our children, then the biological solution of discovering the essential genetic difference between male and female and using this information to satisfy the wishes of parents would appear to be a far more satisfactory solution than infanticide, for the reasons just stated.

If we wish to control the sex of our children, then the biological solution is undeniably more satisfactory than infanticide, whether it is considered innovational or non-innovational progress. In terms of the sociological ethic, *if* we want to control sex then given that the choice is between some form of infanticide or some efficient biological solution the latter clearly satisfies human needs, individual and social, better than the former.

The more difficult question, and one that will surely be asked if and when we arrive at the biological possibility of sex-determination (probably rather soon—a conservative estimate would place it just in the twentieth century),[12] is, do we want to control for sex in this or any other way? Now we are confronted with the issue of what was previously referred to as 'the redefinition of problems'. And this is also a very important part of the activity and theory of progress, for the sociological ethic gives us some criteria on which to judge at least the relative merits of problems as well as of their solutions.

This can be illustrated obliquely by the argument that if the probable consequences of the solution of a particular problem, in science, politics, health, personal relationships or any other area, serve to frustrate individual and social needs *more* than the original problem, then serious consideration must be given to the view that the problem itself must be redefined. At this juncture there often occurs a curious interplay between innovational and non-innovational solutions.

The sex-determination problem, involving preferences rather than any other individual or social need on the simplest level of what parents want, nevertheless could become an explosive social issue if, for example, too few females were being chosen thus creating a shortage of potential mothers, or too few males thus creating a shortage of, say, production workers. In fact, as these last examples show, such problems seem less problematic in industrially advanced societies, but no doubt other unwanted consequences of a largely unbalanced sexual distribution would manifest themselves. This might not happen, as it might not happen that the world will be destroyed by an uncontrollable epidemic as Burnet and others fear, but there surely must be stated reasons why we should not militate for its prevention. The virologists, especially those engaged in military 'defence' work, at Fort Detrick in the United States and Porton Down in England to mention only some of those that have come under criticism recently, rarely offer justifications of their work,[13] and until more information is released it is not possible to pass a reasoned judgment.

Those who wish to market the skill of sex-control of children must justify the actions of research and dissemination of this knowledge on at least two counts. First, it accords with the preferences of many people, and second, it will not interfere with the preferences or any other needs of more people. In this case, this information is not available, and one might be forgiven for being sceptical and suggesting that in the main this knowledge and ability might best be kept for special cases like the control of certain diseases, rather than be given or more likely sold over the counter. But these problems, important and potentially more important as they may turn out to be, pale before the vision of man's exploration of space, and it is to this that I now turn.

The space race

The space race refers specifically to the contemporary competition between the United States and the Soviet Union to accomplish various objectives in space. The first real blow, in the public imagination at least, was the successful launching of the Russian Sputnik in 1957, an event which by all accounts galvanized the United States to the most concentrated and certainly the most expensive scientific and technological programme in recorded history.[14] To put the space race in perspective is difficult, precisely because of its immensity and complexity, but no better short statement sums it up so well as a non-technical article in *The Sunday Times* on the tenth anniversary of the original Sputnik flight. Under a four column headline, '$100,000,000,000 The Great Space-race Extravaganza', the piece continues:

> "I want to be the firstest with the mostest in space, and I just don't want to wait for years—how much money do we need to do it?" a member of a U.S. Congressional committee asked the head of the National Aeronautics and Space Administration when Sputnik 1 was still a recent and humiliating memory.
>
> Even after a 10 per cent cut in its latest budget, NASA is spending about $4,800,000,000 this year, almost double the budget of the Belgian Government. The US Air Force and other departments bring the current bill to about $7,000,000,000 a year.
>
> The absorption of manpower has been equally staggering. More than 400,000 people work on the space programme either for Government agencies or for private firms, among them 5 per cent of the country's scientists and engineers. The demand has created a steady drain of qualified men from other countries where they are badly needed.
>
> Taking $30,000,000,000 as the cost of the Apollo programme, Dr Warren Weaver, the American scientist, has calculated that it would pay for: a 10 per cent rise for all teachers in the United States, a $10,000,000 gift for 200 small colleges, seven-year fellowships for 50,000 scientists and engineers, 10 new medical schools, three new Rockefeller Foundations, new universities for 53 underdeveloped countries—leaving $100,000,000 over for the popularization of science . . .
>
> The enormous expenditure on space is, of course, almost duplicated by the Soviet programme.
>
> There are already signs in America of a revulsion against this extravagance . . .[15]

And not only in America are there signs of revulsion. In 1967 one Soviet astronaut was killed on re-entry to the Earth, and this tragedy, in spite of the attempts of the Soviet govenment to glorify the sacrifice, evoked hostile and bitter comments.[16] World opinion is difficult to assess for the question is pathetic, and it is almost macabre to pose it to the starving and homeless millions.*

A recent article by Nigel Calder, a science journalist, argues that irrespective of the cost and the dubious scientific 'fallout' from the space race, the fact that lives will almost certainly be lost is reason enough to abandon the race, if not the whole project. President Kennedy, who on 25 May 1961 committed America for the race to the moon with the target date of 1970, was responsible for, in Calder's words, 'a grotesque perversion of human skills and courage. Many have judged it folly, but in my opinion it is nothing less than a scandal.' Three American astronauts have already died in their space capsule while on *ground* tests, and 'it is not really a question of whether astronauts will be killed, but simply how many, before the goals of the Apollo programme are achieved or abandoned'.[17]

As probably most people in the world know, the most symbolic goal of the Apollo programme—the landing of Americans on the surface of the moon—was first accomplished on 21 July 1969, before a television audience of hundreds of millions. Though there have been no more American casualties to date, various reports of Russian space tragedies appear from time to time in the Western press.

I do not pretend competence to judge whether Calder's fears are *scientifically* justified or whether he is a Jeremiah or a latter-day cosmic Luddite, though I am of the opinion that the latter are less likely than the former. There would seem to be an argument, however, that if men were prepared to sacrifice their lives for good causes then the sacrifices might be justified. The American and Soviet astronauts are presumably willing to risk their lives, so the problem for any theory of progress will be to assess how worthy is the cause involved. If the space race gave positive help to solving any or all of the great problems of our age then the cause might indeed seem worthy in a social and moral sense. How then does the space race affect the population explosion, world famine, the prevention and cure of disease, problems of engineering and mechanics that affect our lives, and those problems of biology hinted at in the last section?

Robert C. Seamans, Jr., the Associate Administrator of NASA, in a paper in *Science Journal*, stresses the point that we really can never tell what great advances in any field will result from the massive space effort, but that, in any case, those who decided on which projects will be financed 'are guided by what will offer the greatest

---

* The matter was summed up in a cartoon that showed an emaciated peasant and child with empty food bowls looking up to the sky where American and Russian satellites competed for prominence.

return for the applied effort, and represent a broad segment of the nation's intellectual talent'.[18] This is not particularly revealing, nor is his one specific example of the 'fall out' of space research (spotting unhealthy trees from great heights) particularly significant. He hints at the possible repercussions of the space programme for the benefit of humanity, but obviously has no particular and expected benefits in mind.

The American and Soviet attitudes to the possible pay-off for technology, etc., from space science have shown some interesting variations over the past few years. Howard Simons, the American correspondent of the British weekly, *New Scientist*, provides a convenient barometer of views in mid-1965 and late 1966. At the earlier date he wrote: 'There was a time when Administration officials were defending the man-on-the-Moon effort by crowing about the "spin off" in terms of goods and services translatable from the space programme. . . . [Now it] is doing well enough on its own,'[19] and went on to report on a pamphlet which threw large doubts on any widespread applications from the space race. At the end of the next year, Simons wrote, in a very different vein, 'America's civilian space programme is fast becoming the hardiest scapegoat for the frustrations of the Great Society . . . Senator Clinton Anderson, chairman of the Senate space committee . . . [recently] repeated his earlier view that it really does not matter who gets to the Moon first.'[20] This last statement speaks for itself, though the budgetary cuts faced by the space programme have not been great.

After the euphoria of the early Russian and American successes, as the financial and human costs start to mount the manifest aim of space research must swing back to its utility in helping to solve human problems. As a report from the Eighteenth International Astronautical Congress, held in Belgrade in 1967 states: 'This Congress also made it clear that the emphasis has largely swung from scientific investigations of space to commercial applications of the research. Communications . . . [and] Weather satellites, also, have already shown their value.'[21] As far as one can tell from the more popular scientific journals the commercial applications of space research, apart from communications and weather satellites, seem at this stage somewhat limited.[22] The military significance of these activities may well be an entirely different matter. Predictably, there is not a great deal of readily available information on the military uses of space—for all one knows there may be some devastating weapon poised in an apparently innocent 'satellite' circling the Earth at this very moment.[23]

The answer, therefore, to my queries as to the likely contributions of space research and the current space race to the solution of humanity's most pressing problems, is that either those involved do not know and can only suggest generalities, or that they have a good idea but are not broadcasting to any great extent. If there were great benefits forthcoming, one would expect those responsible and knowledgeable to speak out and to justify further their costly activity—their comparative silence suggests that space research is simply a fantastically expensive luxury for a troubled world.* As an editorial in *New Scientist* comments: 'While such terrestrial challenges of hideous urgency, such as poverty and hunger, are met half-heartedly or blotted out in a cloud of wishful thinking, the contracts will go out for rockets of great lift and capsules capable of holding a football team.'[24]

In a sense, this discussion, an evaluation of the space race as a social problem, is entirely vitiated by the widespread belief that it is such activities as the space programme, paradoxically, that maintain the prosperity of the United States, and by implication the Soviet Union. An American aircraft executive, in a brutally frank and simplistic paper, sums up this view by pointing out that in some of the most advanced sectors of industry and those subsidiaries servicing them, economic and social chaos would follow from a serious cut-back in NASA funds.[25] Only the most confident revolutionary could wish for the economic collapse of America *and* Russia!

However, this aspect apart, an analysis of the space race in terms of the theory of progress I have been constructing focuses on the satisfaction of individual and social needs. If, on a very basic level, the American people (or rather the American *government* as recent surveys tend to suggest)[26] have a preference for showing that they are as technically competent as the Russians, then it must be concluded that there are other far less expensive and potentially more significant solutions to this problem than present space efforts. If the problem is denied on the level of national prestige, with the deduction that the original goal of John F. Kennedy has been replaced, and is conceived at the technical level, then much urgently needed money is being spent for not a great return. Even an argument on purely cognitive or quasi-spiritual grounds seems unconvincing, for there are a multitude of unfulfilled needs, both individual and social, on Earth. As was suggested above, the space race is a *luxury*, and nothing offends morality in any society more than the luxury of some in the face of the deprivation of other. The onus is on those engaged in space

* Dr Robert Jastrow, the influential American space scientist, at a meeting in the U.S. embassy in London in November 1969, claimed that the economic returns on the $4 billion annual expenditure on space during the 1960s had been in the region of $6–8 billion per annum. His claim was not documented. An earlier paper by Jastrow that emphasizes the scientific value of space research is 'Science, the Scientist and Space Developments', in H. Taubenfeld (ed.), *Space and Society*, Dobbs Ferry: Oceana, 1964, pp. 31-41. This whole symposium is an interesting account of American thinking at the time.

research, especially at a policy level, to show that their activity is not at this time a luxury.

The complete history of the Apollo project, to say nothing of the genesis of the American and Russian space programmes as a whole, has not yet been written, although some accounts, mainly from well-informed journalists, are appearing. A view with which I would have some sympathy pending the exposure of all the evidence, is that the preceding discussion has been a little naïve in its underestimation of the role of the commercial and industrial interests involved in this costly business. Indeed, even a cursory glance at the contracting system for NASA projects indicates that certain favourably placed industries and particular firms are making large sums of extremely risk-free profits out of the space programme in the United States. One may speculate that as long as the Apollo mission, for example, continued to be tied up with national prestige and not very seriously with scientific or technical objectives, then public and political support would be maintained at a high level. This was certainly the case as far as the *first* 1969 moon landing was concerned. This enormously publicized event appeared to stimulate great worldwide interest and American pride. The *second* moon landing in November 1969, however, seemed to pass off as an almost routine matter— reports indicated that not even large numbers of Americans bothered to watch the actual landing this time on early morning television and the level of coverage and interest (not, of course, independent factors) had declined considerably. If this trend continues, and no new exploit is achieved, then we may expect to find that more and more pressure would build up to cut short the American space programme. The ability of the space establishment to defend itself against this type of pressure cannot be better exemplified than by the events surrounding the 'failure' of Apollo 13 in April 1970, when the moon landing had to be aborted and the three astronauts appeared to be in real danger of death in space. This failure was turned quickly into a success, namely the magnificent achievement involved in bringing the men and the spacecraft back safely to earth. This is not entirely a closed system, of course, for factors in the wider American and international society will clearly influence the future of the space programme. What the Soviet Union achieves in this field could, paradoxically, provide the motivation for even greater American efforts in the future as Sputnik is said to have done in the past.[27]

It may be difficult to assess when any particular activity becomes a luxury, how many artists or poets or sociologists a society can afford when people are starving and homeless, but where there are as many artists as workers in basic industries or if the total costs of entertainment exceed those of health and welfare, then we might be faced with a situation where basic needs were not being met. This is the case with space research; if its practitioners do not or cannot successfully justify it, then it must be condemned.

This example is one of the empiricization of progress, or the autonomy of innovational progress, where new things, ideas and processes, gloriously illustrated by the fascinating and novel world of space and interplanetary travel, take on a quality of their own. They present themselves as justification in themselves and innovation as a slogan is offered as sufficient and necessary reason for the whole endeavour.

It was argued that in the last resort no consistent principle could be applied to guide a choice between innovational and non-innovational solutions to problems in society. The ultimate choice between innovational and non-innovational progress was, in this sense, arbitrary. However, where some solution to a problem-complex seems so completely out of touch with the real needs of human society, and where the problems may be redefined and solved in some other and more acceptable fashion, then we can choose between innovational and non-innovational progress where one patently satisfies more individual and social needs than the other. It will not always be possible to deal in this way with important problems and their potential solutions, but in this case—the space race—the sociological theory of progress suggests that the initial problems be redefined, and that many features of the total activity be abandoned.

This is *not* to say that man should *never* attempt to conquer space or to explore the scientific and technological possibilities of so doing, but only that at this juncture of human history there are many problems which are more pressing. There is also an argument that the space race as it now proceeds is aggravating the already great gap between rich and poor nations, and can cause nothing but resentment and increasing bitterness in international relations.

It must be strongly reiterated that no conclusive answers to such problems exist, but that this should never dissuade us from trying to improve upon past answers. Roscoe Pound makes this point force-fully in the context of his sociology of law:

Einstein has taught us that we live in a curved universe in which there are no straight lines or planes or right angles or perpendiculars. Yet we do not on this account give up surveying. Straight lines and planes and so forth do not exist. But as postulates of a practical activity they are near enough to the truth for the practical needs of a practical activity. So it is with the measure of values postulated or accepted in modern systems of law. If we cannot prove them, we can use them, as sufficiently near to the truth for our practical purposes.[28]

Pound's stress on the use of certain notions for practical activity, with the implication that people generally are content to operate with things that 'do not exist' for the convenience of communication and action, is exactly the note that needs to be struck here.

The arguments of this chapter have utilized the sociological ethic to a greater extent than the distinction between innovational and non-innovational progress. This was to be expected in any discussion of the sociology of science and technology, for these activities, as I have often noted, are the paradigm cases of innovational progress, the innovational solution to problems. The nature of innovation is that the new idea, thing or process should have the maximum possible impact on the society in which it occurs. The hallmark of innovational progress is that the burden of proof is on those wishing to restrict the application of innovations, while the hallmark of non-innovational progress is that the burden of proof is on the innovators. This is a constant running battle in almost every society and it is often difficult to predict where certain social groups will stand on any particular issue. The innovators on one problem may well be the anti-innovators on another. For example, the scientists or scientific manager may favour widespread innovation in scientific or business methods, and oppose innovations in social welfare methods.[29]

The intent of the innovational/non-innovational progress distinction has been to avoid the confusions of identifying the institutional spheres in which progress, on a very basic level, takes place. Progress, the most satisfactory solution to problems in terms of the sociological ethic, takes place in *society*, rather than in science or the economy or the polity or in morality as such.

In the next chapter this study of the theory and practice of progress will be concluded with a brief account of some of the conclusions, the limitations and the implications of the preceding analysis.

XIV   Conclusion

There are three parts to this conclusion. First, the actual conclusions of the research and theory will be set out. Next, some of the limitations of the book will be discussed, in the sense that I shall attempt to make clear those things that I have *not* been trying to do. Last, the main implications of the study will be suggested in order that the intentions, both theoretical and empirical, of the work are entirely clear and open. Indeed, if there is one main point in this *Conclusion* it is that the 'sociology of progress' can never be a closed question for its persistence as a problem for social theory is guaranteed by the persistence of social life.

In the belief that the history of social thought is important for the understanding not only of contemporary social thought but also of contemporary society and the ways in which it changes, I set out to trace the history of the idea of progress. It was found that although many diverse ideas and theories of progress have emerged in Western thought it was possible and even fruitful to study these ideas chronologically. Thus, as the chapter headings indicate, six rough groupings emerge to give six periods through which the development of progress as a social and moral concept can be traced.

I introduced the notions of innovational and non-innovational progress at the earliest opportunity, namely in the *Introduction*, in order that my selection and treatment of the vast array of social thought on progress might be more easily fitted into the overall pattern of this book. Thus, as was pointed out especially in Chapters I, II and VI, it is useful and (I should argue) essential for a proper understanding of social thought and social change to consider two opposed concepts of progress, rather than one central idea with certain peripheral variations as is the view of most historians of progress. In this context, then, Western social thought is interpreted as a struggle between innovational and non-innovational views of progress. This is especially clear with respect to those who have often been regarded as enemies of progress, from Rousseau to Jacques Ellul. This same split between innovational and non-innovational progress, albeit in different expressions, also emerges from some of the more complex theories of progress, like those of Comte and the social evolutionists.

The major link between non-innovational and innovational progress, the variable that differentiates the ideas in Chapters I and II from those in Chapters III to VI, is the institutionalization of science and technology. As I argue in many places, the main consequence of this latter process on the idea of progress is that matters tend to be defined in such a way that non-innovational progress is no longer seen as progress at all. The empiricization of progress takes place, progress is measured in terms of the successes of science and technology, and non-innovational progress becomes regression, reaction, primitivism or traditionalism. And these are all pejorative terms in the modern world. The reaction against innovational progress takes the form of anti-technological thought, the rejection of scientism, and the condemnation of the machine civilization. The defenders of science can only conceive of these outbursts as part of an attack on progress itself.

The way out of this vicious circle is to draw a firm distinction between innovational and non-innovational progress, but a distinction that is not so firm that it obscures the fact that they are both forms of progress. This latter fact is the crux of the matter, and it is discussed in detail in Part Two.

Some other conclusions are drawn from the review of social thought in the first six chapters. It is clear that the classical roots of the idea of progress have contributed more to the non-innovational than to the innovational concept of progress, and even as late as the eighteenth century what I have characterized as the innovational concept of progress was not fully established. Some little evidence has been presented to suggest that the institutionalization of science and technology took place during the decades around 1800, and so it is with the nineteenth-century progress theorists, particularly Comte and Marx, that a truly innovational concept of progress is established and developed.

A specific contribution of Marx, through Hegel, to the theoretical disjunction between innovational and non-innovational progress lies in the notion of oppositional thinking, and this plays an important part in the Marxist theory of progress as I have selectively interpreted it.

A comprehensive history of the idea of progress and its widespread misfortunes in the twentieth century has still to be written, and in Chapters V and VI I present the picture in a somewhat gloomy light.

My conclusions on twentieth-century social thought might appear to be excessively pessimistic, but this is only because no strong non-innovational concept of progress has replaced the innovational concept of progress that has taken such punishment in the name of science and technology. Innovational progress articulates the great promises of science and technology and tends to foster the 'Utopian Mentality',* which suffers greater disillusionment for smaller defeats than more realistic mentalities. Therefore, the decline of optimism that is found is to be understood in this relative sense.

The historical events and the theories about these events, theories about progress and regress, and the theoretical formulation of Part Two of this study, interact in important ways. This is not the place to discuss at length the relationship between empirical and/or documentary evidence and social theory, however, as I have tried to make clear in the body of the work, the 'theory' of the second part and the 'history' of the first part cannot be considered separately for long; the one nourishes the other.

The distinction between innovational and non-innovational progress is elaborated in Chapter VII where the analysis is carried out on the three interrelated levels of history, theory and aspirations of men in society. A typology of societies is also presented here. This takes cognizance of the distinction between innovativeness and inventiveness and could be a useful guide to the orientations to progress of past and present societies.

At this point a possibly polemical conclusion may be pointed out. The sociology of development, with its unmistakable goal of discovering the processes necessary for the transformation of 'developing' countries into modern, industrial 'developed' countries, appears to operate with an implicit concept of innovational progress. More than one scholar has claimed that the institutionalization of science and technology through education and foreign aid schemes, etc., is the key to modernization. Few if any have conceived of non-innovational progress in this context and the assumption is that there is one and only one path into modernity. My book is an attempt to modify this view.[1]

The difference between traditional and non-innovational social action, in ideal-typical terms, is drawn to emphasize that non-innovational action is potentially progressive in so far as it represents an effort to solve problems. Traditional behaviour is more likely to be automatic and not suitable for problem-solving in changing societies, and it is the antithesis of progressive activity in any society in which there are people whose basic needs are not being fulfilled.

* This is, of course, the title of Ch. IV of Mannheim's *Ideology and Utopia*, where he discusses the decline of utopian thought to a sceptical relativism.

This brings us to the moral aspects of the sociological theory of progress that is constructed in this study. Progress is defined, understood and treated as a moral concept as well as a social concept. That is, progress implies that moral decisions are taken about events in societies, and activities in social life. From the analysis of Chapters VIII to XI certain morally relevant conclusions are evident. These can be summed up in the construct that is termed the *sociological ethic*.

The sociological ethic is the value standard that distinguishes progress from regress or stagnation. It is the criterion that decides which of two or more solutions to a problem of men in society is the more satisfactory. From the arguments around traditional and modern moral philosophy it is concluded that the only basis for such an ethic is in the requisites of social life—the needs of individuals and societies. A list of requisites is presented in Chapter XI.

In the last two chapters the sociological theory of progress is put to work to answer some criticisms in general against the idea of progress, and in particular around the sociology of science. Thus the two concepts of progress, innovational and non-innovational, evaluated in terms of the sociological ethic, is an approach to the problems of social change both for the sociologist and for man in society.

The limitations of this study that are self-imposed are threefold. Its scope may obscure details, and perhaps extremely important details, of the development of Western thought. It is restricted to Western thought and thus ignores most of the world in terms of population and size. Finally, the structure of the sociological theory of progress is loose.

I have attempted to paint a bold picture of the development of the idea of progress and I have selected theories and theorists mainly on the basis of sociological interest, defined as widely as possible. A more serious limitation in this connection is that I have necessarily strayed into specialist areas where the non-specialist, though he may attain a general idea of the current state of the field, must inevitably miss many of the finer points. A good case in point is the recent movement in the study of eighteenth-century French thought that implies a greater degree of pessimism to enlightenment thinkers than has hitherto been the case.[2] My presentation of the *philosophes* is perhaps a little too optimistic in the light of these researches, though the warnings of Rousseau did not go unheeded in Chapter II.

Much the same might be said for the interpretations of Durkheim and Weber in Chapter V, but here again I am concerned more with sketching in the broad outlines of thought rather than becoming involved in precise textual exegesis, however valid this enterprise is. Perhaps the one exception to this general rule in the foregoing pages, the more detailed analysis of Comte's theory of progress, is justified because of the complexity of progress as he developed it and the relevance it has in suggesting the possibility of a distinction between innovational and non-innovational progress, as I go on to develop it.

The second limitation of this study is that, in spite of the number of theories of progress it attempts to discuss, however briefly, it is entirely restricted to Western thought. Indeed, in terms of the process of the *institutionalization* of science and technology this is not altogether surprising, for the process has been almost entirely a Western phenomenon.[3] Although there appear to be many types of non-Western philosophies of history, and perhaps some evidence of what I have called the non-innovational concept of progress,[4] this study has not ventured into the vast area of non-Western thought.

The last self-imposed limitation of this study is the loose structure of what has been called the sociological theory of progress. This stems from the fact that I have here been concerned with macro-sociological problems—problems on a high level of generality about the nature of social change and the moral meaning of social life. Subjects such as these do not normally lend themselves to strict theory-building where sets of propositions are logically interrelated in a consistent fashion and where testable hypotheses are directly deducible from the body of the theory. There are good arguments to support the view that theories of this kind are not yet available to the social sciences and to sociology in particular. Whether or not this is so, it has not been my intention to construct such a theory.

What has been attempted here is to cast a long and fairly comprehensive look over the development of ideas and theories of progress, and to interpret these in terms of some sociological and ethical categories. From this investigation into the past of the idea of progress, several theoretical recommendations are made for dealing with the social and moral concept of progress in the present and in the future. As has been pointed out many times, the arguments are nearer the persuasive than the demonstrative pole on the continuum of sociological explanation.

As with all endeavours of this kind, prior acceptance of certain concepts and relations between concepts is necessary. The assumptions made, especially the assumptions surrounding the sociological ethic, are not generally those of most social scientists, as my review of some textbook criticisms of progress suggested. This point leads on directly to some of the intended implications of the sociology of progress that has been developed here.

The first and most general implication is that progress as a social and a moral concept is an essential tool for sociological analysis and particularly where the sociologist examines and attempts to explain the aspirations of men in the context of social change. The analysis

235

of social change not only involves the study of value-judgments, but also involves the *making* of them. The initial step in a sociology that is to be valuable, both scientifically and on grounds of humanity, is to expose the value-judgments of the sociologist. The next step is for the sociologist to give his reasons for the value-judgments that he makes and to show how these reasons are justified by his special skills as a sociologist. This is, in a curious fashion, a technical point, but it is also more than a technical point precisely because the technique of social life is morally relevant. It is part of the task of the sociologist to show that certain social actions lead to progress and that others do not, and to identify them in each case.

There are other, more specific implications of this study that should be pointed out. These concern the role of science and technology in the contemporary world, and in its development. The sociology of science, though some distinguished sociologists have given attention to it, is a critically undernourished field. Few would doubt that science and technology are most vital factors in the modern world and some would even go on to argue that all else in modern life depends on them.[5] The category of innovational progress, of which science and technology constitute the paradigm case, is intended to throw some light on science as a social institution and to suggest a framework for the sociology of science and technology.*

Yet another implication in this context, specifically linked to the history of the attacks on the idea of progress that were discussed in Chapters V and VI, involves what might be termed 'the history and sociology of anti-science'. Part of this has been started with reference to the opposition between science and religion, and this was raised in Chapter IV when the impact of Darwinism and Darwinisticism were discussed. However, the history of anti-science and anti-technology has yet to be fully recorded, and these phenomena have yet to receive proper sociological attention.[6] Such projects are implied by this study, and perhaps the same comment can be made here as was made about the theories of progress of the eighteenth century: just as the enlightenment was too close to the institutionalization of science and technology to appreciate it fully, so perhaps the present generation is too close to the reaction against science and technology to appreciate it fully.

The last point to be made concerns the notion of non-innovational progress and the sociology of development, and I shall use this as a

---

* It is curious that the distinction between normal science and scientific revolutions in Kuhn's *Structure of Scientific Revolutions* (op. cit.) is close in some respects to my non-innovational and innovational change distinction. For discussion of Kuhn's increasingly sociological account of science see I. Lakatos and A. Musgrave (eds.), *Criticism and the Growth of Knowledge*, Cambridge: Cambridge University Press, 1970, esp. the chs. by Lakatos and Kuhn.

vehicle to illustrate a main strand of this investigation. The history of social thought, the activity of social theorizing and the judgment that the sociologist passes on his own and other societies cannot be held to be entirely separate. For the sociologist, as I have defined his role, inquiring into the history of social thought and putting together theories about the social world are not ends in themselves, though they are worthy activities. They are for the sociologist means to a further end, and this is as has been argued extensively throughout this work, the end of making and defending value-judgments about social life.

Non-innovational progress in certain problem areas, or generalized to describe a whole way of life, is, where truly progressive on the basis of the sociological ethic, as morally commendable as similarly progressive innovational progress. As was mentioned above, the notion of non-innovational progress implies that societies do have options if they wish to progress, and that perhaps there are alternative paths to modernity. The precise forms of these paths to modernity, like the precise forms of non-innovational progress, depend largely upon the social organization of the society in question, on its history, its myths and its ability to absorb and assimilate outside influences. It is for the sociologist, in this case the sociologist of development, to ensure that the aspirations of those he is studying play an important part in his analysis.

In this way a sociology of progress will be possible, for it will recognize both the variety of social life and the common elements all men share in social life.

References

Chapter I

1 Robert Flint, *History of the Philosophy of History*, Edinburgh and London: Blackwood, 1893, pp. 87 ff. For Horace, see *Odes*, Book II, 15, and Book III, 6.

2 Ludwig Edelstein, *The Idea of Progress in Classical Antiquity*, Baltimore: Johns Hopkins Press, 1967.

3 Marcus Aurelius, *The Meditations*, New York: Burt, n.d. (trans. by G. Long), p. 149.

4 Lucretius, *Of the Nature of Things*, New York: Dutton, 1957 (trans. by W. Leonard), pp. 245-6.

5 George Sarton, *A History of Science*, New York: Wiley, 1964-5 (2 vols.); and S. Sambursky, *The Physical World of the Greeks, Physics of the Stoics* and *The Physical World of Late Antiquity*, London: Routledge and Kegan Paul, 1956, 1959 and 1962.

6 Edelstein, op. cit., p. 155.

7 Sambursky (1962), op. cit., p. 175.

8 Aristotle, *Nicomachean Ethics*, London: Scott, n.d. (trans. by D. P. Chase), p. 324.

9 Edelstein, op. cit., p. 126. This is from the *Nicomachean Ethics*.

10 Jules Delvaille, *Essai sur l'histoire de l'idée de Progrès*, Paris, 1910, p. 92.

11 Augustine, *The City of God* [Vols. I and II of *Works*], Edinburgh: Clarke, 1871-2 (trans. by Rev. M. Dods), esp. Book XXII.

12 See Ernest Lee Tuveson, *Millennium and Utopia*, New York: Harper Torchbooks, 1964.

13 George Boas, *Essays on Primitivism and Related Ideas in the Middle Ages*, Baltimore: Johns Hopkins, 1948.

14 Flint, op. cit., p. 103.

15 For what follows, see the excellent discussion in Julian H. Franklin, *Jean Bodin and the Sixteenth-Century Revolution in the Methodology of Law and History*, New York: Columbia, 1963.

16 Francis Bacon, *The Advancement of Learning and New Atlantis*, London: Oxford University Press, 1956, pp. 93-4.

17 Lord Macaulay, *Critical and Historical Essays*, London: Longmans, Green, 1883, pp. 346-414, at p. 399.
18 Benjamin Farrington, *Francis Bacon*, London: Lawrence & Wishart, 1951, p. 144.
19 Delvaille, op. cit., p. 163.
20 R. F. Jones, *Ancients and Moderns*, St. Louis: Washington University, 1936, p. 279.
21 René Descartes, Letter-Preface to the 'Principles of Philosophy', in *Discourse on Method and Other Writings*, Harmondsworth: Penguin, 1960 (trans. by A. Wollaston), p. 186.
22 Blaise Pascal, *The Living Thoughts of Pascal*, London: Cassell, 1941 (presented by F. Mauriac), p. 24.
23 Quoted in Flint, op. cit., p. 215.
24 Ronald S. Crane, 'Anglican Apologetics and the Idea of Progress, 1699-1745', *Modern Philology*, 31 (1933-4), pp. 273-306, 349-82.
25 Quoted in Friedrich Klemm, *A History of Western Technology*, New York: Scribner's, 1959 (trans. by D. W. Singer), p. 197.
26 Crane, op. cit., p. 299.
27 The debate over the Weber thesis with reference to the rise of science is very relevant here. For a recent paper comprising an excellent summary and an interesting view of the specifically Anglican *via media*, see Douglas S. Kemsley, 'Religious Influences in the Rise of Modern Science: A Review and Criticism, particularly of the "Protestant-Puritan Ethic" Theory', *Annals of Science*, 24 (1968), pp. 199-226.
28 Crane, op. cit., p. 381. See also Tuveson, op. cit., chs. 3 and 4.

Chapter II

1 J. Bronowski and Bruce Mazlish, *The Western Intellectual Tradition*, London: Hutchinson, 1960, p. 246.
2 Klemm, op. cit., p. 231.
3 R. G. Collingwood, *The Idea of History*, Oxford: Oxford University Press, 1963, p. 76.
4 W. E. Lecky, *History of the Rise and Influence of the Spirit of Rationalism in Europe*, London: Longmans, Green, 1884, II, p. 60.
5 Flint, op. cit., p. 240.
6 J. B. Bury, *The Idea of Progress*, New York: Dover, 1955, p. 128.
7 See F. H. Hinsley, *Power and the Pursuit of Peace*, Cambridge: Cambridge University Press, 1963, esp. ch. 2.
8 Voltaire, *A Philosophical Dictionary*, London: Lewis, 1849, I, p. 64.
9 Quoted in H. Becker and H. E. Barnes, *Social Thought from Lore to Science*, New York: Dover, 1961 (expanded and revised), II, p. 472.
10 Bury, op. cit., p. 167.
11 Flint, op. cit., p. 308.
12 See Arthur O. Lovejoy, *Essays in the History of Ideas*, Baltimore: Johns Hopkins, 1948, p. 24.

13 Ibid. p. 32.
14 Maurice Cranston, B.B.C. Typescript, 1966, pp. 6-7. As F. C. Green notes in *Rousseau and the Idea of Progress* (Oxford: Oxford University Press, 1950), Rousseau warned against the *dangers* of science rather than science itself.
15 See Condorcet, *Sketch for a Historical Picture of the Progress of the Human Mind*, London: Weidenfeld & Nicolson, 1955; this is quoted in Becker and Barnes, op. cit., II, p. 474.
16 R. V. Sampson, *Progress in the Age of Reason*, London: Heinemann, 1956, p. 40.
17 Carl Becker, *The Heavenly City of the Eighteenth Century Philosophers*, New Haven: Yale, 1932, p. 31.
18 Sampson, op. cit., p. 129.
19 Kant, 'Idea of a Universal History from a Cosmopolitan Point of View' (1784), in P. Gardiner (ed.), *Theories of History*, Glencoe: Free Press, 1959, pp. 22-34.
20 W. H. Walsh, *Philosophy of History*, New York: Harper Torchbooks, 1960, p. 134, n. 2.
21 F. M. Barnard, *Herder's Social and Political Thought*, Oxford: Clarendon, 1965, p. 113.
22 Quoted in G. A. Wells, *Herder and After*, s' Gravenhage: Mouton, 1959, p. 133.
23 Barnard, op. cit., pp. 137-8.
24 Ibid., p. 130.
25 Isaiah Berlin, 'J. G. Herder', *Encounter* (July 1965), pp. 29-48, and (August 1965), pp. 42-51.
26 Barnard, op. cit., p. 131.
27 Bury, op. cit., pp. 217-18.
28 Samuel M. Levin, 'Malthus and the Idea of Progress', *Journal of the History of Ideas*, 27 (1966), pp. 92-108.
29 See, for example, Gladys Bryson, *Man and Society*, Princeton: Princeton University Press, 1945; W. C. Lehman, *Adam Ferguson and the Beginning of Modern Sociology*, New York: Columbia, 1930; David Kettler, *The Social and Political Thought of Adam Ferguson*, Ohio: Ohio State, 1965; and D. G. MacRae, 'Adam Ferguson, Sociologist', *New Society* (24 Nov. 1966), pp. 792-4. A recent and detailed study is Alan Swingewood's unpublished Ph.D. thesis, 'The Scottish Enlightenment and the Rise of Sociology', London University 1968.
30 Adam Ferguson, *An Essay on the History of Civil Society*, London: Miller & Cadell, 1768, pp. 247-50.
31 See Kettler, op. cit., ch. 1, and the interesting discussion in Lewis Feuer, *The Scientific Intellectual*, New York: Basic Books, 1963, pp. 209-17.
32 Kettler, op. cit., p. 164.
33 David Hume, *Essays: Literary, Moral and Political*, London: George Routledge, 1894, p. 66 (italics in original).
34 Dugald Stewart, *Outlines of Moral Philosophy*, Edinburgh: Creech, 1808, p. 318.

35 See Bryson, op. cit., p. 89.
36 See John B. Stewart, *The Moral and Political Philosophy of David Hume*, New York: Columbia, 1963, ch. XI and esp. p. 297.
37 This is discussed in Lois Whitney, *Primitivism and the Idea of Progress in English Popular Literature of the 18th Century*, Baltimore: Johns Hopkins, 1934, pp. 280-90; and in Bryson, op. cit., p. 93.
38 Ibid., pp. 14-15.
39 See Karl Popper, *The Logic of Scientific Discovery*, New York: Science Editions, 1961.
40 Maurice Crosland, *The Society of Arcueil*, London: Heinemann, 1967; and Charles C. Gillispie, 'Science in the French Revolution', *Behavioral Science*, 4 (1959), pp. 67-73. The intricate relations between science and politics during the French Revolution are further discussed in papers by Gillispie, Williams, Hill and Guerlac in Marshall Clagett (ed.), *Critical Problems in the History of Science*, Madison: University of Wisconsin Press, 1959, pp. 255-320; and by R. Taton, 'The French Revolution and the Progress of Science', *Centaurus*, 3 (1953), pp. 73-89.
41 The story is traced out in W. Armytage, *The Rise of the Technocrats*, London: Routledge & Kegan Paul, 1965, Part II. A more general account is E. J. Hobsbawm, *The Age of Revolution: 1789-1848*, New York: Mentor, 1964, esp. chs. 9 and 15. D. S. L. Cardwell's *The Organisation of Science in England: A Retrospect* (London: Heinemann, 1957) is particularly useful for the history of the development of scientific and technical education in the nineteenth century.

Chapter III

1 Auguste Comte, *System of Positive Polity*, London: Longmans, Green, 1875 (trans. by J. H. Bridges), II, p. 35.
2 Auguste Comte, *The Positive Philosophy*, London: Bell, 1896 (freely translated and condensed by Harriet Martineau), I, pp. 1-2.
3 Ibid., p. 5.
4 Comte (1875), op. cit., II, p. 4.
5 Ibid., p. 2.
6 Auguste Comte, *Preliminary Discourse on the Positive Spirit*, London: Positivist Library, 1883 (trans. by W. Call), p. 32.
7 Comte (1875), op. cit., I, pp. 555-6.
8 Comte (1896), op. cit., II, p. 188.
9 Ibid., p. 190.
10 Ibid., p. 196. See also Comte (1875), op. cit., I, p. 83, for the same claim made for both 'Progress' and 'Order'.
11 Comte (1875), op. cit., III, p. 56.
12 Ibid., II, pp. 356-7.
13 Ibid., III, p. 57.
14 Ibid.; and compare I, p. 86, and II, p. 147.

15 Ibid., III, p. 10.
16 Morris Ginsberg, 'The Idea of Progress: A Revaluation', in *Essays in Sociology and Social Philosophy*, London: Heinemann, 1961, III, pp. 29-34.
17 H. B. Acton, 'Comte's Positivism and the Science of Society', *Philosophy*, 26 (1951), pp. 291-310.
18 See especially W. M. Simon, *European Positivism in the Nineteenth Century*, Ithaca: Cornell University Press, 1963; D. G. Charlton, *Positive Thought in France during the Second Empire, 1852-70*, Oxford: Oxford University Press, 1959, and *Secular Religions in France, 1850-1870*, London: Oxford University Press, 1963; and John Eros, 'The Positivist Generation of French Republicanism', *Sociological Review*, 3 (1955), pp. 255-77.
19 Simon, op. cit., chs. 7 and 8; J. E. McGee, *A Crusade for Humanity, The History of Organized Positivism in England*, London: Watts & Co., 1931; and Mary E. Farmer, 'The Positivist Movement and the Development of English Sociology', *Sociological Review*, 15 (1967), pp. 5-20.
20 Simon, op. cit., ch. 9. As Simon points out, Comtean positivism had little impact on Germany.
21 See R. L. Hawkins, *Auguste Comte and the United States, (1816-57)*, [and *(1853-61)*], Cambridge: Harvard University Press, 1936 [and 1938].
22 Joao Cruz Costa, *A History of Ideas in Brazil*, Berkeley and Los Angeles: University of California Press, 1964 (trans. by Suzette Macedo), pp. 82-176; Leopoldo Zea, 'Positivism and Porfirism in Latin America', in F. S. C. Northrop (ed.), *Ideological Differences and World Order*, New Haven: Yale University Press, 1949, ch. 8; and Zea, 'Ideas and Ideologies in Latin America', in Guy S. Metraux and François Crouzet (eds.), *The Nineteenth Century World*, New York: Mentor Books, 1963, pp. 485-508, esp. 501 ff.
23 Charlton (1959), op. cit., p. 5.
24 John Wellmuth, S. J., *The Nature and Origins of Scientism*, Milwaukee: Marquette University Press, 1944, p. 2.
25 F. A. von Hayek, *The Counter-Revolution of Science*, Glencoe: The Free Press, 1964, p. 15.
26 Quoted in Simon, op. cit., p. 31.
27 Quoted in Charlton (1959), op. cit., p. 70.
28 Charlton (1959), op. cit., p. 116 and ch. 6, *passim.*
29 See Irving Babbitt, *The Masters of Modern French Literature*, London: Constable & Co., 1913, pp. 218-56.
30 Interesting in this connection is the discussion of Comte and Hegel in Hayek, op. cit., Part 3. See also the stimulating recent work of Z. A. Jordan, *The Evolution of Dialectical Materialism*, New York: St. Martin's Press, 1967, esp. ch. 4, 'French Positivism and the Philosophy of Marx and Engels'.
31 H. A. Taine, *History of English Literature*, Edinburgh: Edmonston & Douglas, 1871 (trans. by H. Van Laun), vol. I, pp. 18-19.
32 Quoted in Simon, op. cit., p. 188.

33 John Stuart Mill, *Autobiography*, New York: Columbia University Press, 1960, pp. 116-17.
34 Mill, *Auguste Comte and Positivism*, London: Trübner & Co., 1865, p. 86.
35 McGee, op. cit., pp. 232, 234.
36 Frederic Harrison, 'The Limits of Political Economy', *Fortnightly Review*, I (1865), p. 375; also his 'The Iron-Masters' Trade Union', ibid., pp. 96-116, for a passionate attack on lock-outs.
37 Noel Annan, *The Curious Strength of Positivism in English Political Thought*, London: Oxford University Press, 1959, p. 15.
38 James H. Billington, 'The Intelligentsia and the Religion of Humanity', *American Historical Review*, LXV (1959-60), p. 815.
39 Simon, op. cit., p. 263.
40 Zea (1963), op. cit., p. 504.
41 Cruz Costa, op. cit., p. 85 and ch. 5, *passim*.
42 For an interesting view on this, see Sydney Eisen, 'Herbert Spencer and the Spectre of Comte', *Journal of British Studies*, 7 (1967), pp. 48-67.
43 Ginsberg, *On the Diversity of Morals*, London: Heinemann, 1956, pp. 227-8.
44 Basil Willey, *Nineteenth Century Studies*, Harmondsworth: Penguin, 1964, p. 217, and ch. 7, *passim*.
45 See F. Engels, 'Preface to German Edition of 1890', in K. Marx and Engels, *The Communist Manifesto*, Moscow: Foreign Languages Publishing House, 1957 (trans. by S. Moore), pp. 34-5, for a succinct statement of the objections to the 'Socialists'.
46 For an account of these forerunners, see G. D. H. Cole, *History of Socialist Thought*, London: Macmillan, 1953, vol. I; and the old-fashioned, though straightforward, Thomas Kirkup, *A History of Socialism*, London: Black, 1909, chs. 2, 3 and 4. On Godwin, see also F. Rosen, 'Progress and Democracy', unpublished Ph.D. thesis, London University, 1965.
47 A sympathetic treatment of Saint-Simon on progress is Sidney Pollard, *The Idea of Progress*, London: Watts, 1968, pp. 96-107.
48 Marx and Engels, op. cit., p. 85.
49 Engels, in Marx and Engels, *Selected Works*, Moscow: Foreign Languages, 1958, II, pp. 49-50.
50 Sydney Hook, *From Hegel to Marx*, Michigan: University of Michigan Press, 1962, p. 61.
51 Walter Kaufmann, *Hegel: A Reinterpretation*, London: Weidenfeld and Nicolson, 1966, p. 190. See also George Lichtheim, *Marxism*, London: Routledge & Kegan Paul, 1964, p. 7 and esp. note 2.
52 Engels, in Marx and Engels (1958), op. cit., I, p. 369.
53 Marx and Engels (1957), op. cit., p. 88.
54 See Marx and Engels, *The German Ideology*, Parts I and II, London: Lawrence and Wishart, 1938 (ed. by R. Pascal), esp. p. 22; V. I. Lenin, *The State and Revolution*, Moscow: Foreign Languages, n.d., ch. 5; and Leon Trotsky, *Literature and Revolution*, Michigan: Michigan University Press, 1960. See also Lichtheim, op. cit., pp. 152-3.

55 See T. B. Bottomore, 'An Examination of Some Recent Theories of Social Progress', unpublished M.Sc. thesis, London University, 1950. See also, Abram L. Harris, 'Utopian Elements in Marx's Thought', *Ethics*, 60 (1950), pp. 79-99.
56 This essay, Martin Nicolaus, 'The Unknown Marx', is reprinted in Karl Oglesby (ed.), *The New Left Reader*, New York: Grove Press, 1969, pp. 84-110. The quotation is from p. 107.
57 Bury, op. cit., pp. 255-6.
58 Kaufmann, op. cit., p. 175.
59 Ibid., p. 258. Contrast this to the last of the 'Theses on Feuerbach', in Marx and Engels (1958), op. cit., I, p. 405.

Chapter IV

1 Phyllis Greenacre, *The Quest for the Father*, New York: International Universities Press, 1963.
2 Samuel Butler, 'Evolution, Old and New', in *Works*, London: Cape, 1924, vol. 5, p. 27.
3 Charles Darwin, *On the Origin of Species by means of Natural Selection*, London and Glasgow: Collins, n.d., p. 97 (orig. pub. 1859). For an interesting discussion of this, see S. F. Mason, 'The Idea of Progress and Theories of Evolution in Science', *Centaurus*, 3 (1953), pp. 90-106, esp. p. 103.
4 Engels, in Marx and Engels (1958), op. cit., II, pp. 82-3.
5 Darwin, *The Descent of Man*, London: John Murray, 1871, vol. 2, p. 384.
6 Darwin (1859), op. cit., p. 497. See also the fascinating details in Francis Darwin (ed.), *Charles Darwin: His Life Told in a Biographical chapter and in a selected Series of his Published Letters*, London: John Murray, 1908.
7 Erik Nordenskiöld, *The History of Biology*, New York: Tudor, 1949 (trans. by L. B. Eyre), p. 574.
8 William Irvine, *Apes, Angels and Victorians*, London: Weidenfeld and Nicolson, 1955, pp. 20, 50.
9 J. S. Wilkie, 'The Idea of Evolution in the Writings of Buffon', *Annals of Science*, 22 (1956), pp. 48-62, 212-27, 255-66; at p. 227.
10 See C. D. Darlington, *Darwin's Place in History*, Oxford: Blackwell, 1959.
11 Irwin Primer, 'Erasmus Darwin's *Temple of Nature*: Progress, Evolution, and the Eleusinian Mysteries', *Journal of the History of Ideas*, 25 (1964), pp. 58-76; at p. 61.
12 Gertrude Himmelfarb, *Darwin and the Darwinian Revolution*, London: Chatto and Windus, 1959, p. 325. Some necessary correctives to this view are contained in Alvar Ellegard, 'Darwin and the General Reader', *Acta Universitatis Gothenburgensis*, 7 (1958), vol. LXIV.
13 Asa Gray, *Darwiniana*, Cambridge, Mass.: Harvard, 1963, p. xxi.

14 Herbert Schneider, 'The Influence of Darwin and Spencer on American Philosophical Theology', *Journal of the History of Ideas*, 6 (1945), pp. 3-18; at p. 13.

15 John Dillenberger, *Protestant Thought and Natural Science*, London: Collins, 1961, ch. 8.

16 See D. G. MacRae, *Ideology and Society*, London: Heinemann, 1961, ch. XI.

17 Morse Peckham, 'Darwinism and Darwinisticism', *Victorian Studies*, 3 (1959), pp. 19-40; at p. 29.

18 Herbert Spencer, 'The Development Hypothesis', in *Essays: Scientific, Political and Speculative*, London: Williams and Norgate, 1891, p. 3.

19 Robert M. Young, in 'Malthus and the Evolutionists: The Common Context of Biological and Social Theory' (*Past and Present*, 43 (May 1969), pp. 109-45), gives Malthus a very important and diffuse role. For a more detailed and more mature account of his theory of evolution, see Spencer's *First Principles*, London: Williams and Norgate, 1910 (sixth edition), vol. 2, esp. chs. XII, XVIII and Appendix A.

20 'Progress: Its Law and Cause', Spencer (1891) op. cit., p. 10. The context of the following remarks is well set out in J. W. Burrow's 'Herbert Spencer' (*History Today*, 8 (1958), pp. 676-83) and *Evolution and Society* (Cambridge: Cambridge University Press, 1966, esp. ch. 6). John C. Greene, in his essay 'Biology and Social Theory in the Nineteenth Century: August Comte and Herbert Spencer' (in Clagett, op. cit., pp. 419-46), deals more critically with Spencer.

21 Spencer, *The Study of Sociology*, London: Kegan Paul, Trench and Trubner, 1904, pp. 342-3.

22 Ibid., p. 438.

23 Ibid., pp. 343, 346, 350. See the critical essay of Lester F. Ward, 'Political Ethics of Herbert Spencer', *Publication of the American Academy of Political and Social Sciences*, no. III (1894), pp. 90-127.

24 Irvine, op. cit., p. 346.

25 Darwin (1871), op. cit., I, p. 177. Emile Durkheim throws an interesting light on this in *Suicide*, London: Routledge & Kegan Paul, 1952 (trans. by J. Spaulding and G. Simpson), esp. pp. 171-85.

26 Darwin (1871), op. cit., I, p. 184; and II, p. 405.

27 See the enthusiastic editorial introduction by Robert L. Carneiro, to Herbert Spencer, *The Evolution of Society*, Chicago: University of Chicago Press, 1967, pp. ix-lvii; and my brief review of this in *The British Journal of Sociology*, 19 (1968), p. 351.

28 Frank Hankins, article on 'Darwin', *Encyclopaedia of the Social Sciences* (1931), vol. 5, p. 5.

29 Enrico Ferri, *Socialism and Positive Science*, London: Independent Labour Party, 1905 (trans. by Edith Harvey), p. 47.

30 Ellegard, op. cit., p. 17.

31 See, for example, the complex story in Max Rouché, 'Herder precurseur de Darwin', *Publications de la faculté des Lettres de l'Université de Strasbourg*, Fasc. 94 (1940).

32 This is argued by George E. Simpson, 'Darwin and "Social Darwinism" ', *Antioch Review*, 19 (1959), pp. 33-45. See also the suggestive

analysis of Eric Bentley, *The Cult of the Superman*, London: Robert Hale, 1947.

33 Richard Hofstadter, *Social Darwinism in American Thought, 1860-1915*, Boston: Beacon Press, 1955, p. 57. Morton G. White's review of Hofstadter's book (in *Journal of the History of Ideas*, 6 (1945), pp. 119-22) further clarifies the 'imperialism issue'.

34 Thomas Cowles, 'Malthus, Darwin, and Bagehot: A Study in the Transference of a Concept', *Isis*, 26 (1936-7), pp. 341-8.

35 Whether this was actually so or only appears to be so is still a matter of historical controversy; for example, see, E. J. Hobsbawm and R. M. Hartwell, 'Standards of Living in the Industrial Revolution: A Discussion', *Economic History Review*, 2nd Series, 16 (1961), no. 1. E. P. Thompson's monumental *The Making of the English Working Class* (London: Gollancz, 1965) provides a wealth of information on early nineteenth-century conditions.

36 See the juxtaposition of views in T. H. and Julian Huxley, *Evolution and Ethics, 1893-1943*, London: Pilot Press, 1947. For the impact of evolution on ethics see C. M. Williams, *A Review of the Systems of Ethics founded on the Theory of Evolution*, New York, 1893.

Chapter V

1 Durkheim, *The Division of Labour in Society*, Glencoe: Free Press, 1949 (trans. by G. Simpson), p. 337.

2 Ibid., p. 399

3 Ibid., p. 251.

4 A good account of this is by Emile Benoit-Smullyan, 'The Sociologism of Emile Durkheim and His School', in H. E. Barnes (ed.), *Introduction to the History of Sociology*, Chicago: University of Chicago Press, 1961, ch. 27.

5 In spite of the defence of Robert K. Merton, *Social Theory and Social Structure* (Glencoe: Free Press, 1963, pp. 37-46), this issue is a focus for attack. See, for example, John Rex, *Key Problems in Sociological Theory*, London: Routledge & Kegan Paul, 1961, esp. ch. 6; and Ralf Dahrendorf, 'Out of Utopia: Toward a Reorientation of Sociological Analysis', *American Journal of Sociology*, 64 (1958), pp. 115-27.

6 Durkheim (1952), op. cit., p. 258 and ch. 5, *passim*.

7 Max Weber, *Methodology of the Social Sciences*, Glencoe: Free Press, 1949 (trans. by E. Shils and H. Finch), pp. 38-9.

8 Ibid., pp. 54, 57. See the remarks of Everett C. Hughes in a review of Bendix, *Comparative Studies in Society and History*, 3 (1960-1), pp. 340-8.

9 Weber, op. cit., p. 60.

10 H. Stuart Hughes, *Consciousness and Society*, New York: Vintage, 1961, p. 328.

11 Weber, op. cit., p. 90.

12 There is considerable controversy over this issue. Marx wrote a *Preface* to *A Contribution to the Critique of Political Economy* in 1857 which he changed when the work was published in Berlin in 1859. The 1857 *Preface* suggests that some aspects of the ideological super-structure may have a degree of autonomy. This is also the impression given by Engels in *Selected Works* (op. cit., vol. II), in the last few letters reproduced there. This has recently assumed a new importance, as Alan Swingewood has pointed out to me, in the context of a Marxist sociology of literature; see Lucien Goldman, *The Hidden God*, London: Routledge & Kegan Paul, 1964 (trans. by P. Thody).

13 Weber, *The Theory of Social and Economic Organisation*, Glencoe: Free Press, 1947 (trans. by A. Henderson and T. Parsons), p. 328.

14 R. Bendix, *Max Weber: An Intellectual Portrait*, Garden City: Doubleday, 1960, p. 306.

15 Ernest Gellner, in *Philosophy*, 36 (1961), p. 256.

16 Hans Gerth and C. Wright Mills, *From Max Weber: Essays in Sociology*, London: Kegan Paul, 1948, pp. 51, 55.

17 H. Stuart Hughes, op. cit., p 290.

18 Gerth and Mills, op. cit., p. 224.

19 Quoted in H. Stuart Hughes, op. cit., p. 290.

20 Weber (1949), op. cit., p. 38.

21 I have discussed this in 'Moral Progress and Social Theory', *Ethics*, 79 (1969), pp. 229-34 (see Chapter VIII below). Julian Freund, *The Sociology of Max Weber*, London: Allen Lane, 1968 (trans. by Mary Ilford), ch. 1, 'Weber's Vision of the World', appears to support the views herein expressed.

22 There is of course a vast critical bibliography on Weber, as well as on Durkheim, which has been drawn upon but has not specifically been cited. See especially Parsons, *The Structure of Social Action*, Glencoe: The Free Press, 1949, and more recently Robert Nisbet, *The Sociological Tradition*, New York: Basic Books, 1967. See also the collection of critical essays edited by Nisbet, *Emile Durkheim*, Englewood Cliffs: Prentice-Hall, 1965.

23 Oswald Spengler, *The Decline of the West*, New York: Knopf, 1926-8 (trans. by C. Atkinson); and Arnold Toynbee, *A Study of History*, London: Oxford University Press, 1947 (abridged to 2 volumes by D. C. Somervell).

24 See Grace Cairns, *Philosophies of History*, London: Peter Owen, 1963, p. 368.

25 These are the last words of Spengler, op. cit., II, p. 507.

26 Toynbee, op. cit., I, p. 123.

27 Pitirim Sorokin, *Sociological Theories of Today*, New York: Harper, 1966, p. 202. Toynbee's work has been widely criticized on many counts; see, for example, Pieter Geyl, *Toynbee's Answer*, Amsterdam, 1961, and *Debates with Historians*, The Hague, 1955, chs. V-VIII; and H. R. Trevor-Roper, 'Arnold Toynbee's Millennium', *Encounter* (June 1957), pp. 14-28.

28 Hans Speier, in Barnes, op. cit., p. 890.

29 Sorokin, *Social and Cultural Dynamics*, Boston: Porter Sargent, 1957 (one volume edition), p. 646.
30 Ibid.
31 See the paper by Schneider and the reply by Sorokin in George Zollschan and Walter Hirsch (eds.), *Explorations in Social Change*, London: Routledge & Kegan Paul, 1964.
32 Ibid., pp. 407-8. Sorokin (with Walter Lunden) makes some positive proposals in *Power and Morality* (Boston: Porter Sargent, 1959).

Chapter VI

1 Becker's thesis did not go unchallenged; see R. O. Rockwood (ed.), *Carl Becker's Heavenly City Revisited*, Ithaca: Cornell University Press, 1958.
2 David W. Noble, *Historians against History*, Minneapolis: University of Minnesota Press, 1965, p. 11.
3 See, for example, Rutherford E. Delmage, 'The American Idea of Progress, 1750-1800', *Proceedings of the American Philosophical Society*, 91 (1947), pp. 307-14; and Daniel J. Boorstin, *The Americans: The Colonial Experience*, Harmondsworth: Penguin, 1965. Leo Marx's *The Machine in the Garden* (New York: Galaxy, 1967) gives a fascinating account from the point of view of the literary critic.
4 Introduction to Bury, op. cit., pp. xxiii, xxiv, xl.
5 See J. Thomas, 'What the Machine is doing to Mankind', *Journal of the Franklin Institute* (March 1933), pp. 247-72; H. A. Wallace, 'The Social Advantages and Disadvantages of the Engineering-Scientific Approach to Civilization', *Science* (N.S.), LXXIX (1934), pp. 1-5; D. Marshall, 'War of the Machines: Enemies of the Modern World', *Catholic World*, CXLV (1937), pp. 66-73, 184-91.
6 See Barnes, *Introduction to the History of Sociology*, op. cit., chs. 6 and 7.
7 Ibid., p. 788.
8 W. Warren Wagar, 'Modern Views of the Origins of the Idea of Progress', *Journal of the History of Ideas*, 28 (1967), pp. 55-70.
9 W. R. Inge, *Outspoken Essays*, London: Longmans, Green, 1922, vol. 2, ch. 3; at p. 163.
10 Ibid., p. 169.
11 Ibid., p. 175.
12 Ibid., p. 239.
13 Christopher Dawson, *Progress and Religion*, London: Sheed and Ward, 1929, p. 239.
14 Ibid., p. 66-7.
15 Wagar, op. cit., pp. 64-7.
16 Quoted in ibid., p. 65.
17 Ibid., p. 69.
18 See the Introduction above for the definitions of these terms and Chapter VII for their development.

19 Vilfredo Pareto, *The Mind and Society*, London: Cape, 1935 (trans. by A. Bongiorno and A. Livingston). See also H. Stuart Hughes, op. cit., pp. 4, 264-9.
20 Pareto, op. cit., I, § 299, and II, § 1102-32, 1462, 1980.
21 Ibid., II, § 1463.
22 Ibid., I, § 304.
23 Sigmund Freud, *Complete Psychological Works*, London: Hogarth Press, 1961 (trans. and ed. by James Strachey), vol. 21, p. 7.
24 Ibid., p. 134 (from 'Civilisation and its Discontents').
25 Ibid., p. 145.
26 See Philip Rieff, *Freud: The Mind of the Moralist*, New York: Viking, 1959, *passim*.
27 L. P. Jacks, *The Revolt against Mechanism*, London: Allen & Unwin, 1934, p. 38.
28 Sir J. Stamp, 'Must Science Ruin Economic Progress?', *Hibbert Journal*, 32 (1933-4), pp. 383-99; at p. 384. The opposite view, that science should be harnessed to social change, was forcefully argued by others. See Henry Elsner, *The Technocrats*, Syracuse: Syracuse University Press, 1967.
29 See the controversy over biological research in Chapter XIII below.
30 N. I. Osmova, 'The "Cultural Lag" Theory', *The Soviet Review*, 2 (1961), pp. 39-53.
31 Gina Lombroso, *La Rançon du Machinisme*, Paris: Payot, 1931 (trans. by H. Winckler), p. 10.
32 Ibid., pp. 10, 352.
33 Ibid., p. 394.
34 Georges Friedmann, *La Crise du Progrès*, Paris: Gallimard, 1936, pp. 183 ff.
35 Quoted in ibid., p. 187. For the curious circumstances concerning the origins of this quotation, see my paper, 'The Revolt Against the Machine', *Journal of World History*, (in press), note 13.
36 Ibid., p. 188.
37 Alfred Sauvy, 'Progrès technique, emploi et chômage', in John Habakkuk et al. (eds.), *Lectures in Economic Development*, Istanbul, 1958, pp. 39-59.
38 For an imaginative development of the argument, see Sauvy's 'The Information of Machines and of Men: Wizards and Technocrats', *Diogenes*, 62 (1968), pp. 1-24.
39 F. G. Juenger, *The Failure of Technology*, Illinois: Henry Regnery, 1949 (trans. by F. O. Wieck), pp. 124, 184-5, and *passim*.
40 Gabriel Marcel, *The Decline of Wisdom*, London: Harvill, 1954 (trans. by M. Harari), p. 7.
41 Jacques Ellul, 'The Technological Order', in Carl E. Stover (ed.), *The Technological Order*, Detroit: Wayne State University Press, 1963, pp. 10-37; at pp. 10-12.
42 Ellul, *The Technological Society*, London: Cape, 1965 (trans. by J. Wilkinson), p. 390.
43 Ibid., p. 29.
44 Ellul (1963), op. cit., pp. 24-5.

45 Ibid., pp. 25-8.
46 Ellul, *The Political Illusion*, New York: Knopf, 1967 (trans. by K. Kellen).
47 Jean Meynaud, *Technocracy*, London: Faber and Faber, 1968 (trans. by P. Barnes).
48 Herbert Marcuse, *One-Dimensional Man*, London: Routledge & Kegan Paul, 1964, p. xii.
49 E. M. Zhukov, 'Concepts of Progress in World History', *The Soviet Review*, 2 (1961), pp. 40-52; at p. 52. See also M. Walzer, 'The Only Revolution', *Dissent*, XI (1964), pp. 432-43.
50 Marcuse, op. cit., pp. 78, 114.
51 Marcuse, 'Philosophy and Critical Theory', in *Negations*, London: Allen Lane, 1968 (trans. by J. Shapiro), p. 156.
52 Gellner, *Thought and Change*, op. cit., p. 221.
53 Ibid., p. 179 and ch. 8, *passim*. See also pp. 68-73.
54 Ibid., pp. 69, 71.
55 For a more detailed account of Ellul's views see my paper 'The Sociology of the Opposition to Science and Technology: with Special Reference to the Work of Jacques Ellul', *Comparative Studies in Society and History* (forthcoming).
56 George Hildebrand in 'Introduction' to F. J. Teggart (ed.), *The Idea of Progress*, Berkeley: University of California Press, 1949, p. 30.
57 See Ellul, 'Western Man in 1970' in B. de Jouvenal (ed.), *Futuribles I*, Geneva: Droz, 1963, pp. 27-64.

Chapter VII

1 See Frank Manuel, *The Shapes of Philosophical History*, Stanford: Stanford University Press, 1965.
2 Gellner (1964), op. cit., ch. 1.
3 See Popper (1961), op. cit.
4 Merton, 'The Unanticipated Consequences of Purposive Social Action', *American Sociological Review*, 1 (1936), pp. 894-904.
5 Kingsley Davis, 'The Myth of Functional Analysis', *A.S.R.*, 24 (1959), pp. 752-72.
6 See my analysis in 'Comte and the Idea of Progress', *Inquiry*, 11 (1968), pp. 321-31; (and above, Chapter III)
7 A recent example is Manuel (ed.), *Utopias and Utopian Thought*, Boston: Houghton Mifflin, 1966.
8 H. G. Barnett, *Innovation*, New York: McGraw-Hill, 1953, p. 8.
9 W. C. Kneale, 'The Idea of Invention', *Proceedings of the British Academy*, (1955), pp. 85-108; at p. 87.
10 Ibid., p. 90.
11 Ibid., p. 95.
12 Ibid., p. 100.
13 Ibid., p. 102.
14 Ibid., p. 108.

15 Popper, *The Poverty of Historicism*, London: Routledge & Kegan Paul, 1961, sections 3 and 30.
16 Barnett, op. cit., pp. 19-20.
17 M. R. Cohen, *Reason and Nature*, Glencoe: Free Press, 1964, p. 123.
18 Barnett, op. cit., p. 9.
19 Ibid., p. 42.
20 S. C. Gilfillan, *The Sociology of Invention*, Chicago: Follet, 1935, p. 10.
21 A good account of this controversy is Steven Lukes, 'Methodological Individualism Reconsidered', *B.J.S.*, 19 (1968), pp. 119-29.
22 See A. Etzioni, *A Comparative Analysis of Complex Organizations*, New York: Free Press, 1961.
23 See Dore, 'Japan as a Model of Economic Development', *European Journal of Sociology*, 5 (1964), pp. 138-54.
24 Weber, *The Religion of China*, New York: Macmillan, 1964 (trans. by H. Gerth), p. 151.
25 Marcel Granet, *Chinese Civilization*, London: Kegan Paul, 1930 (trans. by K. Innes and M. Brailsford), p. 429.
26 See, for example, Paul Radin, *The World of Primitive Man*, London: Abelard-Schuman, 1953, *passim*.
27 Many theories of social change suggest certain elements of the theory put forward here. See, for example, Toynbee, op. cit., on challenge and response; Pareto, op. cit., on rentiers and speculators; and perhaps more directly, Howard Becker, 'Sacred and Secular Societies: Retrospect and Prospect', ch. 5 in his *Through Values to Social Interpretation*, Durham: Duke University Press, 1950, and his ch. 6 in Becker and Alvin Boskoff (eds.), *Modern Sociological Theory*, New York: Holt, Rinehart & Winston, 1966. Two further items, seen after this was written, can be mentioned. The first is the work of my colleague Michael Hill whose notion of 'the revolution of tradition' in the analysis of monastic orders has many points of contact with the idea of non-innovational change. The second is Aharon Ben-Ami's fascinating book, *Social Change in a Hostile Environment* (Princeton: Princeton University Press, 1969)—a study of the Crusaders' kingdom of Jerusalem in the twelfth century. The intent of Ben-Ami's notions of 'institutional lag' and 'innovative functions' are extraordinarily close in some respects to my non-innovational and innovational change. The main difference between my formulations and these others is, however, that I am talking not only about social change but also about progress.
28 Marcuse (1964), op. cit., pp. 51-2.
29 John Jewkes, David Sawers and Richard Stillerman, *The Sources of Invention*, London: Macmillan, 1958, p. 108. A second, expanded, edition of this work was published in 1969.
30 W. M. Grosvener, 'The Seeds of Progress', *Chemical Markets*, 24 (1929), pp. 23-6, speaks of 'intellectual property'.
31 Joseph Rossman, *The Psychology of the Inventor*, Washington: Inventors Publishing Co., 1931.
32 William F. Ogburn, *Social Change*, New York: Huebsch, 1922, pp. 90-122.

33 Bernard Barber, *Science and the Social Order*, New York: Collier, 1962, p. 252.
34 Tom Burns and G. M. Stalker, *The Management of Innovation*, London: Tavistock, 1961, p. 25.
35 Merton (1963), op. cit., ch. 16.
36 Talcott Parsons, *The Social System*, London: Tavistock, 1951, pp. 335-48.
37 See also the research reported in Barber and Hirsch (eds.), *The Sociology of Science*, New York: Free Press, 1962, esp. Parts 4 and 5; W. Hagstrom, *The Scientific Community*, New York: Basic Books, 1965; and Storer, *The Social System of Science*, New York: Holt, Rinehart & Winston, 1966.

Chapter VIII

1 See W. K. Frankena, *Ethics*, Englewood Cliffs: Prentice-Hall, 1963, chs. 1 and 2, for a clear discussion of this usage.
2 This is particularly emphasized in Burns and Stalker, op. cit.
3 Weber (1947), op. cit., pp. 115-18; at p. 116.
4 Parsons, in intro. to ibid., p. 60.
5 For a picture of such a society, see Alan Moorhead, *The Fatal Impact* (London: Hamilton, 1966), on Tahiti before the arrival of the Europeans.
6 Merton (1963), op. cit., ch. 1.
7 See the suggestive analysis of belief systems in Parsons (1964), op. cit., ch. 8. Also relevant is T. S. Kuhn's influential book, *The Structure of Scientific Revolutions*, Chicago: University of Chicago Press, 1962.
8 See C. H. Waddington, *The Ethical Animal*, London: Allen & Unwin, 1960, esp. pp. 7, 59.
9 A. J. Ayer, *Language, Truth and Logic*, London: Gollancz, 1946 (second ed.), Ch. VI.
10 C. L. Stevenson, *Ethics and Language*, New Haven: Yale University Press, 1944.
11 This is Miss Anscombe's translation, quoted from her *Introduction to Wittgenstein's Tractatus*, London: Hutchinson, 1959, p. 18.
12 See Gellner, *Words and Things*, Harmondsworth: Penguin, 1968.
13 Bertrand Russell, in Wilfred Sellars and John Hospers, *Readings in Ethical Theory*, New York: Appleton-Century-Crofts, 1952, p. 1.
14 John Plamenatz, *Man and Society*, London: Longmans, Green, 1963, II, p. 439. This whole chapter 7, 'The Belief in Progress', pp. 409-57, is a sympathetic account of eighteenth- and nineteenth-century theories.

Chapter IX

1 Ginsberg (1956), op. cit., p. 97.

2 Parsons, 1949, op. cit., p. 643 ff. The argument is to be found in Weber (1947), op. cit., pp. 115-118, and *passim*. See also W. Brock, *Introduction to German Philosophy*, Cambridge: Cambridge University Press, 1935, pp. 26-40.
3 Ginsberg (1956), op. cit., p. 98.
4 Marion J. Levy, Jr., *The Structure of Society*, Princeton: Princeton University Press, 1952, ch. 4.
5 Parsons (1951), op. cit., pp. 26-36.
6 Ibid., p. 173.
7 John Rawls, 'Justice as Fairness', in Peter Laslett and W. G. Runciman (eds.), *Philosophy, Politics and Society*, Oxford: Blackwell, 1962 (second series), ch. 7.
8 Carl J. Friedrich and John W. Chapman (eds.), *Justice: Nomos 6* (Yearbook of the American Society for Political and Legal Philosophy), New York: Atherton Press, 1963.
9 Chapman, 'Justice and Fairness', ch. 8 in ibid. See ch. 6 in ibid., John Rawls, 'Constitutional Liberty and the Concept of Justice', p. 102, for the quotation.
10 A. Macbeath, *Experiments in Living*, London: Macmillan, 1952, p. iii.
11 Ibid., p. 33.
12 Ibid., pp. 66, 64.
13 Ibid., p. 451.
14 H. L. A. Hart, *The Concept of Law*, Oxford: Oxford University Press, 1961, p. 41.
15 Ginsberg, *Evolution and Progress*, London: Heinemann, 1961, p. 141.
16 See my 'Comte and the Idea of Progress', op. cit., esp. pp. 328-31.
17 See also Richard Brandt, *Hopi Ethics*, Chicago: Chicago University Press, 1954; Abraham Edel, *Ethical Judgement*, Glencoe: The Free Press, 1955; John Ladd, *The Structure of a Moral Code*, Cambridge: Harvard University Press, 1957; and Kurt Baier, *The Moral Point of View*, Ithaca: Cornell University Press, 1958; all of which address themselves more or less relevantly to these problems. The most satisfactory all-round treatment of the subject is D. Emmett's admirably balanced *Rules, Roles and Relations*, London: Macmillan, 1966.
18 Some remarks that come quite close to my meaning here will be found in the interesting paper by Richard E. Duhwors, 'Social Persistence and Social Change', *Sociologia Internationalis* (Berlin), 1969 (in the press).
19 See the value-judgments outlined by Marcuse in the Introduction to *One-Dimensional Man* (op. cit.), for an interesting comparison.

Chapter X

1 Bronislaw Malinowski, *The Scientific Theory of Culture*, Chapel Hill: University of North Carolina Press, 1944, p. 150.
2 Ibid., pp. 41 ff.
3 Ibid., p. 125, esp. the diagram.
4 Ibid., pp. 91 ff.

5 For a spirited defence of it see Ralph Piddington, 'Malinowski's Theory of Needs', in Raymond Firth (ed.), *Man and Culture*, New York: Harper, 1964, pp. 33-52.

6 See Spencer (1904), op. cit., ch. XIV.

7 This distinction is argued in, for example, C. T. Morgan, *Introduction to Psychology*, New York: McGraw Hill, 1961, Ch. 3.

8 See Thomas Szaz, *The Myth of Mental Illness*, New York: Hoeber, 1961, for this distinction.

9 Gellner, 'Concepts and Society', in *Transactions of the Fifth World Congress of Sociology*, Washington, 1962, vol. 1, pp. 153-84.

10 D. Aberle, A. Cohen, A. Davis, M. Levy and F. Sutton, 'The Functional Prerequisites of a Society', *Ethics*, 60 (1950), pp. 100-11.

11 Levy (1952), op. cit., p. xiv.

12 See the section on Parsons below.

13 Many of the most important contributions to the battle are collected in N. Demareth and W. Peterson, *System, Change and Conflict*, Glencoe: Free Press, 1968.

14 Aberle et al., op. cit., p. 100.

15 In George C. Homans, *Social Behaviour*, London: Routledge & Kegan Paul, 1961.

16 See Melvin Tumin, *Social Stratification*, Englewood Cliffs: Prentice-Hall, 1967.

17 This is hinted in Parsons, 'Some Considerations on the Theory of Social Change', *Rural Sociology*, 26 (1961), pp. 219-39.

18 Levy (1952), op. cit., p. vii.

19 Ibid., p. 37.

20 Ibid., pp. 156-7.

21 Ibid., p. 164.

22 Ibid.

23 Dahrendorf, 'Out of Utopia', op. cit.

24 See C. P. Snow, *The Two Cultures: and a Second Look*, New York: Mentor, 1964.

25 Levy (1952), op. cit., p. 173.

26 Ibid., p. 179.

27 Ibid., pp. 181-2.

28 Ibid., p. 182.

29 Ibid., p. 187. See also p. 154.

30 Parsons, *The Structure of Social Action*, op. cit.; *Toward a General Theory of Action*, New York: Harper, 1962 (with E. Shils, eds.); *The Social System*, op. cit.; *Working Papers in the Theory of Action*, Glencoe: Free Press, 1963 (with R. Bales and Shils); *Essays in Sociological Theory*, Glencoe: Free Press, 1964; *Economy and Society*, Glencoe: Free Press, 1956 (with N. Smelser); *Theories of Society*, Glencoe: Free Press, 1961 (with Shils, K. Naegele and J. Pitts, eds.), pp. 30-79, 239-64, 963-93; and *Societies: Evolutionary and Comparative Perspectives*, Englewood Cliffs: Prentice-Hall, 1966.

31 Parsons, 'The Point of View of the Author', in Max Black (ed.), *The Social Theories of Talcott Parsons*, Englewood Cliffs: Prentice-Hall, 1961, pp. 311-63; at p. 316.

32 See, for example, Popper (1961), op. cit., esp. chs. 3 and 4; and E. Nagel, *The Structure of Science*, London: Routledge & Kegan Paul, 1961, esp. p. 90 ff. The relation between 'theory' and 'empirical reality' has always bothered Parsons, cf. the dedication in *The Social System*.

33 Parsons and Kroeber, engaged in an interesting though unresolved controversy over 'culture' with R. Ogles and Levy, in 'Communications', *American Sociological Review*, 23 (1958), pp. 582-3, and 24 (1959), pp. 246-50.

34 Bales, *Interaction Process Analysis*, Cambridge, Mass.: Addison-Wesley, 1950.

35 See the powerful criticisms by Sorokin (1966), op. cit., pp. 53 ff.

36 An assault on functionalism along these lines is Gideon Sjoberg, 'Contradictory Functional Requirements and Social Systems', in Demareth and Peterson, op. cit., pp. 339-45. See also the papers in this volume by Moore, Homans and Bredemeier for further relevant points.

37 See Alvin Gouldner, 'Reciprocity and Autonomy in Functional Theory', in Llewellyn Gross (ed.), *Symposium on Sociological Theory*, New York: Harper and Row, 1959, pp. 241-70; at p. 263. In Gouldner's and Richard A. Peterson's *Technology and the Moral Order* (Indianapolis: Bobbs-Merrill, 1963) the theory is worked out in practice! Parsons (*Societies: Evolutionary and Comparative Perspectives*, op. cit., p. 11) makes some interesting remarks in this connection.

Chapter XI

1 The recent work of A. Macintyre, *A Short History of Ethics* (London: Routledge & Kegan Paul, 1967), is notable for its attention to such concerns. See also Emmett, op. cit., and Ginsberg, op. cit., I.

2 Jan Narveson, *Morality and Utility*, Baltimore: Johns Hopkins, 1967, p. 19.

3 Ginsberg, op. cit., I, p. 47.

4 Stephen Toulmin, *The Place of Reason in Ethics*, Cambridge: Cambridge University Press, 1961; see, for example, remarks on pp. 170-1, 224.

5 A good account of the difficulties and complexities of research in this area in U. Bronfenbrenner, 'Socialization and Social Class through Time and Space', in E. E. MacCoby, T. M. Newcomb, and E. C. Hartley (eds.), *Readings in Social Psychology*, New York: Holt, 1958.

6 See the fascinating book by Marcel Sire, *The Social Life of Animals*, London: Vista, 1965 (trans. by C. Sherman), esp. pp. 165-71.

7 Noam Chomsky, *Cartesian Linguistics*, New York: Harper & Row, 1966. See also 'The Language Generator', a discussion between Chomsky and S. Hampshire, BBC Typescript, 1968.

8 A comprehensive account of this debate is George A. Huaco, 'The Functionalist Theory of Stratification: Two Decades of Controversy', *Inquiry*, 9 (1966), pp. 215-40. My argument in the following pages has been influenced by Gabriel Newfield, 'Equality in Society', *Proceedings of the Aristotelian Society*, 66 (1965-6), pp. 193-210.

9 See P. Blau, *Bureaucracy in Modern Society*, New York: Random House, 1956, esp. ch. 3.

10 The increasing sensitivity of social reseachers to the moral implications of their work leads me to suspect that this view is gaining momentum in sociology. It is argued in, for example, Sjoberg (ed.), *Ethics, Political and Social Research*, Cambridge, Mass.: Schenkman, 1967; K. Benne (ed.), 'The Social Responsibilities of the Behavioural Scientist', *Journal of Social Issues*, 21 (1965), no. 2; and continually in the Journal *Transaction*.

11 For a critique of this aspect of Marxist thought which my argument attempts to meet, see R. C. Tucker, *Philosophy and Myth in Karl Marx*, Cambridge: Cambridge University Press, 1961, ch. XV.

12 See, for example, Sorokin, *The Ways of Power and Love*, Boston: Beacon Press, 1954.

Chapter XII

1 Henry V. Dicks, 'In Search of our Proper Ethic', *British Journal of Medical Psychology*, 23 (1950), pp. 1-14; at p. 3.

2 K. Soddy and R. Ahrenfeldt (eds.), *Mental Health and Contemporary Thought*, and *Mental Health in the Service of the Community*, London: Tavistock, 1967; and also Soddy (ed.), *Identity, and Mental Health and Value Systems*, London: Tavistock, 1961.

3 E. Gombrich, 'The Idea of Progress in Art', unpublished lecture, Feb. 1968.

4 See Chapter X above.

5 Nisbet (1967), op. cit.

6 See the discussion by Ginsberg in many essays; especially relevant here is 'Basic Needs and Moral Ideas', in *On the Diversity of Morals*, op. cit., ch. VIII.

7 See Meynaud (1968), op. cit.

8 Earl Bell, *Social Foundations of Human Behavior*, New York: Harper, 1961, p. 487.

9 Ogburn and M. Nimkoff, *A Handbook of Sociology*, London: Routledge & Kegan Paul, 1964 (5th ed. rev.), p. 604.

10 R. Bierstedt, *The Social Order*, New York: McGraw-Hill, 1963, p. 557.

11 Ibid., pp. 557-8.

12 R. MacIver and C. Page, *Society*, London: Macmillan, 1955, pp. 522-3.

13 Ibid., ch. 28.

14 C. Panunzio, *Major Social Institutions*, New York: Macmillan, 1948, p. 401.
15 The considerable complexity of this issue is discussed from many sides in S. Hook (ed.), *Determinism and Freedom*, New York: Collier, 1958, esp. Parts III and IV.
16 See Karl Mannheim, *Ideology and Utopia*, London: Routledge & Kegan Paul, 1948 (trans. by L. Wirth and E. Shils), for the possibilities of such loopholes for the intelligentsia.
17 See Chapter III above.
18 Ginsberg (1956), op. cit., ch. IV, 'Durkheim's Ethical Theory'.
19 G. Plekhanov, 'The Place of the Individual in History', in Gardiner, *Theories of History*, op. cit.
20 Berger and Luckmann, *The Social Construction of Reality*, op. cit., p. 30.
21 For the heights of the metaphor, see G. Roppen, *Evolution and Poetic Belief*, Oslo, 1956. For a more general use of *metaphor* in this context, see Nisbet, *Social Change and History*, op. cit.
22 P. Landis, *Sociology*, Boston: Ginn, 1957, p. 177.
23 J. Fichter, *Sociology*, Chicago: University of Chicago Press, 1957, p. 394; Barnett, op. cit.; and Merton (1963), op. cit., ch. IV, esp. pp. 141-9.
24 Bell, op. cit., p. 489.
25 Ogburn and Nimkoff, op. cit., p. 606.
26 K. Young, *Sociology*, New York: American Book, 1949, p. 581.
27 MacIver and Page, op. cit., p. 619.
28 Bottomore, *Sociology*, London: Unwin, 1962, p. 268.
29 Bottomore (1962), op. cit., ch. 7, 'Some Recent Theories of Social Progress'.
30 W. Sprott, *Sociology*, London: Hutchinson, 1961, p. 165.
31 H. Odum, *Understanding Society*, New York: Macmillan, 1947, pp. 513, 522, and ch. 29, *passim*.
32 Bottomore (1962), op. cit., p. 268.
33 Toulmin, *The Place of Reason in Ethics*, op. cit., p. 165, n. 2.
34 Some interesting criticisms of these arguments are given by G. Nakhnikian, 'An Examination of Toulmin's Analytical Ethics', *Philosophical Quarterly*, 9 (1959), pp. 59-79.
35 See the confusions of this type in D. Hodges, ' "Moral Progress" from Philosophy to Technology', *Philosophy and Phenomenological Research*, 28 (1968), pp. 430-36, and my reply, 'Moral Progress Revisited', ibid. (forthcoming), Hodges' (terminal) reply following merely restates his views, in my opinion.

Chapter XIII

1 Van Doren, op. cit., chs. 18-25, treats progress in terms of institutional spheres, with very little success.

2   F. M. Burnet, 'Men or Molecules? A Tilt at Molecular Biology', *The Lancet* (1 January 1966), pp. 37-9.
3   G. Rattray Taylor, *The Biological Time Bomb*, London: Thames and Hudson, 1968, pp. 10-11, and *passim*.
4   'Genetics: Are There Things We Should Try Not to Know?', *The Sunday Times* (9 January 1966).
5   Ibid.
6   Anthony Tucker, 'A New Breed of Men?', *Guardian* (22 February 1966). We must allow here for journalistic hyperbole.
7   H. Kahn and A. Wiener, *The Year 2000*, New York: Macmillan, 1967; and *Science Journal* (October 1967), issue on 'Forecasting the Future'. A very sober and concise account is Office of Health Economics, *Medicine in the 1990's*, London: O.H.E., 1969.
8   Taylor, op. cit., pp. 222-6.
9   Figures quoted in the CIBA symposium, G. Wolstenholme and M. O'Conner (eds.), *The Health of Mankind*, London: Churchill, 1967, p. 38.
10 A. Storr in *The Sunday Times* (21 April 1968).
11 See, for example, the account in Raymond Firth, *We, The Tikopia*, London: Allen & Unwin, 1957, pp. 527-30.
12 This is the view of Kahn and Wiener, op. cit., p. 53, items 40-2.
13 See the review of these problems in Robin Clarke, *We all Fall Down*, London: Lane, 1968.
14 An interesting sociological treatment of the 'Sputnik trauma' in the United States is N. Smelser, *Theory of Collective Behaviour*, London: Routledge & Kegan Paul, 1962, pp. 67-90.
15 *The Sunday Times* (1 October 1967).
16 See the article 'Soviet Scientists Split by Space', *Daily Telegraph* (16 June 1967).
17 Nigel Calder, in *The Sunday Times* (14 July 1968).
18 R. C. Seamans, Jr., 'Space', *Science Journal* (October 1967), pp. 82-8.
19 H. Simons in *New Scientist* (12 August 1965), p. 383.
20 'NASA Enfiladed', ibid. (29 December 1966), p. 733.
21 'The Second Decade of Space Research', ibid. (5 October 1967), p. 16.
22 The following articles in *Scientific American* give this impression: O. King-Hele, 'The Shape of the Earth' (October 1967), pp. 67-76; R. Scott, 'The Feel of the Moon' (November 1967), pp. 34-43; and E. Ellis et al., 'The Lunar Orbiter Missions to the Moon' (May 1968), pp. 58-78.
23 See L. Beaton, 'The Military Significance of Space', *New Scientist* (19 November 1964), pp. 499-501; also the papers by Gatland and Shepherd.
24 'Editorial', *New Scientist* (28 December 1967), p. 741.
25 Earl Johnson, 'The Aerospace Industry', in E. Ginzberg (ed.), *Technology and Social Change*, New York: Columbia, 1964, pp. 60-81. This argument, with respect to the military basis of the American economy, is put in Leonard Lewin (ed.), *Report from Iron Mountain*, New York: Dial, 1967; and variously dismembered by a clutch of social scientists in *Transaction*, 5 (1968), 3, pp. 8-20.

26 See the Harris poll reported in *The Sunday Times* (1 October 1967).
27 The most thorough account of the Apollo project so far comes from *The Sunday Times* team, Hugo Young, Brian Silcock and Peter Dunn, *Journey to Tranquillity*, London: Cape, 1969. This paper has been an excellent source of information on the space programme for the last few years. I have extended this discussion in my forthcoming book on the sociology of science, to be published by MacGibbon and Kee in 1971.
28 Roscoe Pound, *Social Control Through Law*, New Haven: Yale University Press, 1942, p. 109.
29 Some interesting research is reported by Peter Dodd, 'The Slow Pace of Change in the Space-Centered Communities', *Journal of World History*, X-3 (1967), pp. 567-80.

Chapter XIV

1 It is interesting in this connection to note that the *tradition/modernity* dichotomy is being critically re-examined. See, for example, Joseph R. Gusfield, 'Tradition and Modernity: Misplaced Polarities in the Study of Social Change', *American Journal of Sociology*, 72 (1967), pp. 351-62; S. N. Eisenstadt, 'Review Article', *Economic Development and Cultural Change*, 16 (1968), pp. 436-50; and Henry Bernstein, 'Modernization Theory and the Sociological Study of Development', *Journal of Development Studies* (forthcoming).
2 This is argued in Henry Vyverberg, *Historical Pessimism in the French Enlightenment* (Harvard: Harvard University Press, 1958). A comprehensive review of this movement in thought is Lester Crocker's 'Recent Interpretations of the French Enlightenment', *Journal of World History*, 8 (1964), pp. 426-56.
3 Once again, this is not to say that only the West in recent centuries has developed science and technology. Joseph Needham's *Science and Civilization in China* (Cambridge: Cambridge University Press, 1953) has for ever disabused us of this ethnocentric view. The institutionalization of science, as I have argued, is quite another matter.
4 In Grace Cairns' *Philosophies of History* (London: Peter Owen, 1963) many such theories are discussed which suggest this.
5 D. J. de S. Price has suggested that science has grown exponentially from his findings on the growth of the scientific literature. From this he concludes that the 'scientific doomsday is therefore less than a century distant' (*Little Science, Big Science*, New York: Columbia, 1963, p. 19). Though Price's inferences have been questioned in an incisive note by Jacob Schmookler in *Invention and Economic Growth* (London: Oxford University Press, 1966, pp. 60-1), there is no doubt that the rate of growth of science is worthy of careful study.
6 This I have attempted in my paper, 'The Sociology of the Opposition to Science and Technology', *Comparative Studies in Society and History* (forthcoming).

Name index

Subject index